Trading Commodities and Financial Futures

Trading Commodities and Financial Futures

A Step-by-Step Guide to Mastering the Markets

George Kleinman

FINANCIAL TIMES

Prentice Hall

An imprint of **Pearson Education**

Boston • San Francisco • New York • Toronto • Montreal • London • Munich
Paris·• Madrid • Capetown • Sydney • Tokyo • Singapore • Mexico City

Library of Congress Cataloging-in-Publication Data: 2004107810

Publisher: Tim Moore
Executive Editor: Jim Boyd
Editorial Assistant: Richard Winkler
Development Editor: Russ Hall
Marketing Manager: Martin Litkowski
International Marketing Manager: Tim Galligan
Cover Designer: Alan Clements
Managing Editor: Gina Kanouse
Project Editor: Christy Hackerd
Copy Editor: Specialized Composition
Senior Indexer: Cheryl Lenser
Compositor: Gloria Schurick and ICC
Manufacturing Buyer: Dan Uhrig

© 2005 Pearson Education, Inc.

Publishing as Financial Times Prentice Hall

Upper Saddle River, NJ 07458

Financial Times Prentice Hall offers excellent discounts on this book when ordered in quantity for bulk purchases or special sales. For more information, please contact: U.S. Corporate and Government Sales, 1-800-382-3419, corpsales@pearsontechgroup.com. For sales outside the U.S., please contact International Sales at international@pearsoned.com.

Printed in the United States of America

Third Edition

ISBN 0-13-147654-8

Pearson Education LTD.
Pearson Education Australia PTY, Limited
Pearson Education Singapore, Pte. Ltd.
Pearson Education North Asia Ltd.
Pearson Education Canada, Ltd.
Pearson Educación de Mexico, S.A. de C.V.
Pearson Education—Japan
Pearson Education Malaysia, Pte. Ltd.

FINANCIAL TIMES PRENTICE HALL BOOKS

For more information, please go to www.ft-ph.com

Business and Society

John Gantz and Jack B. Rochester

Pirates of the Digital Millennium: How the Intellectual Property Wars Damage Our Personal Freedoms, Our Jobs, and the World Economy

Douglas K. Smith

On Value and Values: Thinking Differently About We in an Age of Me

Current Events

Alan Elsner

Gates of Injustice: The Crisis in America's Prisons

John R. Talbott

Where America Went Wrong: And How to Regain Her Democratic Ideals

Economics

David Dranove

What's Your Life Worth? Health Care Rationing...Who Lives? Who Dies? Who Decides?

Entrepreneurship

Dr. Candida Brush, Dr. Nancy M. Carter, Dr. Elizabeth Gatewood, Dr. Patricia G. Greene, and Dr. Myra M. Hart

Clearing the Hurdles: Women Building High Growth Businesses

Oren Fuerst and Uri Geiger

From Concept to Wall Street: A Complete Guide to Entrepreneurship and Venture Capital

David Gladstone and Laura Gladstone

Venture Capital Handbook: An Entrepreneur's Guide to Raising Venture Capital, Revised and Updated

Thomas K. McKnight

Will It Fly? How to Know if Your New Business Idea Has Wings... Before You Take the Leap

Stephen Spinelli, Jr., Robert M. Rosenberg, and Sue Birley

Franchising: Pathway to Wealth Creation

Executive Skills

Cyndi Maxey and Jill Bremer

It's Your Move: Dealing Yourself the Best Cards in Life and Work

John Putzier

Weirdos in the Workplace

Finance

Aswath Damodaran

The Dark Side of Valuation: Valuing Old Tech, New Tech, and New Economy Companies

Kenneth R. Ferris and Barbara S. Pécherot Petitt

Valuation: Avoiding the Winner's Curse

Tom Osenton
Customer Share Marketing: How the World's Great Marketers Unlock Profits from Customer Loyalty

Bernd H. Schmitt, David L. Rogers, and Karen Vrotsos
There's No Business That's Not Show Business: Marketing in Today's Experience Culture

Yoram J. Wind and Vijay Mahajan, with Robert Gunther
Convergence Marketing: Strategies for Reaching the New Hybrid Consumer

Personal Finance

David Shapiro
Retirement Countdown: Take Action Now to Get the Life You Want

Steve Weisman
A Guide to Elder Planning: Everything You Need to Know to Protect Yourself Legally and Financially

Strategy

Edward W. Davis and Robert E. Spekmam
The Extended Enterprise: Gaining Competitive Advantage through Collaborative Supply Chains

Joel M. Shulman, With Thomas T. Stallkamp
Getting Bigger by Growing Smaller: A New Growth Model for Corporate America

"It is literally true millions come easier to a trader after he knows how to trade, than hundreds did in the days of his ignorance."

Jesse Livermore (1923)

This book is for Sherri

Contents

8 The advanced futures trading course (or how to analyze the markets technically) **119**

9 The most valuable technical tool (TMVTT) **175**

10 How I use "TMVTT" **187**

11 A day trader's secrets **205**

12 Your state of mind (trader's psychology) **213**

Acknowledgments

My sincere thanks to these people. The finished product is far superior due to their help.

Sal (William G. Salatich, Jr.) from the cattle pit, Joe Orlick from the corn pit, and Joseph Santagata and James Gallo from the copper pit. Their stories made for great contributions.

Mary Ellen Scanlin and the professionals at the superb clearing firm of R.J. O'Brien, one of the last privately owned.

Ginger Szala and Gary Kamen from Futures. It is with their permission that I was able to include the "Day Trader's Secrets" in Chapter 11.

The editors of Wall Street Winners: Elliot Gue, Ivan Martchev, and Yiannis Mostrous.

CQG, Inc. for a superb technical analysis program. It is their charts you see throughout this book.

My favorite clients, Bruce, Ivan, and Wayne, for remaining cool and calm during both the good and bad times, and John Baird. (I'm sure you must be trading in heaven with Jesse Livermore.)

Without my people at Commodity Resource, Nancy Torok and Greg DeLong, it would be impossible to function effectively. Thanks for putting up with me. I know how difficult I can be.

My beloved wife, Sherri, also has to put up with me. And, of course, to Rebel & Rocky for daily stress relief, because as Will Rogers said, "If there are no dogs in heaven, then when I die, I want to go where they went."

George Kleinman
Incline Village, Nevada

Disclaimer of liability

Preface

Why trade commodities?

In recent years, I've seen more market moves of significance take place in commodities than anywhere else—*moves that can literally make the financial difference of a lifetime* (for better or for worse). Because of the leverage inherent in commodity futures, more fortunes are made and lost more quickly than in any other markets. Yet, with all the potential that the commodity futures markets have, few really make out well. Do you wonder why that is?

Why this book?

I've been trading for more than 25 years now. As head of a trading firm working with individuals and corporations alike, I've witnessed thousands of trades and participated in thousands more. I've seen fortunes won and lost. After awhile, you do learn a few things, and it's my goal to share some of what I've learned with you. Hopefully, I can save you some of the grief I've experienced and give you a jump-start on the road to success. Of course, I'm still learning and still have a lot left to learn. This, the third edition of *Trading Commodities and Financial Futures,* is probably my last book (I'm a trader, not a writer) and no doubt my best work. I call it my best work (with all due modesty) because I've grown older, and as you grow older, you learn more. Some call trading a young man's game; however, I can honestly say that after 25 years in the business, I now trade with less stress and better results than I did when I was younger and more impulsive. This is because the older one gets, the less important ego becomes—and I've seen the disasters that can result when ego takes precedence over the major prevailing trend of the marketplace.

Without trying to be all things to all people, I've written this book for both novice *and* seasoned traders. It is meant to be a primer and reference source for those of you who are seriously considering, but have not yet taken, the plunge into the shark-infested commodity waters. This book is also designed to help those of you who are currently trading and want to perform better. What will it take to succeed? You'll need patience, guts, discipline, and vision. I cannot infuse these qualities into you; instead, I can tell you only what to look for and what to watch out for. We'll start slow and then build up to a master trading plan. Along the way, I'll share some good stories with you.

Why trade commodities now?

I entered this crazy business during the commodities boom of the late 1970s. The Hunt brothers were attempting to corner the silver market, the Carter Administration couldn't get a grip on inflation, the currency markets were in turmoil, the Russians were invading Afghanistan, the world was running out of food due to a series of weather disasters, the Iranians were holding American citizens hostage, and there was an energy crisis. Hard assets were in vogue. Paper assets were just that. During the 1970s, the CRB Index (basket of commodities) appreciated well over 100%. The Dow Jones Index (basket of "blue chip" U.S. stocks) literally went nowhere for more than 10 years.

Here's an interesting (and frightening) statistic: The world is adding to its population at the rate of the country of Mexico every year—that's more than 80 million people. If we could shrink the earth's population to a village of precisely 100 people, with all the existing human ratios remaining the same, it would look approximately like this:

- Just 14 people would be from the western hemisphere (only 5 from the United States).

- 27 would be from Africa, Australia, Europe, and the Middle East combined.

- 57 would be Asian (38 from China and India).

The rapid movement of China and India into the mainstream of the world economy is generating new demands for commodities, the likes of which have never been experienced. As just one example, take a look at oil. Today, the United States consumes approximately one quarter of all the oil produced; this is approximately 25 barrels per capita per year. When Japan accelerated its economic growth (from 1950 to 1970), Japanese oil consumption rose from 1 barrel per capita per year to more than 17 barrels. China and India are now in the early stages of a similar growth curve, today consuming just over 1 barrel per capita per year. China and India's combined populations are 18 times that of Japan. As their consumer economies continue to expand, it's hard to fathom the stress that will be placed on the world's limited and diminishing capacity to produce crude oil (or metals, or food for that matter).

China, in particular, is in the back of investor's minds these days because it is driving the most powerful investment trend witnessed since the tech bubble burst in 2000. Look at food consumption trends. China has a huge population with a rapidly growing economy and a growing middle class. As its population becomes richer, subsistence-level eating just isn't good enough. China can't grow enough food to feed its people (which is behind the huge exports of soybeans and wheat to China). All nations face a crop failure every decade or so. What happens when one of the world's major food producers such as the United States, Brazil, or China has the next one? In 1995, due to a poor domestic crop, China turned from the largest corn exporter in Asia into a corn importer. It was no coincidence that this was the year of the greatest bull corn market in history, with corn prices surging from less than $2 per bushel to more than $5.

Chinese agriculture brings about other demands. For example, a large part of increasing the efficiency of Chinese agriculture is fertilizer. Good fertilization could dramatically increase China's ability to produce the basic foodstuffs it needs, and most fertilizers contain a mineral known as potash—a mineral China simply doesn't have enough of. In fact, industry estimates put China's requirements at about 10 million tons five years from now, of which it is able to produce only about a million tons domestically. When I wrote the first edition of this book, nobody had ever heard of the Dalian Commodity Exchange in China. Today, it is the ninth largest exchange in the world—and growing. The Chinese factor is not going away. Instead, it is accelerating the demand for commodities—everything from gold to copper to soybeans to wheat—and as a result, this decade and beyond will be the era of a new and sustained mega-bull market for commodities.

For now, think of this as a game

Financial markets come in many flavors. Think of commodity futures and options trading as a *game*—the highest stakes money game in the world, where fortunes are made and lost daily. Sure, there's a loftier purpose. Governments allow the traditional financial markets to operate for the purpose of capital formation. Futures markets are allowed to operate as a vehicle of risk transference for commodity producers and users. However, this book is not a scholarly treatise, and it is not about investing for your retirement. It is a guide to winning the game.

A game with consequences

If you choose to play the game, be forewarned that it can dramatically affect your lifestyle. For every buyer of a gold, copper, bond, cattle, or Euro contract, there is someone unseen (but out there) on the other side of the transaction. The buyer is known as *the long* and the seller as *the short*. At any point in time, except for the split second when a new trade is initiated, someone is winning, and someone is losing. You should understand from the outset that commodity futures are a *zero sum* game. For every dollar won by one player, someone else loses that same dollar. Accurate statistics are not available, but it generally is agreed that the great majority of players lose this game. Because this game is *zero sum*, by definition, the great minority are winning what this majority is losing. This is one of the reasons the stakes are so high. Fortunes are made in commodity futures, in some cases starting with an extremely small stake. Luck might play a part in the short run, but in the end, only those players who play the game better will triumph. No method is foolproof, so the best I can do is help you to place the odds in your favor. If I am able to accomplish this, and you are able to act in a disciplined manner, success is assured. Sound simple? If it were so simple, most people wouldn't lose, and the nature of the markets is to punish the majority. The purpose of this book is to place you in the minority, because it is the minority who will reap the rewards!

George Kleinman
2004

Introduction

Do you have what it takes?

A floor broker who is a friend of mine once told me the following story; he swears it's true.

In the 1960s, there was a corn speculator who traded in "the pit" at the Chicago Board of Trade. He was known for **plunging**, or taking big positions.

Early one summer, he put on a large, short corn position for his own account (a position that makes money if prices fall but is costly if prices rise). Soon after, the weather began to heat up in the midwestern United States, where the corn is grown. The corn crop needed rain, and prices began to rise.

Day after day, the sun shone, not a cloud in the sky, and the corn crop was burning up. The market continued to rally against this guy. He knew if this continued, he'd go broke.

Late one trading session, the big trader started a rumor in the corn pit. His rumor was that it was going to rain the next morning at 10:30 A.M.; however, the next morning, the sun shone with not a cloud in the sky, and the market opened higher. Then, almost miraculously, at precisely 10:30 A.M., rain started pouring down the windows that looked onto the grain trading room. (The old grain room was located on the fourth floor of the Chicago Board of Trade Building, which had tall windows you could see from La Salle Street.) Inside in the corn pit, a selling panic developed as the traders scrambled to sell out their corn futures. The market went down the limit! The speculator covered his entire short position on this break and was saved from bankruptcy.

How did the trader know it would rain at 10:30 that morning? It seems he was owed a favor from his drinking buddy, the Chief of the Chicago Fire Department. The Chief brought out the hook and ladders and decided it was a good day to wash those tall windows that looked out on La Salle Street!

So you're thinking of trading, but you don't know the chief?

Let's assume you've just finished reading a private newsletter hot off the presses, a firsthand report of how the witch's tail disease is devastating the cocoa crop in the Ivory Coast. Cocoa sounds like a moneymaker, but you have no way of knowing for sure how true all of this is. You do like chocolate, but you didn't know it all starts with a bean called the cocoa bean. (You thought it came out of a can.) Hey, you don't even know where the Ivory Coast is, and you're thinking of trading this bean against the likes of Hershey and Nestlé and whoever else really does know what's going on. Why would you do something like this? To make money, of course!

You do know one thing, however; the cocoa market is moving up, and it's moving fast. Although you aren't exactly losing money by doing nothing, it's starting to feel that way. Do you have the guts to act? Do you have the money? Is now the time?

You assume the **shorts** (those betting on lower cocoa prices) are beginning to experience financial pain. The **longs** (those betting on higher cocoa prices) are experiencing the opposite emotions—elation and the satisfaction that comes from being right. The accounts of the longs are growing bigger. Money from nothing. The shorts are watching their money evaporate.

Let's stop this commentary for a moment, because it's time for your first lesson: *Trading is a human game.*

As a result, emotions affect price as much, perhaps more, than the news. You will learn that price movements themselves are a fundamental and, in turn, they affect future price movements. It's all a function of who is being hurt and who is benefiting. It's a function of which side of the market is being "sponsored" by the "strong hands." Shorts and longs act differently based on price movements, which affect their emotions as much as their pocketbooks.

Your job as a trader is to identify what happens next. To do that, I want you to start thinking about how others feel, because feelings affect actions. People who are generally right tend to do certain things (on balance). People who are generally wrong tend to act differently. The majority acts a certain way, but be warned, the majority is usually wrong at major turning points (although it can be right at times).

So, back to our scenario. Find out whether the majority is now long or short cocoa. The shorts are in pain, the longs are not; but then again, this can change just as fast as the market's tone changes.

Here's lesson number two: On balance, when talking about futures trading, the uninformed majority will not win.

Because the profitable minority acts in a completely different manner, you must learn what makes these people tick and how to act like them. One fact is certain, and this is that people make markets, and generally people tend to act the way they did in the past. With certain stimuli, they could act opposite of how they generally act, but you are playing the odds here. You need to identify what manner of move the market is in now. Is it a "normal" move in which the market acts in a normal way, or is it extraordinary? (At times, the market acts in an extraordinary manner, and these can be the best times to play.) If you, as a trader, are able to accurately predict what the next pattern will be, your rewards will be substantial.

In this book, I present various methods designed to identify profitable market patterns. No method is foolproof, so the best I can do is try to put the odds in your favor. My goal is to teach you to approach commodity futures and options trading like a business. This is not a casino. In a casino, risk is artificially manufactured for risk's sake, and the odds are engineered in favor of the house. In the commodity futures and options markets, you are dealing with natural risks associated with the production and consumption of the materials that make life possible and worthwhile—food, metals, financials, and energy products. You cannot bend these risks to your will, but you do have tools to manage them. Unlike a casino, I believe you can move the odds to your side of the table. To do this, you must be disciplined.

You will need patience, and you will need guts. I cannot force these qualities upon you, but I can describe how the successful trader acts. It will then be up to you to act the right way. To profit in the commodity futures and options, you will need a *systematic* approach, a well-thought-out strategy. I will present you with some good ideas, but it's up to you to implement them systematically. After all, a strategy is just a consistent approach to trading.

Do you have what it takes?

So you've decided to risk some of your hard-earned cash, go for the big bucks, and trade commodities. This is a **zero sum game**, meaning that for every dollar someone makes, someone else loses it. Some of the money goes to your commodity broker in the form of commissions, and a small amount goes to the Exchanges for their fee. Then, if you are lucky or skillful enough to win, you owe the taxman some of your profits. When you lose on any particular trade, most of your loss is transferred electronically to someone else's account (and you still pay that commission). You will never see this person on the other side of your trade, but he (or she, or it if a corporation) is out there somewhere.

You will be pitted against some of the best financial minds in the world. Professionals on the Exchange floor, professional traders who are Exchange members off the floor, CTAs (Commodity Trading Advisors) and CPOs (Commodity Pool Operators) hedge fund managers, commercial firms that use and other commercial firms that produce commodities. Then there are those other individuals with more experience than you have. Can you hope to compete? The answer is, emphatically, yes! But I didn't say it would be easy, did I? You will need to develop a sensible trading plan and a feel for the markets. This book will help you. You must develop certain human qualities too, which nobody can give to you.

More than 50 years ago, the legendary speculator W.D. Gann discussed the four qualities essential for trading success. His observations are just as valid today, and trust me, you must have these (if you don't, then develop them) if you ever hope to compete and win.

Patience

According to Gann, patience is the number one essential quality for trading success. A good trader possesses the patience to wait for the right opportunity. He will not be over-anxious, because over-anxiousness consumes capital, and over time it will tap you out. When you are fortunate enough to catch a good trade, you need the patience to hold it when it starts to move your way. Perhaps the primary failing of the amateur is to close out a profitable position too soon. In other words, patience is required for both opening and closing a position. Hope and fear need to be eliminated. If you are in a profitable position, instead of fearing the profit will turn into a loss, hope it becomes more profitable. You have a cushion to work with in this case. When you are in a losing position, instead of hoping it will turn around, fear it will get worse. If you see no definitive change in trend, use your essential quality of patience and just wait.

Knowledge

There is no on-the-job training program here. The stakes are too high, and the competition too intense. You need a well-thought-out and thoroughly researched trading plan before you begin, and you need to do your homework.

Your plan should always have a mechanism to cut the losses on the bad trades and to maximize profits aggressively on the good ones. You must be organized and remain focused at all times. If the plan is a good one, you need the consistency to stick with it during down periods.

My personal goal is to make money daily, but when that is not possible, I try not to lose too much. It is a constant trial to maintain the vigilance necessary so as not to let good judgment lapse. If you are a novice, it makes sense to "paper trade" before you trade for real. If you are trading currently, you should keep a logbook. Log your triumphs and your failures. You want to avoid making the same mistakes again, but I must warn you, all traders repeat this same mistake. At the very least, learn not to make the mistake so often. By keeping a record of what you do right and what you do wrong, you can identify areas of weakness and areas of strength. If you are not totally prepared on any given day, don't trade. You can't "wing it" in this business, because the competition will eat you up. Over time, you will develop what I call a "trader's sense." You will know when a trade doesn't feel right, and when this happens, the prudent thing to do is step aside. You cannot ignore the danger signals, and when it's time to act, you must do so without hesitation.

To recap, you must have a game plan and stick to it, but the paradox here is that you also need to be flexible. At times, it is best to do nothing, and you need to fight the urge to play for every pot. And, as I said before, stay focused. At times, I've been distracted by day trades and missed the big moves, because I missed the big picture. By the time I finally saw the light, it was too late.

The legendary trader of the 1920s, Jesse Livermore, once shared one of his secrets, which is that he attempts to buy as close to the danger point as he can and then he places his stop loss. In this way, his risk per trade is low. This makes sense, but how do you know where that danger point is? In normal markets, you need to take normal profits, but on those rare occasions when you have the chance to make, a windfall, you must go for it. But how can you tell when a market is normal as opposed to extraordinary? It takes experience, and it takes knowledge, an essential quality for success. Knowledge takes study and hard work. This book is a good first step.

Guts

Call it nerve, courage, bravado, or heart; I call it guts, and this one quality is as essential as patience and knowledge. Some people have too much guts, and this isn't good because they are too hopeful and tend to overtrade. Some lack the guts to act (either to enter a position when the time is right or to cut a loss when it isn't). This is a catastrophic fault and must be overcome. You need guts to pyramid positions, which is not easy, but it's where the big money is made.

In this book, I am going to teach you to trade without hope, without fear, and with just the right amount of guts. I will instruct you to enter positions on what I believe is the proper basis, and then urge you to remember at all times that you could be wrong. You will need a defensive plan to cut the losses when you are wrong. I've been a student in the School of Hard Knocks too many times, but I've never lost my guts. At times, I know I've had too much and have overtraded, but then there are some people I know who have an inability to pull the trigger, and this is just as deadly. Looking back only brings regrets, so you need to face the future with optimism, knowledge, patience, and guts.

Health and rest

This is the fourth essential quality for trading success. If you don't feel right, you won't trade right, and this is the time to be on the sidelines. When you stick with something too long, your judgment becomes warped. Traders who are continually in the market without a rest get too caught up in the day-to-day fluctuations and eventually get tapped out. At least twice a year, it makes sense to close out all your trades, get entirely out of the market, and go on a vacation. When you return, recharged, your trading will improve.

So there you have it: Gann's four essential human qualities required for success. You need them. Very soon this book delves into specifics that I believe will help you travel this rocky road to trading success. Some of the most important lessons I've learned over the past 25 years are in the pages to come, and they should help you make money. However, if you don't have patience, guts, knowledge, and good health, all the rules in the world are just so many words.

So, with that said, let's get into the meat of the matter. I'm not trying to be all things to all people, but I do believe this book will appeal to the novice and veteran trader alike. We begin at the beginning. If you are new to this game, you need to know how the game is played, what the rules are, and how the money works. I will strive to be as complete as possible, and if I do this right, at times it might actually appear simple. If it were that simple, however, most people wouldn't lose, and the nature of the futures markets is to punish the majority. Let's begin our journey to join the minority, because it is the minority who reap the rewards!

Basic training: a futures primer

Picking up the phone and instructing your broker to buy or sell is relatively simple. Performing a few mouse clicks and transmitting your order to a handheld device in the pit or to a totally electronic marketplace isn't all that hard either. It's really not all that difficult to understand how the money works. What is difficult, however, is extracting profits from the markets (something we'll tackle later in this book), but you have to start somewhere. This chapter is for those of you who need to learn the basics. So here we begin, as good a place to start as any.

Commodities are not only essential to life, but they are absolutely necessary for quality of life. Every person eats. Billions of dollars of agricultural products are traded daily on the world's commodity exchanges—everything from soybeans to rice, corn, wheat, beef, pork, cocoa, coffee, sugar, and orange juice. Food is where the commodity exchanges began.

In the middle of the nineteenth century in the United States, businessmen started organizing market forums to facilitate the buying and selling of agricultural commodities. Over time, farmers and grain merchants met in central marketplaces to set quality and quantity standards and to establish rules of business. In the course of only a few decades, more than 1,600 Exchanges sprung up at major railheads, inland water ports, and seaports. In the early twentieth century, as communications and transportation became more efficient, centralized warehouses were constructed in major urban centers such as Chicago. Business became less regional, more national; many of the smaller Exchanges disappeared.

In today's global marketplace, approximately 30 major Exchanges remain, with 80% of the world's business conducted on about a dozen of them. Just about every major commodity vital to commerce, and therefore to life, is represented. Billions of dollars worth of energy products—from heating oil to gasoline to natural gas and electricity—are traded every business day. How could we live without industrial metals (copper, aluminum, zinc, lead, palladium, nickel, and tin); precious metals such as gold; or platinum and silver, which are considered both industrial and precious metals? How could we live without wood products or textiles? It would be hard to imagine life without them, and yet few people are aware of just how the prices for these vital components of life are set. Unlike 100 years ago, today the world's futures Exchanges also trade financial products essential to the global economic function. From currencies to interest rate futures to stock market indices, more money changes hands on the world's commodity exchanges every day than on all the world's stock markets combined.

Governments allow commodity exchanges to exist so that producers and users of commodities can *hedge* their price risks. However, without the speculator, the system would not work. Anyone can be a speculator, and contrary to popular belief, I do not believe the odds need be stacked against the individual. In this book, I plan to share with you techniques designed to help you make money trading commodities. Actually, you as an individual have one distinct advantage over the big players, and that's flexibility. You can move quickly, like a cat, something a giant corporation can't do. Many times, several of the big commercial operators that utilize the Exchange for hedging literally hand you your profits on a silver platter—they're there for a different reason. So, let's start by looking at how the futures contract works and the various participants in the marketplace. We'll also look at what they are attempting to accomplish and how they interact with each other.

Futures markets and the futures contract

Futures markets, in their most basic form, are markets in which commodities (or financial products) to be delivered or purchased at some time in the future are bought and sold.

The **futures contract** is the basic unit of exchange in the futures markets. Each contract is for a set quantity of some commodity or financial asset and can be traded only in multiples of that amount. The futures contract is a legally binding agreement that provides for the delivery of various commodities or financial entities at a specific time period in the future. (Prior to the time I was in this business, I envisioned the parties sitting at a table and actually signing paper contracts. It's nothing like that.)

When you buy or sell a futures contract, you don't actually sign a contract drawn up by a lawyer. Instead, you're entering into a contractual obligation that can be met in only one of two ways. The first method is by making or taking delivery of the actual commodity. This is by far the exception, not the rule. Less than 2% of all futures contracts are concluded with an actual delivery. The other way to meet this obligation, which is the method you most likely will be using, is offset. Very simply, **offset** is making the opposite (or offsetting) sale or purchase of the same number of contracts bought or sold sometime prior to the expiration date of the contract. Because futures contracts are standardized, this is accomplished easily.

Every contract on a particular Exchange for a specific commodity is identical except for price. The specifications are different for each commodity, but the contract in each market is the same. In other words, every soybean contract traded on the Chicago Board of Trade is for 5,000 bushels. Every gold contract traded on the New

York Mercantile is for 100 troy ounces. Each contract listed on an Exchange calls for a specific grade and quality. For example, the silver contract is for 5,000 troy ounces of 99.99% pure silver in ingot form. The rules state that the seller cannot deliver 99.95% pure. Therefore, the buyers and sellers know exactly what they are trading. Every contract is completely interchangeable. The only negotiable feature of a futures contract is price.

The size of the contract determines its value. To calculate how much money you could make or lose on a particular price movement of a specific commodity, you need to know the following:

- Contract size

- How the price is quoted

- Minimum price fluctuation

- Value of the minimum price fluctuation

The contract size is standardized. The minimum unit tradable is one contract. For example, a New York coffee contract is for 37,500 pounds, a Chicago corn contract is for 5,000 bushels, and a British Pound contract calls for delivery of 62,500 Pounds Sterling. The contract size determines the value of a move in price.

You also need to know how prices are quoted. For example, grains are quoted in dollars and cents per bushel: $2.50 per bushel for corn, $5.50 per bushel for wheat, and so on. Copper is quoted in cents per pound in New York, and dollars per metric ton in London. Cattle and hogs are quoted in cents per pound, whereas gold is quoted in dollars and cents per troy ounce. Currencies are quoted in the United States in cents per unit of currency. As you begin trading, you will quickly become familiar with how this works. Your commodity broker can fill you in on how prices are quoted on any particular market you decide to trade.

The minimum price fluctuation, also known as a "tick," is a function of how prices are quoted and is set by the Exchange.

For example, prices of corn are quoted in dollars and cents per bushel, but the minimum price fluctuation corn can move is 1/4¢ per bushel. So if the price of corn is $3.00/bushel, the next price tick can either be $3.00 1/4 (if up) or $2.99 and 3/4 (if down). Prices can trade more than a tick at a time, so in a fast market, the price could jump from $3.00 to $3.00 1/2, but it could not jump from $3.00 1/2 to $3.00 and 5/8 because the minimum price fluctuation for corn is a quarter penny. Therefore, the next minimum price tick for corn from $3.00 1/2 up would be $3.00 3/4, or down would be $3.00 1/4. The minimum price fluctuation for a gold contract is 10¢/ounce, so if gold is trading for $425.50 per ounce, the minimum it can move in price would be $425.60 if up, or $425.40 if down. Once again, in a fast market, or if the bids and offers are wide, it might jump from $425.50 to $426, but in liquid and quiet markets, many times the market moves from one minimum tick fluctuation to the next.

The value of a minimum fluctuation is the dollars and cents equivalent of the minimum price fluctuation multiplied by the contract size of the commodity.

eg **For example, the size of a copper contract traded in New York is 25,000 pounds. The minimum price fluctuation of a copper contract is 5/100 of one cent per pound (or 1/20 of one cent). By multiplying the minimum price fluctuation by the size of the contract, you obtain the value of the minimum price fluctuation, which in this case is $12.50 (1/20¢ per pound times 25,000 pounds). In the case of the grains and soybeans, a minimum price fluctuation is 1/4¢ and a contract is for 5,000 bushels, so the value of a minimum fluctuation is also $12.50 (1/4¢ per bushel times 5,000 bushels).**

Except for grains, minimum fluctuations are generally quoted in points.

eg **For example, sugar prices are quoted in cents and hundredths of a cent per pound. The minimum fluctuation is 1/100 of one cent, or one point. If the price is quoted at 15 1/2 cents per pound, your broker would say it is trading at 1550, and if it moves up by a quarter of a cent per pound, this would be a move of 25 points, to 1575.**

In some cases, the value of a minimum move may be more than a point. In the copper example, the minimum move is 1/20¢ per pound. A penny move is 100 points (for example, if copper prices rise from $1 per pound to $1.02 per pound, the market has moved up 200 points), but because the minimum fluctuation is for 1/20¢, a minimum move is 5 points, or $12.50 per contract. A move of 1¢ is worth $250, which is 100 points. You must understand what the value of a move is for the commodity you are trading. For example, if you are trading soybeans, you should know that a move of 1¢ is worth $50 per contract (either up or down), and if you buy three contracts and the market closes up 10¢ that day, you would make $1,500, or $500 per contract. If the market closes down 10¢, you would lose the same amount. Although this might seem confusing at first, you'll quickly understand the value of a minimum fluctuation and the value of a point at the time you write that check for your first margin call. That reminds me of an amusing true story told to me by my favorite copper broker.

On the floor of the COMEX (the world's largest metals Exchange), where copper is traded, the pit brokers always talk in terms of points instead of dollar values. You might hear a trader saying, "I made 300 points today," or "I lost 150 points on that trade." A number of years ago, there was a big commission house broker (a floor broker who makes his living filling buy and sell orders from customers who call in from off the floor) who was pressured by his wife to hire his brother-in-law. The brother-in-law wasn't all that bright, but the broker felt his brother-in-law couldn't do that much damage if he were on the phone as a clerk. After all, the clerks just take the buy and sell orders over the phone and run them into the pit to be filled.

Well, everything went reasonably well for a few weeks, and then the first inevitable error occurred. Apparently, the brother-in-law took an order to buy five contracts, and he wrote "sell" on the order ticket. By the time the error was discovered, it had resulted in a loss of 370 points ($925) that the commission house broker had to make good. After the market closed, the broker took the brother-in-law aside and carefully spoke to him.

The broker said, "Look, mistakes happen and, fortunately, this error was for only 370 points. It could have been much worse, but you have to be more careful. We cannot afford to have any more errors like this one."

The brother-in-law replied, "What are you getting so hot under the collar for? Sure I made a mistake, but it's only points."

To this day, whenever anyone makes an error in the copper pit, the guys on the floor say, "Hey, what's your problem? It's only points!"

Some contracts have associated daily price limits, which measure the maximum amount that the market can move above or below the previous day's close in a single trading session. Each Exchange determines whether a particular commodity has a daily trading limit and for how much. The theory behind the **limit-move rule** is to allow markets to cool down during particularly dramatic, volatile, or violent price moves. For example, the rules for the soybean contract state that the market can move up or down 50¢ per bushel from the previous close if it did not close "limit" the previous day. (Limit moves result in expanded limits). So if the market closes at $8.10 per bushel on Tuesday, then on Wednesday it can trade as high as $8.60 or as low as $7.60. Contrary to popular belief, the market can trade at the limit price; it just cannot trade beyond it. At times of dramatic news or price movements, a market can move to the limit and "lock." A **lock-limit move** means that there is an overabundance of buyers (for "lock limit up") versus sellers at the limit-up price, or that there is an overabundance of sellers (for "lock limit down") at the limit-down price.

eg **For example, suppose that in a drought market, the weather services are forecasting rain one weekend, thereby causing the market to trade lower on a Friday. However, the rain never materializes, and on Monday morning, the forecast is back to drought with record-high temperatures predicted for the week. Conceivably, the market could open "up the limit" as shorts scramble to buy back contracts previously sold, and buyers would be willing to "pay up" for what appears to be a dwindling future supply of soybeans. Let's say the market closed on Friday at $7.50 and that it opened at $8 on Monday. Now it could trade at that price, or it could trade even lower that day. But suppose 20 million bushels are wanted to buy at the limit-up price of $8, with only 10 million bushels to sell. The first 10 million would trade at $8, with the second 10 million bushels in the "pool" wanting and waiting to buy. If no additional sell orders surface, the market would remain limit up that day, with unsatisfied buying** ▶

demand at the $8 level. However, there is nothing to say the market has to open higher on Tuesday (it could unexpectedly rain Monday evening), but all other factors remaining equal, this unsatisfied buying interest would most likely "gap the market" higher on Tuesday morning.

In fact, some markets have what are called **variable limits**, which is where the limits are raised if a market closes limit up or limit down during a trading session. Cattle is one of the markets with variable limits. If one or more contract months close at the 3¢ (300-point) limit for two successive days, the limit is raised to 5¢ on the next business day. (You can consult the Web sites of the various Exchanges for the daily price-limit rules for each market.) Limit moves are rare, but they do occur during shocks to a market. Pork bellies, for example, are notorious for moving multiple limit days after an unexpectedly bullish or bearish "Hogs and Pigs Report."

Here's a true story of how gutsy some of the floor traders at the Board can be at times.

Bill, who works our soybean orders, told me about one summer day when the soybean market was down the limit. It wasn't just down the limit; it was "locked down the limit," with five million bushels offered to sell down the limit and no buyers in sight. It was very quiet. Then, out of nowhere, one large "local" wanders into the pit and utters, "Take 'em." "How many?" they ask. "*All* of 'em!'"

The other brokers in the pit literally fell over themselves selling the entire five million to this guy. What could he be thinking? But then, as soon as the five million were bought, and the quote machines around the world tuned into soybeans showed this, the telephones around the pit started to ring. Off the floor, traders around the world assumed with such a big buyer at limit down that something was up, and they started to buy, too. The market immediately started to rally. When it moved 5¢ per bushel off the limit-down price, the large local stepped back in and sold his five million bushels. It was a quick $250,000 profit, and it took only 20 seconds!

Trading hours are set for each individual market by the Exchange. Cattle opens at 9:00 A.M. Chicago time on the Chicago Mercantile and closes at 1:00 P.M. sharp. (If your order to sell reaches the cattle pit at 1:01 P.M., you're out of luck, at least for that trading session.) As more and more markets become completely electronic, trading hours won't matter as much as they used to. Many markets, particularly the financials, trade on virtually a 24-hour basis. Most of the major markets have after-hours trading, but some don't. If you miss the Live Cattle close at 1:00 P.M. Chicago time, for example, you have no choice but to wait until the next trading day. If you miss coffee, however, you can trade it in London, but there is an eight-hour period where coffee futures are not traded anywhere in the world. If you miss corn, on the other hand, which closes at 1:15 P.M. central standard time (CST), you can trade it electronically at night from 5:30 P.M. until 4:00 A.M. the following morning.

To review thus far, before you trade in any market, you need to know, at minimum, the Exchange the market is traded on, the trading hours, the contract size, and the delivery months traded. You need to know how prices are quoted, so that you can put them in the right priced order, the minimum fluctuation, the dollar value of the minimum fluctuation, and if there are any daily trading limits. You also need to know the types of orders accepted at that particular marketplace. Finally, you want to know what the margin requirement is for the market you are trading, and what commission your broker will be charging. These topics are covered in the following sections.

It is as easy to sell short as to buy long

If you're an experienced trader, feel free to skip this section. For the rest of you, the concept of selling short is an important one. After you begin to trade, selling short will become second nature, but experience has shown that many novices initially have trouble with the concept.

Everyone knows that if you buy something at one price and sell it for a higher price, you make money. If you sell it at a lower price than what you paid for it, you lose money. When you trade futures, you can buy or sell in whatever order you like. You can buy and then sell, or sell and then buy. Whichever you choose, the idea is that the selling price should be higher than the buying price. One question I've often heard is "How can you sell what you don't own?" Well, here's how: A buyer of a futures contract is obligated to take delivery of a particular commodity or—and this is what happens most of the time—sell back the contract prior to the delivery date. The process of selling back, which can be done anytime during normal market hours (assuming the market is not "locked limit down" in those markets with limits, which is a rare occurrence), in effect, wipes the slate clean. People seem to have no trouble understanding that if you buy 200 shares of General Electric stock that you can sell back 200 shares of General Electric stock at the stock exchange. Again, if you buy at one price and sell at a higher price, you make money, and vice versa.

eg **For example, if you buy soybeans at $8 per bushel and sell them at $8.20 per bushel, your profit is 20¢ per bushel, which is worth $1,000 for a soybean contract. (A penny move is a profit or loss of $50.) If you buy a contract of beans at $8 and sell them back at $7.80, you lose 20¢, or $1,000 per contract. If you buy 10 contracts of July soybeans, you could cancel your obligation to take delivery by selling back 10 contracts of July soybeans. You would then be out of the market, and the difference between the price at which you bought and sold would determine your profit or loss on the trade.**

When trading futures, because you are trading for future delivery, it is just as easy to sell first and then buy back later. Selling first is referred to as **shorting** or **selling short**. To offset your obligation to deliver, all you need to do is to buy back your contract(s) prior to the expiration of the contract(s). This process of buying back is known as **covering**. You "covered your short position" to wipe the slate clean. The purpose of shorting is to profit from a fall in prices. If you believe the price of a particular commodity is going down, due to an oversupply or poor demand, you want to go short. The objective is to cover at a lower price than you sold.

eg **In the soybean example, if you believe prices at $8 are too high and are heading for a fall, you could go short at $8. If prices fall to $7.80, you might want to cover your position and take the 20¢ profit. A short sale at $8, covered at $7.80, is a profit of 20¢, or $1,000 per contract. Of course, if prices rise and you have to cover at $8.20, you would have a loss on the short sale of 20¢ per contract, or $1,000. "Sell high, buy back low" can be just as profitable as "buy low, sell high."**

Kevin 'Mac,' who leased my COMEX seat, once told me a humorous (and true) story: Kevin traded in the copper pit, as did Al, a big commission house broker. Al was big in more ways than one, and his weight seemed to roller coaster depending on which diet he was on at the time. Diet or not, Al was a big guy, and this was an advantage that would get him noticed in the pit. Al was also a colorful guy who liked to play the horses, but at heart he was a shy man. Still, you wouldn't know it when you saw him in the pit because he moved frenetically and possessed a gruff voice. He "filled paper" for a living, meaning he executed customer orders in the pit.

This happened in the copper market of 1987–1988, a particularly wild time. The day of the stock market crash, the market spiked downward 10¢ per pound, a huge single-day move, to less than 80¢ per pound. (Interestingly, just a few months later, it was more than $1.40 per pound). The market was wild and noisy that day, and Al was summoned to the phone to take a large buy order from a New York client. Al was on one of his diets, and that day he had forgotten his belt. He rushed into the pit, raised his arms to bid for the copper, and his pants fell to his ankles. It was a wild day, but for a few seconds, no one could believe their eyes. Everyone stopped trading to stare at Al's boxer shorts. Al turned as red as the hearts on his boxers. (He had gotten them for Valentine's Day.) Then Kevin broke the silence. As Kevin tells it, he didn't stop to think. It just came out.) Kevin yelled, "Look at Al! He's covering his shorts!"

Now there's a story only commodity traders find funny.

Margin and leverage

One of the big attractions—and what makes futures exciting—is leverage. **Leverage** is the ability to buy or sell $100,000 of a commodity with only a $5,000 security deposit so that small price changes can result in huge profits or losses. Leverage gives you the ability to either make a killing or get killed. You need to understand how this important concept works before you trade, and a thorough understanding of the powers and pitfalls of leverage is imperative to sound money management principals, which we'll discuss later in the book.

Each contract bought or sold on a futures Exchange must be backed by a good-faith deposit called **margin**. This is not like buying on margin in the stock market. When a stock market investor buys on margin, he is, in effect, borrowing half of the purchase price of the stock from his broker. (Stock exchange rules prohibit borrowing more than 50%.) The investor is charged interest on the balance. This provides a degree of leverage, but nothing like commodities.

To see how powerful leverage can be, let's compare a futures purchase with a stock purchase for cash. If a stock investor buys 200 shares of a stock trading at $10, his purchase cost is $2,000. If the stock moves up by 10% to $11 per share, the investor has made $200 on his $2,000 investment, or 10%. Margin in commodity trading is like a good-faith deposit. It is a small percentage, generally in the neighborhood of 2 to 10%, of the value of the underlying commodity represented by the contract. Margin deposits are set by the Exchange, and they can change with price movements and market volatility. Because you are trading for future delivery and not borrowing anything, no interest is charged on the balance. Margin is not a partial payment or a down payment, and it's not even considered a cost. If you make money on the trade, upon liquidation, your total margin deposit is returned, along with your profits. Commissions are deducted, and they are a cost. Margin is money deposited in your brokerage account that serves to guarantee the performance of your side of the contract. Margin is a form of "earnest money" deposited by both the longs and the shorts, and it serves to ensure the integrity of every futures transaction. In effect, margin ensures that you are paid when you win, and that whoever is on the other side of your transaction is paid if you don't.

When you enter a position, you have deposited (or will deposit) the margin money in your account, but your brokerage house is required to post the margin with a central Exchange arm called the **clearinghouse**. The clearinghouse is a nonprofit entity that, in effect, manages the daily process of debiting the accounts of the losers and redistributing the money to the accounts of the winners.

 Now back to the leverage example. The margin requirement for a 5,000-ounce silver contract has been running $2,000 on average in recent years. At $6 per ounce, a contract is worth $30,000 ($6 per ounce times 5,000 ounces). If the price of silver rises by 10% to $6.60, the same contract is worth $33,000. However, suppose the same investor puts up his $2,000 and instead buys a silver contract. If the price of silver rises by 10%, or 60¢, he makes $3,000 on his contract. This is 150% on margin, not 10%. It's powerful leverage, but also a double-edged sword. If prices fall by 10%, the investor's $2,000 is now worth a *negative* $1,000. When you trade futures, you are responsible for the total value of a move of any position you hold. In most cases, if a market moves against you, you have time to liquidate before the account shows a deficit; however, this is not always the case. If you don't use adequate risk-control measures, or if a market moves very quickly against you, your account could go into a deficit situation, and *you are obligated by contract to pay the difference.*

There are two types of margin: initial margin and maintenance margin.

Initial margin is the amount that must be in the account before you place a trade. If you do not have enough initial margin in your account, you incur a *margin call.* Most brokerage firms require the initial margin to be in the account before they allow a trade to be placed. Some might issue credit for good customers, but they generally require that the margin call be met within one to three business days. Any firm has the right to require same-day deposit by bank wire transfer at any time and might request this during volatile markets. **Maintenance margin** is the amount that must be maintained in your account as long as the position is active. If the equity balance in your account should fall below the maintenance margin level, because of adverse market movements, you incur a margin call as well. After the margin call is issued, you are required to meet the call or liquidate the position. If you fail to meet a margin call in a timely manner, the broker has the right (and will use it) to liquidate the position for you automatically. This is done to protect the broker from additional adverse movements in the market, because he is responsible for meeting your margin call, even if you're a deadbeat and don't.

If you fail to meet a margin call, and the position is ultimately liquidated at a loss that leaves a deficit in the account, the broker is immediately responsible for the deficit, but you are legally responsible. In other words, initial margin might not be the extent of your liability. You are responsible for all losses resulting from your trading activities. If the market moves against you five, six, or seven days and you do not get out, if the market moves limit against you and eats up your margin, you are still responsible for any and all losses. Later in the book you'll learn ways to manage the risk, but at this point be aware that whenever you trade futures, your risk is not limited to the initial margin or your account balance. It can go further than that. (Options work differently; they will be discussed later in the book.)

eg **Here's a typical example. Assume silver is trading at $6 per ounce, and the initial margin requirement is $2,000. A silver contract has a size of 5,000 ounces, so at $6 per ounce, the total value of the contract is $30,000. However, all that is required to purchase or sell a contract is $2,000 (in this example, about 6%). A rule of thumb for maintenance margin is that it will be at the 75% level of initial. If the initial is $2,000, for example, maintenance might be $1,500. If you have an account value of $20,000 with no other positions on, you *could* buy 10 contracts without a margin call; however, this is not recommended because you would be overtrading, or too highly leveraged, and a relatively minor price movement would move you into margin call territory.**

For illustrative purposes only, let's assume your account balance is at $20,000 and that you buy 10 silver contracts. Your maintenance level is at $15,000. If the market starts to move your way immediately, you're OK. Because a silver contract is for 5,000 ounces, a 1¢ move results in a profit or loss per contract of $50. In this example, the 10 contracts give you a profit or loss of $500 per penny move. Suppose you buy the 10 contracts at $6, and the market closes that same day at $6.05. Your account balance is $22,500 on the close of business that day. You have an *unrealized* profit of $2,500. The profit is unrealized because the

position is still open. The increase in equity value of $2,500 is the result of the 5¢ move in your favor (5¢ times $50 per contract times 10 contracts). Suppose the next day, the price falls 10¢ to close at $5.95. Your account value decreases by $5,000 to $17,500. You would *not* have a margin call, because your value still would be above the maintenance level. If on the next day prices rose 5¢ to $6, your equity value would move back to $20,000.

Basically, the futures is the process of generating a credit or debit daily against your initial position until you close it out. If you make money on any particular day, the unrealized credit balance is credited immediately to your account and debited from the people on the other side of the transaction. (You will never know who they are because it's completely anonymous, but they are out there.) If the market closes against your position on any particular day, the loss would be immediately debited from your account.

Now, let's get back to the example. On the fourth day, the market drops 25¢ to close at $5.75. Your account is debited $12,500 (25¢ times $50 per contract times 10 contracts). Your equity balance is now down to $7,500, which is below the maintenance margin level, so it's margin call time. You now get a communication from your broker, who informs you about your $12,500 margin call. You see, after your equity level falls below the maintenance margin level, you are required to bring your balance up to the initial margin level. You now have two choices: You can either liquidate the position in whole or in part, enough to move your equity back above the initial margin level, or you can meet the call. In this case, you could sell out seven contracts, realize your loss on those seven, hold onto the three, get your initial margin down to $6,000, and hope the market recovers. If you feel strongly about the position, you could opt to meet the call. Let's say you send in a check, or if required, wire transfer the $12,500 to your account. Your account balance now shows $20,000, so you are "off call." You have deposited $32,500 into your account at this point, but if you close out the position at the current price of $5.75, you have a balance remaining of $20,000 minus any transaction costs. If your thinking is correct, and the silver market recovers to $6, your account balance would grow back to $32,500. You now have the right to request that the $12,500 (the amount over the initial margin) be sent back to you. If the market falls again, however, you could certainly be issued another margin call.

It is important to leave a cash cushion in the account so that you have the ability to ride out normal market fluctuations without receiving a margin call. My general rule of thumb is to *never margin yourself higher than 50%.* In other words, if your account value is $25,000, I would not put on positions that, at most, would require more than $12,500 in initial margin.

Each market has its own margin requirement. This requirement is based on the volatility of the particular market and also the volatility of the markets as a whole. Greater volatility equals greater risk and higher requirements. The S&P 500 index and the NASDAQ are two of the more volatile contracts, and it is not uncommon to have a daily range of $5,000 per contract or more in value. The margin requirement for the S&P can be in a normal period from $7,000 per contract on up. I have seen the NASDAQ in the high-priced days with $20,000 range days and $30,000 margin for a single contract. On the other hand, corn is traditionally less volatile, and in a normal market, it might have a price range of $250 per contract. The initial margin might be $400 in a quiet market, but it could move up to $1,000 in a volatile environment for corn prices.

Here's another important point on margins: Although the Exchange sets a minimum margin requirement, individual brokerage houses have the right to charge higher than "Exchange minimum." This protects the brokerage house from overtraders who tend to **plunge** (trade in excess of prudent speculation, even in excess of their ability to pay), which would require the broker to make good on his commitment to the clearinghouse.

The entire point of this margining system is that all positions are "marked to the market" by the clearinghouse daily and revalued to the current market price. As such, profits and losses are paid daily.

One last point about margins: The Exchange allows initial margins to be posted either in cash or (in the United States) U.S. government obligations of less than 10 years to maturity. If an investor wishes to post T-Bills for margin, he can do so; most commodity brokers will pass the interest back to the customer. So, in effect, the initial margin earns interest.

Delivery months

Every futures contract has standardized months that are authorized by the Exchange for trading. For example, wheat is traded for delivery in March, May, July, September, and December. If you buy a March contract, you need to sell a March contract to offset your position and meet your contractual obligation. If you buy a March wheat contract, and you sell a May wheat contract, you have offset nothing. You are still "long" March and now "short" May. Some commodities are traded in every month, but by convention, some contract months are traded more actively than others. For example, gold trades in every month of the year, but the active months are February, April, June, August, October, and December. On the London Metal Exchange, or LME (where aluminum, copper, zinc, nickel, lead, and tin are traded), a different system, known as **prompt dates**, is used. The active contract on any particular day is the 3-month. If you buy or sell a new 3-month on say, May 10, you are in the August 10 contract (assuming August 10 does not fall on a weekend or holiday). Then, to offset your position, you need to sell the August 10 contract. You can do that prior to August 10, but your buy or sell price is based on an interpolation of the cash (or spot contract) to 3-month differential on the day you liquidate. The margining procedure is different for the LME as well, so if you are thinking of trading in these markets, talk to your commodity broker about how it works.

Which month should you trade? This is a general rule of thumb only, but unless you have a specific reason for trading a specific month, trade the active month—for example, if in May you want to be short December corn because this is the first new crop month and, despite tight supplies, you think there's a big crop coming and predict this month will fall faster. The active month is the one with the highest open interest, and your broker can tell you which month this is for any particular commodity at any point in time. This is because the active months have the greatest number of players and, therefore, the most liquidity. Because of this, you can get in and out with a smaller degree of slippage. **Slippage**, in effect, means having your order filled at a price different from that which existed as the last trade.

For example, let's say you want to buy gold and the last quoted price is $401.10, but the best bid is $401.10 and the best offer is $401.30. It is a fast-moving market, and you want in. You buy at the market, and even though the last trade is $401.10, your price fill comes back at $401.30. These 20 points represent $20, and they're likely to go into the pocket of a floor broker. It is legal, and as long as there are no lower offers in the pit, it is the price you pay for the liquidity the floor brokers provide.

You'll learn more about this later in the book, but the point is, for minimum slippage, it is best to trade in high-volume, active markets. I've also found a good commodity broker, who uses the better floor brokers in the pit-traded commodities (there are good and bad floor brokers) who tend to, on average, get you better fills, thereby reducing the costs associated with slippage.

In most cases (and there are exceptions to this rule as well), it doesn't make sense to trade in a delivery month. Therefore, you want to avoid entering positions that are close to delivery, because you'll need to "roll over" into the next contract sooner. The rules are different for each market, but in many cases, a contract enters actual delivery the last day of the month prior to the delivery month. For example, with March wheat, the **first notice day**, or first possible day the shorts can make a delivery, is the last trading day in February. What happens if you fail to sell out and are still in the contract on first notice day? Well, there is a *possibility* you will get actual delivery of the wheat because the shorts are not required to make delivery the first day or the next. A short is required only to make delivery if you have not covered your contract prior to the last trading day. The last trading day for March wheat is in the third week of March, so the delivery period lasts about three weeks. A long can receive delivery, at the discretion of the shorts, on any one of the days in the delivery period. If the cash price is above the futures on first notice day, the shorts may not find it lucrative to deliver and wait. If the cash price is below the futures, odds increase for deliveries. Now, just because deliveries are made on any particular day does not mean you will get delivery on any particular day. Early in the delivery period, the number of open contracts exceeds the deliverable supply. If open interest in the March wheat is, say, 100 million bushels, and the deliverable supply in the elevators licensed for delivery is 20 million bushels, the odds of delivery are high only if you purchased the contract months ago instead of days ago. This is because deliveries are assigned to the oldest date first. The oldest long is first in line for delivery. However, as the delivery period progresses, the odds for receiving a delivery increase as the number of outstanding contracts is liquidated downward and your date becomes "fresher."

So what happens if you do get delivery? Contrary to popular belief, you do not get a load of wheat dumped on your doorstep—or worse yet, a load of hogs.

Instead, you receive a warehouse receipt that shows you now own 5,000 bushels of wheat in, for example, a Toledo elevator. Because you are now in a cash contract (the delivery offsets your futures), you're now required to post the full value of the contract. Your leverage is gone. If your margin deposit was $700 for the futures, you now need to pony up an additional $19,300 if you received delivery at $4 per bushel. If you don't have the money in your account, your broker will have to post this amount on your behalf, and he will charge you interest on the balance. Other fees include an additional commission, insurance, and storage costs. You can pass your delivery receipt on to someone else. Because only the shorts can make delivery (and you are *long* a warehouse receipt), you first need to sell a contract short and then instruct your broker to make your delivery on your short contract. This is the way to sell back your warehouse receipt. In most cases, there is no good reason to be trading in a delivery month unless, of course, you have a good reason. A good reason might be a belief that there is not enough of the commodity available to deliver, which could cause a **short squeeze**, a panic situation for the shorts. However, be aware that this is generally a game for sophisticated traders. Of course, as a short, you have no chance of receiving a delivery (because it is at your discretion as to when to make it), but then your chance of being squeezed increases with each day you are in the contract during the delivery period. If you are in on the last day, and your broker hasn't forced you out, good luck in making the delivery. This is a game for the commercials.

When I was at Merrill Lynch, I remember one of the commodity brokers had a client who refused to liquidate a long sugar position prior to the delivery period. The client thought there was no sugar but, alas, there was. (The sugar contract is written so that you can receive delivery at any one of a hundred ports around the world.) He got his sugar on a barge off Bangkok, and it cost him plenty for Merrill Lynch to find a cash operator and dispose of this **distress merchandise** in the cash market. (The commercials knew he had no use for 112,000 pounds of sugar on a barge.)

One last point: Most financial futures (stock indices and currencies) and even some of the agricultural futures (feeder cattle and lean hogs) are **cash settled**. Any positions still open when the contract expires are closed at the settlement price. The amount paid or received is calculated for everyone who remained in at expiration based on this common price.

Brokers and commissions

Although margin isn't a true cost (you get it back at the end of the trade, plus any profits or minus any losses), commissions are. **Commissions** are your broker's fees for his services, and they range across the board and by broker. The two major types of commission firms are the discounter and full service.

Commissions, while important, should *not* be your only consideration when choosing a broker. Low commissions do not always mean the best service. My firm is a full-service firm, and although our commissions are competitive for full service, they are generally a bit higher than discounters. I'm not trying to say there isn't a place for discount brokers. My firm also offers online trading at reduced rates for self-directed traders. If you are relatively sophisticated, know exactly what you want to do in the marketplace, do not require advice or additional services, and only need order execution (especially in the electronic markets where execution does not vary from broker to broker), then you should certainly consider using a discount or online futures broker. However, you need to evaluate what you're receiving. With some firms, discount commissions equal cheaper service, particularly when you have a problem. All firms use brokers in the open outcry pits to execute trades. Some use company brokers, but most use independents, which are members of the Exchange who fill 'paper,' or public orders.

Not all independents are equally talented. Larger firms with bigger orders tend to attract the bigger (and better) floor brokers because the floor brokers are paid a small fee per contract executed. If a floor broker is a bit louder, more aggressive, or is known to hold a large **deck** of orders, he tends to do a better job than the novice floor broker with a smaller deck. At my firm, we pay floor brokers who do an outstanding job an additional or higher-than-standard fee per contract executed. I do not believe any discount brokers do this. We do this because when a floor broker can be a bit faster, he can at times buy the bid for us or sell the offer and get us a slightly better price fill for our customers, and this means more money in for our customer and can be more important than a low commission. The bottom line? Whichever broker you ultimately choose, you should evaluate how accurate and proficient your price fills are. You also need to see how fast your broker gets back to you with price fills. Additionally, you need to evaluate how much help your broker is providing you with versus how much help you require. A knowledgeable full-service broker who provides you with profitable recommendations is worth many times the commissions charged. Just as important, is your broker helping you to control your risks properly on the bad trades? Is he helping you to avoid the classic mistakes such as overtrading? These are factors you'll need to evaluate. A brokerage relationship is extremely personal, and whom you trade with can mean the difference between profit and loss.

One last thought about commissions. When talking commodity futures, the fee per contract traded is low when compared with many other types of investments. The fee can be one-half of a percentage point of the total contract value. It is a higher percentage when compared to the margin deposit, but it's still small. The other side of the coin is that futures traders are much more active than more traditional investors, and *total* commission costs for an active trader can run up substantially over time.

One last thought about brokers: There are brokers who do both securities (stocks) and commodities business. I'm sure there must be some of these dual types who excel at both, but I've personally never met one. Many of our clients who previously had troubles in commodities seem to have drifted to us from brokers, in many cases from a major wire houses, who were these "'Jacks of all trades." On the other side of the spectrum are those traders who know what they're doing and trade only electronic markets, for example, the S&P "E-minis." Price fills (the quality of order execution) are generally uniform for the electronic markets. However, if you need help, remember that commodity trading is an intense, full-time business, and you should go with a specialist.

The players

The two major classes of participants in the futures and options markets are the hedgers and the speculators.

Hedgers can account for from 20 to 40% of the volume and open interest in the major futures markets and up to half or more in some of the smaller contracts. Hedgers use exchange traded contracts to offset the risk of fluctuating prices when they buy or sell physical supplies of a commodity.

For example, a copper mining company might sell copper futures to lock in a sale price today for its future production. In this way, the company protects its profit margins and revenue stream should future copper prices drop. Should future copper prices rise, the company loses on its futures position; however, the value of its physical metal rises. The copper mine is a producer and is just trying to offset, or *hedge*, its price risk. A hedger can be a buyer or a seller.

A tube manufacturer, which buys copper as a raw material in the production of copper tube used for plumbing, might buy copper futures to lock in its copper cost for future purchase. If the price of copper rises, the manufacturer has a profit on its hedge, which can be used to offset the higher price of physical copper it needs to purchase in the marketplace. If copper prices fall, the manufacturer shows a loss on the futures side of the transaction, but it is able to buy the copper cheaper in the marketplace.

In either case, the copper mine or the tube manufacturer has the ability to hold its contracts into the delivery period. They then have the option to make or take copper delivery through the Exchange at an approved warehouse licensed to do business on the Exchange. This option is as important in theory as in practice because it is what allows physical commodity prices and the Exchange traded contracts to come together in price. If the price of the commodity is too high in relation to the futures price, then those people involved in the usage of a particular commodity buy the low-priced futures contracts and take delivery. Their buying, in effect, pushes futures prices up to meet the physical price. If the price of a futures contract is too high in relation to the actual commodity, then producers of that commodity sell the contract to make delivery, because the higher-priced futures (in relation to the physical) just might be their best sale. Their selling pushes the price of the futures down to the cash price. This entire process is known as **convergence**. This potential process of convergence is what makes the system work; however, in practice only, one to two percent of all commodity contracts end in delivery. Odds are that you, as a speculator, will never get involved in a delivery, and there's no need to. In fact, even the majority of hedgers do not use the markets to actually make or take delivery; they are using the futures as a pricing tool to help stabilize their revenues and their costs.

I have a client, a major manufacturing firm that publishes a biannual catalog with prices they honor during the catalog date. They use copper and zinc in their manufacturing process, and they know what their profit margin is based on today's price of copper and zinc. If they don't hedge and lock in the six-month price of copper today, and the price goes up during the time the catalog is distributed, their entire profit margin could be wiped out. The other side of the coin is that if copper prices fall and their published price remained based on the published higher prices of the raw materials, they could reap a windfall profit. However, they are not in the business of speculation; they are in the manufacturing business. They are more than willing to forego the chance of a windfall to be assured of a profit margin that allows them to keep the plant running and avoid layoffs.

A few times each year, I sit down with them and determine where to buy copper and zinc futures to lock in a price they can live with for the next six months. After they know this price, they can publish their catalog with peace of mind knowing that their profit margin is secure. If the price of copper rises, they will have to pay the higher price in the cash copper market; however, their futures contracts will rise in value as well, and the profits from the futures offset the higher price that must be paid in the physical market. If the price of copper falls, they will show a loss on their futures, but this will be offset by the lower price they will enjoy in the cash market when they buy their copper. In this particular case, this firm has documented an additional cost savings by using futures.

In the past, they used to lock in their price by buying six months worth of copper and zinc and storing the metal in large warehouses. At times, there were so many tons of metal that they had to rent space in warehouses they didn't own. Not only does this involve the rent and the cost of maintaining these warehouses (you have to pay forklift operators to move the goods), but think of the cost of money to finance thousands of tons of heavy metal. Now that they are assured of a future price, they maintain just two to four weeks worth of physical metal on location, and they have eliminated the need for many of these warehouses. The savings in interest alone is in the hundreds of thousands of dollars. This firm has never taken delivery on the futures. Actually, they do not even use the type of copper specified in the futures contract (the pure, or virgin, metal); they use scrap copper. However, because the price of scrap moves in the same direction as the price of the virgin metal, this is a good *cross-hedge* that works well in their risk-management program.

Many of the products hedged on a futures Exchange are actually cross-hedges. For example, jet fuel is similar to heating oil, which often is priced within a few cents different from each other. A major airline might use the heating oil contract to hedge its jet fuel requirements, and a trucking company might use the same contract to hedge its diesel fuel needs.

Basis risk

The definition of **basis** is the difference between the cash, or spot price, and the futures price. Every contract traded has what are termed specifications, which make the contracts fungible and standardized.

 For example, let's look at the contract specifications for heating oil traded on the New York Mercantile Exchange:

Trading Unit
42,000 U.S. gallons (1,000 barrels).

Price Quotation
U.S. dollars and cents per gallon.

Trading Hours (All times are New York Time)
Open outcry trading is conducted from 10:05 A.M. until 2:30 PM.
After-hours futures trading is conducted via the Internet-based trading platform beginning at 3:15 P.M. on Mondays through Thursdays and concluding at 9:30 A.M. the following day. On Sundays, the session begins at 7:00 P.M.

Trading Months
Trading is conducted in 18 consecutive months, commencing with the next calendar month.

Minimum Price Fluctuation
$0.0001 (0.01¢) per gallon ($4.20 per contract).

Maximum Daily Price Fluctuation
$0.25 per gallon ($10,500 per contract) for all months. If any contract is traded, bid, or offered at the limit for five minutes, trading is halted for five minutes. When trading resumes, the limit is expanded by $0.25 per gallon in either direction. If another halt is triggered, the market will continue to be expanded by $0.25 per gallon in either direction after each successive five-minute trading halt. There will be no maximum price fluctuation limits during any one trading session.

Last Trading Day
Trading terminates at the close of business on the last business day of the month preceding the delivery month.

Settlement Type
Physical.

Delivery
F.O.B. seller's facility at New York harbor, ex-shore. All duties, entitlements, taxes, fees, and other charges have point paid. Requirements for seller's shore facility: capability to deliver into barges. Buyer may request delivery by truck, if available, at the seller's facility, and pays a surcharge for truck delivery. Delivery

also may be completed by pipeline, tanker, book transfer, or inter- or intra-facility transfer. Delivery must be made in accordance with applicable federal, state, and local licensing and tax laws.

Delivery Period
Deliveries may be initiated only the day after the fifth business day and must be completed before the last business day of the delivery month.

Grade and Quality Specifications
These generally conform to industry standards for fungible No. 2 heating oil.

Inspection
The buyer may request an inspection for grade and quality or quantity for all deliveries, but shall require a quantity inspection for a barge, tanker, or inter-facility transfer. If the buyer does not request a quantity inspection, the seller may request such inspection. The buyer and seller share the cost of the quantity inspection equally. If the product meets grade and quality specifications, the buyer and seller share the cost of the quality inspection jointly. If the product fails inspection, the cost is borne by the seller.

This contract is **standardized**, in that all contracts created are the same. Contract specifications for all contracts traded on the Exchange are available from your commodity broker or the Exchange Web site. (A listing of the Exchanges is included in the Appendix of this book.) As a speculator, you really are not concerned with the delivery specifications, because you will not be involved in delivery—you'll be out long before it starts. What about the hedger? This particular contract calls for delivery of No. 2 heating oil in New York harbor. Of course, not all heating oil is used in the New York area, and prices in other cities will vary due to differences in transportation costs, storage costs, and local supply-and-demand considerations. A wave of Arctic air sweeping through Europe would no doubt raise the price of heating oil globally, but the price would rise faster in Rotterdam than in New York. These differentials are known as the **basis**. The basis can be stable and predictable at times. For example, if it costs 3¢ per gallon to transport heating oil from New York to Boston, the basis in Boston may predictably run at "plus 3¢ per gallon," all other factors remaining equal. However, if Boston is under a deep freeze and New York isn't, the basis might move up to "plus 4¢."

For the manufacturing firm I work with, the price of scrap copper can, at times, be at the price of the virgin metal (when there is a scrap shortage). Other times, it could be as much as 4 or 5¢ per pound under. The point here is that the hedger has what's called **basis risk**. Basis risk is almost always far less than the price risks involved without a hedge. A hedger who does not hedge is just like a speculator, because he is assuming the natural risks of the marketplace. Once again, I want to point out that most hedgers close out their futures positions long before their futures contracts expire, and the majority long before the delivery period even starts. Then they take or make delivery of the physical commodity they are involved in through normal channels by using their standard suppliers. Knowing that each contract is actually keyed into a specific actual grade of the underlying commodity keeps the value true to life. No matter what the underlying commodity is, each Exchange ultimately guarantees the purchase and sale, as well as the delivery grades for quality and quantity. This is why quotations from the Exchanges for most of the commodities traded are used as pricing standards by companies and individuals around the world.

A hedging example

The primary thrust of this book is geared toward the speculator and how he can use the commodity futures and options markets to make money. However, it is important for all traders to understand how a typical hedge might work to see why these markets exist in the first place. Remember, the perfect hedge is rare; there is just about always some basis risk. However, the concept is the same regardless of whether we are discussing a packing plant hedging its live cattle needs or a bank hedging its interest rate risk. Hedges come in two basic forms: the short and the long.

The short hedge

A short hedge is entered into to protect the value of an inventory. Consider an example using crude oil. An inventory of 1,000 barrels of crude oil constantly changes in value from wellhead to consumer, even before it is processed into gasoline or heating oil. A short hedge is used by the owner of a commodity to essentially lock in the value of the inventory prior to the transferring of title to a buyer. *A decline in prices generates profits in the futures market on the short hedge.* These profits are offset by depreciation in the inventory value.

 Let's say an oil producer is afraid of a price decline. In August, he anticipates he will sell his August production in September. His production is 1,000 barrels a day for 25 days. The cash price in August is $20 per barrel, and October futures are quoted in August at $20.10 per barrel. Here's what the producer might do in the futures market: sell 25 October futures (each contract is for 1,000 barrels, so this represents his August production of 25,000 barrels) at $20.10, which locks in a value of his inventory equivalent to $502,500 ($20.10 per barrel times 25,000 barrels.) Suppose he is correct about the price falling. Along comes September 15, and the price of crude falls in the cash market by $2 per barrel. Because the futures mirror the cash fairly closely, the futures also fall in price. Let's say the futures on that date are quoted at $18 per barrel. The cash price on September 15 is now $18, or $2 less than the $20 price at production time. He sells his product in the cash market to the refinery for a total of $450,000 ($18 times 25,000), or $50,000 less than what he could have received in August. However, the futures have also dropped, and he buys back his October futures contracts on September 15 for $18. (This offsets his position; he does not have to make delivery.) Remember, he sells for the equivalent of $502,000, he buys back at the equivalent of $450,000, and the difference of $52,000 is his gain in the futures. The futures gain of $52,000 offsets the cash market loss of $50,000, and he has, in effect, protected the value of his inventory at the August price.

What if the oil producer is wrong, and the cash price rises? Let's say that instead of falling to $18, the cash price rises to $21 by September 15, and the October futures rise to $21.10. His 25,000 barrels realize him $525,000 in the cash market, or $25,000 more than he could have received in August. However, his futures also rise to a total value of $527,500 ($21.10 times 25,000). When he buys his contracts back, he realizes a futures loss of $25,500 ($502,000 minus $527,500). Therefore, the futures loss of $25,500 must be taken into consideration with the extra cash profit of $25,000. He still comes back to approximately the August price. The short hedge has protected the value of his inventory at about $20, which is the number he was happy with.

The Nebraska farmer, who wants to lock in the price of his corn for harvest time in the fall, while it is still in the ground during the summer, would use a short hedge in much the same way.

The long hedge

The long hedge is entered into by a commodity user (buyer) to fix acquisition costs and ensure a certain profit margin.

eg For example, let's suppose an ethanol producer (a corn-based fuel additive) uses 1 million bushels of corn to meet the ethanol requirements for his major customer during the peak summer driving season. It is April, and July corn futures are quoted at $2.50 per bushel. By July, depending on weather, exports, and other unknowns, the price of corn could be much higher or lower. This big customer wishes to enter into a contract with the producer for delivery at today's price in August (for ethanol the producer will manufacture in July). The producer knows he can make a profit at today's ethanol prices *if* the price of corn remains at $2.50. He calculates his gross profit at $2.50 corn to be $50,000. His profit would be greater if corn prices fell. His break-even is at $2.70 corn, and if corn prices rise above this level, he would actually wipe out his profit margin and see red ink (assuming today's ethanol prices, which also could fluctuate).

To keep his customer happy and loyal and to ensure his plant continues to run at capacity, he enters into an agreement to deliver ethanol at today's price to the big customer in August. Rather than take the risk of the marketplace and run the risk of potentially selling his product at a loss in the summer *should* corn prices rise, he foregoes the gamble of a windfall profit (should corn prices fall) and enters a long hedge in the futures market. He buys 1 million bushels of July corn in the futures on April 15. This is the day he also enters into his cash contract for delivery of ethanol to his customer next August. The price of July corn on April 15 is $2.50. A drought develops, and in July, when he needs to go into the cash market to purchase the million bushels, the price of corn has risen to $3.00 in both the cash and futures. It has gone up by 50¢ per bushel, which is an additional cost to him, over and above the April price, of $500,000 (1 million bushels times 50¢ per bushel).

▶

However, the futures have also risen by 50¢, and he sells the July futures contracts he purchased for $2.50 at the then prevailing price of $3.00. He thereby realizes a futures *gain* of $500,000, exactly offsetting the additional cash loss of $500,000. In this way, he assured his $50,000 gross profit on the transaction. If he had not hedged, he would have lost $450,000 on the cash contract instead of realizing a profit of $50,000.

Now if the weather had been good, and it looked as if a large crop was forthcoming, prices might have fallen to, say, $2.20 by July 15th. His cash corn cost in this case would be $300,000 less. If unhedged, and if he had entered into a cash contract for ethanol at the April price, he could have realized a windfall profit of $350,000 versus $50,000, all other factors remaining equal. If hedged, he loses $300,000 on the futures transaction (a fall of 30¢ per bushel times 1 million bushels). However, the ethanol producer makes this decision; if he can always enter into profitable contracts with his users, he knows he will remain in business. Sure, if prices of corn fall, he is out the extra $300,000 profit in this example (and this $300 grand probably was transferred from his account to some speculator(s) he'll never see, but this is OK—he's not in the casino business, his business is ethanol production), but he will gladly forego the chance of a windfall for the ability to keep his plant running profitably.

This simple example demonstrates that the objectives of hedgers and speculators are not the same. The speculator is always looking to make money on his transactions. The hedger, however, is not always looking to necessarily profit on the futures side of the transactions. The hedger's goals are to lock in a price that will assure a profit or prevent a loss for his business, either the production or consumption of some product. The bread baker who wants to lock in his future wheat purchase prices would use a long hedge in much the same way.

The reality

In these examples, I have kept the basis fairly constant, but in reality, it can change. If a short hedger (one who sells futures) experiences a *widening* of the basis (where cash prices have fallen to a greater degree than futures—either cash has fallen faster or risen slower than futures), a basis loss may result. In other words, the short hedger's cash position loss may be greater than the gain realized on the futures side of the transaction. Or, in a rising market, the gain on the cash side of the transaction would not be as large as the loss on the futures side.

Conversely, a basis gain would occur with a **widening** basis on a long hedge. The futures would rise in price to a greater degree than the cash. A **narrowing** basis yields additional gains for a short hedger (the cash falls less, or rises more, in relation to the futures) and incremental losses for the long hedger (the cash falls less, or rises more, in relation to the futures). Basis gains or losses are a risk to the hedger, but they're not nearly as big a risk as what is called **flat price risk**. The price of heating oil may move 20¢ per gallon in a couple of months, whereas the basis might move 1¢ either way. For example, the flat price move was a result of a warmer than normal winter whereas the basis change was due to the fact it was colder in New Haven than New York that particular winter. The speculator might analyze basis changes to help him determine the strength or weakness of a market, but this is really more of a hedger's concern.

It doesn't matter whether the user needs copper or soybean oil or to purchase Euros six months hence; any market in which prices fluctuate creates price risk for commercial participants, which in turn creates the need for a hedging tool. Remember, hedgers are not trying to make a killing in the market; they wish to offset price risks. The speculator, on the other hand, tries to make money by buying low and selling high (or vice versa). A speculator is a marketplace participant who is neither a producer nor a consumer of a commodity or financial instrument. By definition, he does not have or want the underlying commodity, and this participant could be you or me. Without speculators that the system would not work; they add *liquidity.* Speculators often take the other side of the bids and offers in the marketplace put out by hedgers. At times they take the other side of a speculative bid and offer, and at times different hedgers may be on both sides of a transaction. However, a trade cannot be completed unless someone is willing to take the other side, and if there were only hedgers and no speculators, the system would not operate smoothly. By assuming the risks the hedgers are trying to avoid, the speculators will make money when they are right and lose when wrong. In the earlier ethanol example, when the manufacturer made the $500,000 in the futures market, some person or persons lost that money. Those persons could have been speculators betting that the crop would be good and prices would fall. On the other hand, if prices did fall, this hedger's loss might have been made by speculators who were betting on lower prices.

Various types of traders fit the speculator category. **Pit traders** (also called *locals*) and other professional traders stand in the pit and trade for their own account, or trade for their own account from a computer screen. Many of them are *scalpers,* who are trading for ticks, or minor fluctuations. A local may, for example, scalp a small profit by selling five May copper contracts to a hedger who is buying at 98.10¢ per pound and then cover (or buy them back) from a speculator who is selling at 98¢ per pound. The tenth of a cent represents two price ticks (a tick is a minimum fluctuation); for copper this is .05¢ per pound or $12.50 per tick, or $25 per two ticks (or $125) for a two-tick move on a five-contract position. In this example, the local made a profit of $125, and he provided liquidity for both the hedger and the speculator. The hedger wanted to establish a longer-term buy hedge, and the speculator wanted to establish a new short position. The scalper is **making a market** here. At times, without the scalpers, a market can be thin, with buyers and sellers bidding and offering prices away from each other. Therefore, the local who is a scalper is providing an economic service, and this is why he is allowed to exist. I am not trying to say he is a wonderful person or a bad person; he is simply out to make a profit for himself (or herself—about 1% of pit traders are women). I am also not trying to insinuate that being a local on the floor is a license to print money. If a local's judgment is off, he can get caught in an adverse market swing, and his modest scalp will turn into a healthy loss.

When I leased my Exchange seat to a local because I was required to guarantee his performance, I received duplicate account statements. I saw as many losing trades and losing days as winning days, but on balance, he made money. He was a scalper (primarily) who traded hundreds of contracts each day, but it may have been in 2 or 5 or 10 lots at a time and for very short time periods. He was usually out, or flat, by the end of the day. At times he held a small position overnight, but most days he was out by end of the day, win or lose. The local, as an Exchange member, has the advantage of very low fees, just a few dollars per transaction. This is why the pit trader can trade so many contracts and trade them for just a few ticks and still make money. For the rest of us, commissions and **slippage** (the inevitable difference between buying the offer and selling the bid) would eat us up if we tried to scalp. Some pit traders are also **position traders**, which means they hold a position for more than minutes. Most off-the-floor speculators do not try to scalp. Although some speculators may be **day traders** (in and out during the same trading session), more hold a position for a few days, weeks, and in rarer cases months. When trading futures, holding a position for months is generally the exception (although the big money can be made with longer term positions). A speculator can be a big commodity fund manager, a lawyer in Toronto, a farmer in Montana (who is not hedging), a software engineer in London, or you! The risks in these markets can be high, so by definition, so are the rewards for the speculator.

The Exchange, 'open outcry' and the clearinghouse

Much of the public does not understand that the Exchange does not set the prices of the traded commodities. Actually, the prices are determined in an open and continuous auction on the Exchange floor by the members who are either acting on behalf of customers (you and me), the companies they work for (if a hedger), or themselves (for their own account). The process of the auction has been around for more than 100 years is called **open outcry**. (It has already been replaced outside of the United States and is losing market share in the U.S. to electronic trading primarily for financial futures.).

Open outcry is not like the typical auction at Sothebys, where a single auctioneer announces the bids. At the Exchange, people are not only competing to buy, but also to sell, and they all can be doing this simultaneously. Every floor trader is his own auctioneer. The democratic feature of open outcry is that only the best bid and offer are allowed to come forward at any point in time. If a trader is willing to pay the highest price offered, he yells it out, and by Exchange rules, all lower bids are silenced. By Exchange rules, no one can bid below a higher bid, and no one can offer to sell higher than someone else's lower offer. Although each trader in the pit can see who the other floor trader is, customers remain anonymous. At times, customers who are entering or exiting a large position act through multiple floor brokers so as not to tip their hand. Because this is an anonymous auction, prices quoted on futures Exchanges are accepted widely and are used as reference prices for the underlying commodity. This process is known as **price discovery**, because anyone, anywhere, can discover the price. For commodities not traded on the Exchange (tungsten, cobalt, bananas, and onions, for example), a few large players can set the price, and the **bid-to-offer spread** (the difference between where the buyers can buy and the sellers can sell) is generally much wider than the Exchange-traded commodities. As a result, middlemen can take a greater percentage out of the middle, making many of these thinly traded cash markets much less efficient, which is one of the benefits of a futures Exchange to a free society. By helping to manage risks and broadcast prices, a well-run business can bring its goods and services to market at the lowest possible price more efficiently.

How is the price determined?

Conspiracy theorists would tell you price is determined by the big banks or the oil "seven sisters;" a clergyman might tell you that it's God. A simpler explanation is supply and demand, or in other words, buyers and sellers. If the buyers are more aggressive than the sellers, prices go up. If the sellers are more eager, prices go down. In a free market, prices are determined by what the seller can get from the buyer. Prices are made by what someone is willing to pay for a given product. You might think any given price is too low or too high, but at any point in time, the market sets the price, and there's an old adage that says that the market is always right.

How do the participants know they will get paid?

Investors trade futures to make money. Commercial interests use futures to lessen the risks in their businesses. Both groups want to make sure that if they make money on their transactions, they get paid. This is the job of the Exchange—to guarantee each trade. Although a trade may be conducted between two parties on the floor, it is ultimately the Exchange's responsibility to act as the seller to every buyer and the buyer to every seller. Each Exchange is made up of many member firms, some of the largest and best capitalized names in banking, brokerage, and private industry. They all individually and collectively guarantee against default by any one party. Each player in the marketplace, whether he is a farmer from Des Moines or an automobile manufacturer in Stuttgart, must deal through a clearing member. Each participant must post a good-faith deposit (*margin*). If a doctor in Los Angeles buys 10 gold contracts, for example, he is required to have on account (or to quickly send in) the margin money required for 10 gold contracts to his broker. His broker is either a clearing member or dealing through one. Whether he sends the money or not, the clearing member is still obligated to post this margin money at the Exchange. The seller of the 10 gold contracts could be a mine that is hedging or another speculator who believes prices will fall, but regardless, the short is required to post the margin, and so is his clearing firm. The Exchange must know that participants have sufficient funds to handle losses they could potentially experience in the markets.

The margin is determined and set by the Exchange. It is generally stable, but it can be and is changed by the Exchange based on market volatility and risk. **Margin** is generally the amount of money the Exchange determines sufficient to cover any one-day price move. It should be noted that the Exchange determines the *minimum* margin necessary to hold each contract; however, any one brokerage firm or clearing firm can charge an individual customer a higher margin rate than the minimum if it feels it requires additional protection against customer default. As an additional safeguard, the clearing members contribute to a pool of funds, a guarantee fund, that can be used in the event that any one member defaults. Although individual customers of clearing firms, and even clearing firms at time, have defaulted, there has never been an Exchange default. If an Exchange defaulted, it would mean the members collectively defaulted, and we would all be trouble because the entire global financial system would be in jeopardy. The bottom line? Don't be concerned about being paid if you win.

What are they doing on the floor?

You probably have seen photos or films of the Exchange trading floors. These 'floors' have already been replaced in Europe by computer terminals. In the years to come, these trading floors may all become relics of the past, but, for now, some of the world's largest Exchanges based in the United States still use floor traders. Traders, many wearing wildly colored jackets, stand in the trading rings around a bar or in pits arranged like amphitheaters, with steps descending to the center. They gesture wildly, screaming out bids (buys) and offers (sells). Meanwhile, men and women who work for the Exchange are silently punching keys on computer terminals or, in some cases, hand-held computers. These people are reporters, who are listening for completed transactions so that they can broadcast the price to the information vendors who, in turn, transmit the price to quote machines around the world. You'll also see people running back and forth and around the floor, you'll see huge wallboards that flash a series of ever-changing numbers. The shouting, gesturing, and jumping around by the pit traders gives the floor a chaotic appearance to the uniformed. In reality, it is quite orderly. The people who are running are carrying customer orders from the clerks, who receive them by telephone from buyers and sellers around the world, to the floor brokers in the pits who will bid, or offer, the order in the pit to the other floor brokers who also have orders to buy or sell. Also, the "runners" are taking **confirms**, or completed trades, back to the phone clerks, who then report back to their customers.

In some pits, the orders are *flashed* into the pit directly from phone clerks who are using hand signals or, at times, just plain, old-fashioned yelling. In the pits, the floor brokers, who are holding bids, are crying out to other brokers in the ring how much they are willing to pay and at what quantity they are willing to purchase. Sellers are crying out their offers with price and quantity. When a buyer and seller meet, they cry out "Sold," "Done," or "Take it!" These are the words the reporter is listening to hear, and when these words are heard, the reporters report the price (not the quantity), and this price is then transmitted almost simultaneously around the world electronically. Each floor broker wears a badge with a number of letters to identify himself to the other brokers. When a trade is completed, or executed, each selling broker must record each transaction on a card or hand-held computer that shows the commodity, quantity, delivery month, price, and the badge number or name of the buyer on the other side of the transaction. In some of the more active pits, thousands of contracts are bought and sold each and every minute. The transaction then is sent to the data-entry room, where operators key the data into the Exchange's central computer system. Because both sides of the transaction are submitted in the same manner, there is a dual audit trail.

What's the difference between a floor broker and the broker you'll use to place your orders?

A **floor broker** is buying and selling futures on the floor, either entirely for himself or filling orders for his customers, who are the brokerage houses. He cannot take customer orders from the public, but he can fill them. The Exchange has strict rules for floor brokers who trade for their own account or filling customer orders. The basic rule is that brokers can never trade for themselves *ahead* of customer orders. A broker off the floor is licensed by the government to execute trades for the public. Your broker calls the floor (or submits an order via the Internet) to have trades executed on your behalf. The same rule applies to the broker who places orders for you. He cannot trade for his own account ahead of your customer order. The customer always comes first.

Most of the trading is done during the official hours the trading floor is open; however, all the major Exchanges, for most of their major contracts, also have in place after-hours electronic trading systems, which are active after the trading floor is closed. These are computer terminals where transactions can take place electronically, and the contracts created are the same as those created during normal trading hours, so they can be sold or bought the next day or whenever (in other words, offset), on the Exchange floor.

How Do the Floor Brokers Do It?

When you see pictures of the traders in the pit, here's what you're looking at:

- Palms in, or "I'm a buyer."

- Palms out, or "I'm a seller."

- Hands away from body, with arms outstretched, fingers moving, or "Here's my price." (Prices 1–5 are quoted with vertically extended fingers, prices 6–9 are quoted with fingers horizontal, and a closed fist indicates a zero price.)

- Hands held near head, or "This is how many I want."

Of course, these brokers are all yelling, too. Do mistakes ever happen? Well, we're dealing with human beings, right?

Sal, an experienced floor broker, tells the story of a novice floor broker in the deferred cattle futures (the months that are traded thinly) who wrote the book on how *not* to open a market. The day after a bearish Cattle on Feed Report, the broker had orders for 30 contracts to sell and only five to buy. He bid 20 lower for the five and offered 30. A local trader sold the five immediately and, seeing that the other markets were sharply lower, *screamed* an offer to sell 50 contracts 100 lower. The novice panicked and offered his 30 contracts limit down. The local bought his five back (limit down) for a tidy profit. The novice had to answer as to why the opening range was 130 points, and he made both sides of it!

Here's a quote recently heard from a Feeder Cattle broker on a volatile, wide-ranging, whipsawing-type day:
"I've 10 left. I'll pay half on 10, sell 10 at a quarter
[the lower price]. Anybody want 'em?"

Sal tells this other story of what he terms the best order he ever received as a floor broker. He was working for the now-defunct Mitchell-Hutchins. "I was told to go into the bellies, don't bid for the front contract, but just start buying the rest. I was also told to report back to the desk every 15 minutes and report how I was doing. I was told to keep my ears open for any large offers to sell that came into the pit, and if I heard them, I was supposed to buy 'em, and after they were gone, bid higher. My final instructions were, by the end of the day, 'Have the bellies limit up!'"

Here's a quote from a pork belly trader:
"If God told me bellies would be limit up tomorrow,
I would still go home long only five contracts."

Open outcry versus electronic

My first 20 years in this industry were almost wholly involved with the traditional open outcry, auction-style trading methods, and this is evident by much of what I write in this book, as well as in many of the stories from traders' lore. However, as Bob Dylan once said, "The times, they are a changin'," and although just a few years ago all futures trading took place in open outcry pits, today the volume for purely electronic markets has outpaced the traditional. Whereas the physical commodities at the U.S. Exchanges (oil, agricultural, and so on) are still primarily open outcry, virtually the rest of the world's Exchanges are purely electronic. There are no trading pits; instead, computer terminals match up trades. The advantages of the electronic markets include low cost of execution and clearing and a perception of a more level playing field (because it is first-come, first-served with an electronic timestamp). Some industry experts predict all futures trading will eventually go electronic. They just may be right, but this is probably still many years away for the United States.

Although electronic execution of trades may make for better speed and efficiency, the new technology will not help with your trading decisions; that's what this book is designed to help you with.

The regulators and regulations

The first level of regulation is the Exchange. If you recall from earlier in this chapter, the Exchange does not take positions in the market. Instead, it has the responsibility of ensuring that the market is fair and orderly. The Exchange does this by setting and enforcing rules regarding margin deposits, trading procedures, delivery procedures, and membership qualifications. Members who violate the rules can be fined and expelled. A sophisticated, intricate system of safeguards virtually guarantees against counterparty credit risk and default. Although an individual member may default, the party on the other side of the transaction always gets paid. This statement cannot be made for over-the-counter, or non-Exchange, markets. Each Exchange is composed of non-clearing members and clearing members. All members need to meet business integrity and financial solvency standards, and all members can trade on the Exchange, but the standards are higher for clearing members.

Each clearing member (the NYMEX alone has more than 60) must show a minimum working capital of $2 million and own two seats. Clearing members must also deposit 10% of the firm's capital (up to $2 million) into the guarantee fund, which is $160 million for the NYMEX. Still, even if one clearing member goes under, and the guarantee fund cannot cover it (which has never happened), every clearing member has agreed to cover a loss on a prorated basis. The clearing members represent some of the largest firms in the world, from Merrill Lynch to Citibank to Exxon. As a result, the financial strength of the Exchange is based on the combined financial capability of all its clearing members. The clearinghouse ensures that all trades are matched and recorded, and that all margin is collected and maintained. The clearinghouse also is in charge of ensuring that deliveries take place in an orderly and fair manner. The compliance department of the Exchange set capital-based position limits on each clearing member. In addition, the Exchange places position limits on customers. The limits are always lower in the spot, or delivery, month. For example, the maximum number of contracts any customer or entity can hold in crude oil is 10,000 in all months, with 5,000 in any one month and 1,000 in the spot month. There is an exemption from position limits for bona-fide hedge transactions.

Looking over the Exchange regulators are the governmental regulators. In the United States, the Commodity Futures Trading Commission (CFTC) regulates the futures and options markets. Customers who maintain large positions are required to be reported to the Exchange and to the CFTC by the customer's futures commission merchant. The reporting level in crude oil, for example, is 300 contracts. In addition, in the United States, the National Futures Association, a self-regulatory body, oversees its members, which make up the brokerage community. Finally, the world's major Exchanges (in the United Kingdom, for example) have an agreement with the Securities Investment Board (SIB) to share financial information on common members.

How to place an order

Let's do a bit of time traveling and assume you've finished this book, you've done your homework, you've opened an account with a commodity broker, and you're ready to place your first trade. What's the procedure? Very simply, you need to instruct your broker (either by telephone or by Internet order entry) which commodity you want to trade, the quantity (in terms of numbers of contracts), the month, and whether you want to go long or short. You then need to tell your broker how you want your order to be executed.

Market order

This is an order to buy or sell at the prevailing price. By definition, when a commodity is bought or sold "at the market," the floor broker has an order to fill immediately at "the next best price," but in reality, it is the "next price." I've seen advice in trading manuals that effectively states that you should never use a market order. The reasoning has to do with the bid/offer spread.

In an auction market, traders make bids and offers. The **bid** is the price put out for immediate acceptance. The **offer** (sometimes known as the "asked price") is the price at which the seller is "offering" for immediate sale. In most cases, unless the floor broker is able or willing to pass along the edge to the customer, you buy at the offer and sell at the bid. You potentially lose this difference—it may be small—but you can lose it by placing a market order.

I totally disagree with the advice never to use market orders. For one thing, floor brokers are out there who *are* able to buy the bid or sell the offer and pass this along to us, the customers. If I consistently don't like the price fills received by a certain floor broker in a certain market, I go out and find myself a new one, and there are many around. In the markets I trade actively, I personally know the brokers on the floor who are filling our orders. This personal bond, I find, makes for better fills. However, this aside, there's a more important reason to use market orders in many cases, even if you have to give up the bid/offer spread. For one thing, if you use a limit order at a specific price, there is no guarantee you will be filled. The market may have to move away from the direction you think the market is moving to get filled. Most importantly, with a market order, you know you will be filled. This is important in a fast moving market, because these are the ones you most want to be in. By definition, you will be filled on every bad trade at a limit price (because it has to move against your bias first), but you could miss some good trades. If a market is moving at 50, 55, 60, 65, 60, 70, 80 to close at 120, and you place a market order at the 60 level the first time you see 60, you might get 60 or 65 or even 70, but you know you are in a trade that is at least starting out right. If you limit your price to 55, you might never get on a good move. Who knows? The next day it could open at 150.

Limit order

When you place this type of order, you know what you will get in the worst-case scenario (you could get better), but there are strings attached. With a limit order, the floor broker is prevented from paying more than the limit on a buy order, or less than the limit on a sell order. Unless the market is willing to meet your terms, you will not get in. The drawback of a limit order is that there is no guarantee you will get in. You could miss some markets. You are not even assured you will get in if your limit is hit. In the preceding example, if you place a limit order to buy at "50 or better" and the market touches 50, this may be your trade, or it may be someone else's. You can be only reasonably assured you are in if the market trades *lower* than 50. Nothing is more frustrating than to place an order to buy at 50, see the market trade there once, and call the floor to see whether you are filled, only to receive an "unable" just as the market's crossing 75. That's not to say there isn't a place for limit orders. I like to use them in quiet, back-and-forth type markets so as not to give up the slippage seen with a market order. I also use them to take profits on a good position. I try to let the market reach out to my limit price. After all, if the market doesn't reach my limit, I can always revert to a market order.

Stop orders

Stop orders, or stops, are used in two ways. The most common method is to cut a loss on a trade that is not working (also known as a stop loss order). A **stop** is an order that becomes a market order to buy or sell at the prevailing price only if and *after* the market touches the stop price. A **sell stop** is placed under the market, a **buy stop** above the market.

 For example, you buy July Sugar at 11¢ (1100). You buy it because your analysis suggests that the market is going to go higher. However, you do not want to risk more than approximately 50 points, so you give your broker a sell stop, to "sell July Sugar at 1050 stop." As long as the market moves higher—fine and good— your stop will not be elected. However, if the market trades down to 1050, your stop loss automatically becomes a market order to sell. Depending on the speed and direction of the market and the skill and luck of the floor broker who has your order, you will be out at the next best price. It most likely will be 1050 or slightly below, say, 1049. In a fast market, it could be lower, say 1048, or it even could be higher, say 1051 if the market upticks after the stop is hit.

A stop also can be used to lock in a profit and cut a loss. In the sugar example, let's say the market starts to move in your favor, up to 1150. You might decide to cancel your 1050 stop and move it up to 1104, thereby assuring a worst-case break even or a small loss after commissions. The market continues to move up, reaching 1210. You move your stop up to 1150, thereby assuring a profit on the trade, even if it trades back down. This is, at times, termed a *trailing stop*, which occurs when you move your stop with the market. A buy stop is placed above the market to liquidate a losing short position. You go short sugar at 1201 and place your buy stop *above* the market at 1253 to limit your loss. You can always cancel and move your buy stop lower, should the market move in your favor.

Stops also can be used to initiate positions. They're used by momentum traders who want to enter a market moving in a certain direction.

For example, if a trader believes gold can trade above the psychologically significant $400 mark, it will move higher. He places a buy stop at 401. If the market
remains under 401, he never enters the market and potentially avoids a "do
nothing" or worse, a losing trade. If the market reaches the 401 level, he will be
in at the next prevailing price. The hope is that the market keeps moving, to 402,
403, and on up. Once in, the trader can place a sell stop at, say, 396, to limit losses should this turn out to be a false signal. Of course, the risk is that the market
could run up to 401 and back down again. In this case, it would have been better
to limit the price at a lower level or not use the stop to initiate the trade at all.

However, when used correctly, these can be good orders to enter with. A sell stop
would be used under the market to initiate a new short position if not in the market.
There is, in addition, a variation of a stop order called a **stop limit**. With a stop limit
order, if the stop price is touched, a trade must be executed at the exact price (or better) or held until the stated price is reached again. The risk with the stop limit is the
same as with a straight limit. In other words, if the market fails to return to the stop
limit level, the order is not executed, so I normally do not recommend its use. It can,
in a fast moving market, defeat the purpose of the stop (to stop your loss).

Market if touched orders

Also called MITs, these are the mirror image of stops. An MIT is placed above the
market to initiate a short position.

 For example, you are long platinum 405, and you want to take profits at 410. You
could place a limit order to sell at 410, but you cannot be assured that you will
be filled if the price touches 410. The market would have to trade above 410 to
have a reasonable assurance that you are out. An MIT at 410 becomes a market
order if 410 is touched, which will ensure you are out at the next prevailing
price. MITs tend to be filled better on average than stops because you are moving with the prevailing trend. In a market that moves 40950, 410, 41050, 411, an
MIT at 410 would be filled at either 410 or 41050. If the next tick after 410 was
409, you certainly could be filled at 409 (because the MIT became a market
order), but it is more likely that a buy stop at 410 would be filled at 41050 in this
example. An MIT could also be used to initiate a new short position *above* the
market. An MIT to buy is placed *under* the market to exit a short position or
enter a new long. If the market is trading at 100, you might place an MIT to buy
at 99, but you would place a stop to sell at 99. See the difference?

These are the major types of orders you will use. There are other exotic orders I've
not found useful in practice, with the exception of the OCO. OCO stands for *one
cancels the other*. It is used on both sides of the market either to take profits or cut
losses; one cancels the other. For example, you buy silver at 700, you want to take
profits at 750, or cut the loss if the market trades down to 675. You could place
an order with your broker to sell at 750 or 675 stop; one cancels the other. In this
way, you are assured that if one side is hit, the other side will be canceled. This is

significant in volatile markets. If you placed two separate orders, and the market first runs up to 750, takes out your position at a profit, then trades down to 675, you could be sold into a new short position you didn't want.

Conclusion

That concludes our discussion of the basics. If this is your first exposure to commodity trading, you now know just enough to be dangerous. If you're a novice, hopefully this has shed some light on the game. If you've traded awhile, this is probably nothing new, but you'll find a lot of new and exciting stuff in subsequent chapters.

Let's conclude this chapter with a true story that happened to a commodity broker friend of mine. Remember, it is a common practice (and a good one) to place your stop loss order at the same time you place your trade. A good broker will remind you of this. There is a belief that the floor traders will "run the stops." I'll talk more about this later in the book. However, I've found that the proper and judicious use of stops is essential to successful trading. The best markets will never reach your stop. I cannot count the number of times in my personal trading a stop has prevented a bad trade from turning into disaster.

My commodity broker friend Tim tells the story of Elmer, a farmer client of his from rural Minnesota. Tim suspected Elmer was growing a bit feeble, but then again, Elmer had been trading for many years, and he had always been the eccentric type. Tim recounts the day that Elmer called him up prior to the market open.

Elmer to Tim: "Tim, a miracle happened to me this morning."

Tim to Elmer: "What's that, Elmer?"

Elmer to Tim: "Tim, I was shaving this morning, and as I looked in the mirror, the Holy Spirit came to me and said, 'Elmer, today you should buy 50 March wheat market at the open.'"

The way Tim tells it, he didn't hesitate, cross-examine, or stop to pass Go; he immediately asked Elmer, "Elmer, did he tell you where to place your stop?"

2

The intermediate futures trading course (*or just enough knowledge to make you dangerous!*)

A broker took on a customer with whom he was told to be extremely careful. The money was thought to be Mafia. The customer opened the account with $50,000 and initiated a long platinum position. The market went down, and the customer bought more. The market went down even more, and it was margin call time. The broker was becoming a bit nervous with the position, but when he called the customer, the reply was, "Sure, we'll send you more money. No problem." When the margin call went that easy, the broker felt much more relaxed. The market kept going lower, the customer kept adding to the position, the margin calls continued, and the Mob continued to send in the money. The broker was talking with the customer one day and confided that he was not sure platinum was going to rebound any time soon. The response was simple, "Let's get this straight. You can have all the money you want; just remember, we don't take losers!"

Zero sum game

There's an old saying, "To make a small fortune in commodities, start with a big one."

You may be getting the impression that the odds are stacked against you; however, I don't feel that way at all. It's true that most people lose when trading commodities, but it's not because the odds are stacked against them. Every buyer of every losing trade could have been a seller and made money on that same trade, and every seller of every losing trade could have been a buyer and made money on that trade. A profitable minority is doing just that. It's not on every trade, mind you, but on balance. So what's the key? Is it how you analyze the market? We will discuss various analysis methods shortly, but the real determinant of success or failure is the trader's state of mind, the psychology. All winning traders understand this. Trading emotionally, or on gut feelings, will ring your death knell. You need to understand mass psychology because this is the reason markets move in trends. You also need to understand when the trends are turning and why the majority is wrong at turning points. The key to this whole equation is smart money management.

Money management

If emotions can kill you in the markets, then the opposite must be true—to be unemotional enhances your prospects. Years ago, a friend of mine whom I respect as a successful trader cashed in on what I knew was a major score in the wheat market. I saw him in the Members Dining Room, and I said to him something to the effect of, "You must be feeling damn good having cashed in at the top." He was a calm sort of fellow, and I still remember what he said. "George, when the markets treat me well, I don't dance in the streets, and when they do not treat me well, I don't beat myself up. Always remember this: Slow and steady wins the race." Years later, I think I know what he meant by this. What a trader needs to do is not to think about the money, but instead to concentrate on trading correctly. If you trade right, the money will come. If you trade wrong, you're doomed.

A loser hopes too much. He has an inability to get out of a losing trade early enough, because he keeps hoping the market will turn back his way. Sometimes it does, but too often, his broker is the one forcing him out. Invariably, after he's forced out, the market comes back the way he thought it would, but by then it's too late. Why do so many people sell at the bottom or buy at the top? It's because they're acting emotionally instead of intellectually. One simple way to avoid this is not to get attached to any position. Trading should not be an ego thing. There is always another market tomorrow, and yet another the week after.

I've literally witnessed thousands of trades from hundreds of brokerage clients over the years. I've seen what it is those who make money do, and I've seen what the losers do. Invariably, the losers make the same mistakes. They make money initially, and they might even have more winners than losers, but there always seems to be those few large losses that wipe out whatever good came before.

A few years ago, the Chicago Mercantile Exchange had an ad campaign in which it tried to teach the public how to trade—an impossible undertaking. One of the full-page magazine ads pronounced, "Do not risk thy whole wad." How profound. And yet, this is the one major mistake the majority of novice traders make. They bet too much on one trade or on one market, which brings us to the first tenant of good money management:

You must know in advance how much you are risking on a trade, and unless it is a small percentage of your total risk capital, don't take it.

I could go into theoretical probability theory here, but common sense works better. Some of the most important advice I can give you early in this book is to plan for slow and steady gains, and look to minimize the draw-downs. The way to do this is to cut the losses quickly on the bad trades. So, how much should this be? It should definitely not be more than 10% of your total trading capital per trade, and ideally no more than 2 to 5% per trade. Think of it this way: If you risk 5% on each trade when you start trading, you would need to be wrong 20 times in a row to be totally wiped out. You would need to be using a very poor trading system to do this. (I'll be able to give you some ideas that will help you to develop a good trading system that fits your personality.) Consider this: If you win on just half of your trades, but your net profit is 10% on each winning trade, with your net loss of 5% on each losing trade, you're up 50% on your first 20 trades. Not bad for being right only half of the time. On the other hand, if you risk 25% of your capital on each trade, it takes only four losing trades in a row before you're done for. It is a certainty that if you trade long enough, a time will come when you have four losing trades in a row. The key here is to avoid major draw-downs. Plus, I have a couple of other tips.

For one, diversify. Don't put all your eggs in one basket, and don't place all of your chips on a single roll of the dice. This lessens the opportunity for any one trade to be your last. Stick with the trades that are working, and cull the ones that aren't. If you don't have the discipline to get out of the bad trades when you need to, make it your own personal rule to place a stop loss order physically in the market the moment you enter any trade. Tell your broker that if you haven't given him that stop, his job is to twist your arm to get it. Believe me, your stops will not be hit on the very best trades. Then, once you have a reasonable paper profit on a trade, move your stop so that it never turns into a loss.

Contrary opinion theory

At times it pays to be contrary. Because this chapter is about not doing what the losers do, which generally is what the majority is doing, this is a good time to introduce the **contrary opinion theory**. The concept is simple: If all the bulls have already bought, there are no bulls left to buy, and the market falls of its own weight. If a piece of bullish news fails to move the market up, this is your clue. When all the bulls decide to run for the exit door, there will be no cushion of new buyers to soften the decline, and the decline will be particularly severe. The reverse is true if "all the bears" have already sold.

The father of contrary opinion is recognized to be Humphrey Neill, who published *The Art of Contrary Thinking* in 1954. Neill compiled a bullish consensus that gave a percentage estimate of how many newsletter writers, analysts, and traders were bullish or bearish for a particular commodity. You can try to do this yourself, or subscribe to a commercial service. For example, Consensus Inc. of Kansas City, Missouri, publishes a weekly newspaper with its "Consensus Index of Bullish Market Opinion." The consensus is expressed as a percent of a market, with 0% indicating no bulls in a market, and 100% no bears. The lower the reading, the more oversold, or bullish (closer to a bottom), the market is. Contrary opinion is not a hard and fast trading system. The way to use it is to watch closely for signs of a turn in the marketplace when the index is high (more than 80%) or low (less than 20%). I am always on alert when a market is very bullish or very bearish, and when everyone knows the story or when the story is on the front page of the commodity section of *The Wall Street Journal or* the *Financial Times,* on the evening news, or on the cover of a major news magazine. In the summer of 1993, when the floods hit the Midwest and thousands of acres of good cropland were under water, it seemed everyone was bullish soybeans (including myself). The consensus ratings were more than 90%, *Newsweek* ran a cover story on the floods. The cover had a picture of a farmer up to his neck in water. Looking back, we now know that issue came out on the very day the contract high for the next decade was reached in the grains.

Spreads, straddles, and switches

Spreads, straddles, and switches are actually three terms you might hear for the same animal. I'll use the most common—spread—but feel free to substitute the other two if you'd like. Spreads are a more sophisticated way of trading, and they fit well into the game plan of many traders. I know some traders who trade only spreads because they feel spreads are the best way to limit some of the risks inherent in futures and options. Actually, this is the main purpose of spreading: to reduce risk.

When you enter a spread, the objective is not necessarily to make money on a rise or fall in the market in question, but rather to make money from a change in the relationship between different prices. When you put on a spread, you buy one contract while *simultaneously* selling another. You are long and short in either two related commodities, or in two different months of the same commodity at the same time. The relative change between the two determines your profit or loss.

The two major categories of spreads include intramarket and intermarket spreads.

Intramarket spreads

Intramarket spreads consist of buying one month in a particular commodity and simultaneously selling a different month in the same commodity. Examples would be buying July corn and selling December corn, buying March crude oil and selling April crude oil, and buying May cotton and selling December cotton. Because you are trading two different months in the same commodity—one long and the other short—their prices tend to move in the same direction. So how can you possibly make money in a spread? Well, although spreads tend to move in the same direction, they don't have to. And even when the two months move in the same direction, they generally tend to move at different speeds. Many times, when you gain on one side of a spread, you lose on the other. What you're looking for is a bigger gain on the winning side than loss on the losing side.

eg Let's look at an example. Assume you put on a spread between March copper and July copper in December of the previous year. You are buying the March and selling the July. When you buy the near month and sell the distant, it is called a *bull spread*. A *bear spread* (short March and long July) is the mirror image. In a bull spread, you are predicting that the near month either will rise faster than the distant or fall slower. Either outcome is profitable. Spreads can be more reliable and more predictable than outright positions, which is precisely the reason many traders like them. Spreads are not sure things, but they can put the odds in your favor.

Look at this particular example. Most years, the March copper tends to gain on the July because of seasonal considerations. March is historically a high demand time of the year for copper because of inventory rebuilding prior to the peak building season. Suppose that when you "place" the spread in December that March is trading at 102 and July is trading at 101. You have put on this bull spread—long the March and short the July—with the March trading at a 100-points (1¢ per pound) *premium* to the July. (If the March was trading at 100 and the July at 102, you would say you were long the March and short the July, with the March 200 points *discount* to the July.) A few months pass, and in February, copper has risen in price with both months appreciating—but at different speeds. The March is trading at 115 and the July at 110. The spread has now *widened* from 100-points premium the March to 500-points premium the March, and you sense it is time to take your profits. You would give your broker an order to do the reverse transaction—that is, sell the March and buy the July. This offsets both sides of the spread and effectively wipes your slate clean. Let's look at the result. The March has risen from 102 to 115, so you have a 13¢, or 1,300-point profit, on this side of the spread. The July (the short side) has risen from 101 to 110, so you have a 9¢, or 900-point loss, on this side of the spread. The difference between what you gained and what you lost (1,300 minus 900) is your profit, which in this case is 400 points. Note that you don't need to calculate both sides to determine your profit; this works out neatly to be the spread differences: 500 minus 100 is 400. Because one point in COMEX copper is worth $2.50 per contract, this is a gross profit of $1000 per spread, not considering commissions.

You might be asking yourself why you'd want to trade the spread when you could make more money by simply buying the March outright. In this case, March rallied from 102 to 115, a 1300-point move, or $3,250 profit versus $1,000 profit. It all has to do with the risks versus the reward. Spreads generally move slower. Yes, you can certainly lose in a spread as well, but at times you can gain even when the market doesn't move the way you plan. What if the economy weakens and March copper falls 1300 points? If you were long, you would lose $3,250 per contract. The spread could certainly fall 400 points, but it is also possible that traders would turn bearish the whole market, and both months could go down the same amount, thereby resulting in no loss. When spread trading, you are more interested in the difference between the months than the outright flat price movements.

The ability to profit in both an up or down situation is one of the advantages of spread trading. Also, the margin requirements for spreads are generally much smaller than outright positions because the Exchange recognizes that, in most cases, spreads are less risky. If you are long May corn and short September corn, and the President declares a grain embargo, odds are that both months will be down sharply. In other words, you are somewhat insulated from dramatic news with the resulting price shocks when spread trading. In addition, spreads tend to move slower, giving you more time to react, and many traders believe spreads are more predictable.

Intermarket spreads

Intermarket spreads consist of buying one commodity and simultaneously selling a related commodity. Examples would be buying silver and selling gold, buying hogs and selling pork bellies, and buying Minneapolis wheat and selling Chicago wheat. In these examples, the two markets are related, and they generally move in the same direction because the same market forces affect both. They move, however, at different speeds.

For example, you may decide to buy July corn and sell July wheat. Both are grains, both can be used for animal feed, and both are export commodities. They will tend to move in the same direction. However, if the fundamentals are strongly opposed, the two could move in opposite directions. Let's assume it is March, and that you believe the supplies of corn are tight but that wheat supplies will grow larger as the market moves closer to the harvest in the early summer. July corn is at $3.10 and July wheat is at $4.50, so you buy the corn and sell the wheat, with corn at a 140 discount to the wheat. (Be sure to read the order with the long, or the buy side, first.) Intermarket spreads cannot be classified as bull or bear like an intramarket. Suppose a few months go by and both corn and wheat fall in price—corn to $2.80 and wheat, because of harvest selling pressure, to $3.60. You decide it is time to *unwind* the spread. You buy the July wheat and sell the July corn, which offsets both sides of the spread and wipes your slate clean. The long side (the corn side) shows a loss of 30¢, and the short side shows a profit of 90¢. Your gross profit is the difference of 60¢, and because in grains a penny move is worth $50 per contract traded, this is a profit of $3,000. Note that you put the spread on at a 140 discount and took it off at an 80 discount; the difference between 140 and 80 is 60. In this case, you wanted the spread to *narrow*; you wanted the lower-priced corn to gain on the higher-priced wheat, and it did. If the corn fell by 40¢ and the wheat by 20¢, you would have lost 20¢ on the spread. If there were weather problems with the new crop wheat, and the spread widened to 190 (wheat went up 40¢ and corn fell 10¢), you would have lost 50¢, or $2,500 per spread.

Special spreads

Certain spreads are actively and commonly traded. In certain markets, there are spread brokers who only trade spreads and who make a market both ways in these common spreads. The Exchanges generally gives the trader a break on the margin rates for trading the common spreads. For example, although it may cost $700 to margin a wheat contract, because Kansas City and Minneapolis recognize intermarket spreads between their two respective wheat markets, a long Minneapolis wheat and short Kansas wheat spread might require only $500 total (or $250 a "side," not $1,400).

Grains

The new crop/old crop spreads are popular among traders who try to determine how the relationship will change between one crop that has already been harvested and another that is either in the ground or yet to be planted. Here are some common examples:

- Long May or July corn/short December corn

- Long May or July soybeans/short November soybeans

- Long May or July soybean meal or oil/short December soybean meal or oil

- Long May or July oats/short December oats

- Long March or May wheat/short July or December wheat

Popular intermarket grain spreads include these:

- Long or short wheat versus corn

- Long or short corn versus oats

- Long or short soybeans versus corn or wheat

The soybean crush is used by the soybean processors to lock in profit margins when available. This involves the purchase of soybeans (the raw material) and the simultaneous sale of the products: soybean meal and soybean oil. The **reverse crush** involves the purchase of the products and the sale of beans.

Cotton

The new crop/old crop July cotton versus December is popular and can be volatile.

Meats

The hogs versus cattle, cattle versus feeder cattle, and hogs versus pork belly spreads are the most popular. Some traders like to trade the **cattle crush**, which involves a purchase of corn and feeder cattle (the two raw ingredients) versus the sale of live cattle (the finished product).

Energy

By far, the most popular energy spread is the purchase or sale of heating oil versus the unleaded gasoline, because traders try to take advantage of the seasonal tendencies of these two products to move toward or away from each other. The **Crack Spread** is the simultaneous purchase and sale of the crude oil contract versus the products, gasoline, and heating oil.

Metals

The gold/silver ratio spread is calculated by dividing the price of gold by the price of silver. It represents the number of ounces of silver required to equal the price of one ounce of gold. In 1980, when gold was $850 and silver $50, the ratio was 17;

however, in 1996 with gold at $350 and silver at $5, the ratio was 70. I'm not sure there is an average or a correct number here, but recently the ratio has traded between 30 and 70, with the average for the past century at 32.5. The purchase of platinum versus the sale of gold is another popular metal spread, with a margin break for buying one and selling the other.

Interest rates

A popular interest rate spread is the NOB (Treasury Notes versus Treasury Bonds), or the spread between the U.S. Treasuries and the Bund (Japanese Government Bonds), or the Eurodollar versus the Note spread (the relationship between short-term and longer-term rates).

Carrying charges

Other limited risk spreads include carrying charge spreads. **Carrying charges** are the costs to hold a commodity from one month to the next, and include storage costs and interest. For example, if it costs 3¢ per month to hold wheat, and the July/September wheat spread is trading at 8¢ premium, the September, by definition the risk on this one, is low. Unless interest rates rise dramatically, the likelihood September would rise much more above July is minimal. However, should a bull market develop in wheat due to limited nearby supplies, there is no limit as to how far July could rise above September. These are spreads to watch for. Limited-risk carrying charge spreads can be found *only* in storable commodities. There is no limit to how spreads can vary in either direction for perishable commodities such as live cattle.

You should be aware that, *if you ask,* many commodity brokers offer a commission discount if you trade a spread as a spread (meaning you enter both sides simultaneously and exit both sides simultaneously). Yes, you can **leg off** a spread (meaning you can liquidate one side and leave the other intact), but it is generally not a good idea. You normally enter the spread because it is a lower-risk transaction. Novice traders, when a spread isn't working to form, have been known to take off the profitable leg, leaving the unprofitable on, in hopes that it will come back and profits can be realized on both sides. For some unexplained reason, this usually doesn't work. (It would be better, in most cases, to take off the unprofitable side, because this is the side that isn't working.) No matter which side you take off, however, if you exit one side of a spread, you immediately incur the risk of an outright transaction. You can think of this like splitting sixes in blackjack, because you don't like a 12 against a dealer's ace. Although it might work at times, in the majority of situations, you're just asking for trouble. Incidentally, when you leg off a spread, you immediately lose your margin advantage, and your account is charged full margin for the remaining outright position.

Normal or inverted?

For this discussion, note that spreads can trade with the front month higher than the back, and vice versa. You can use this fact as a valuable forecasting tool, a discussion best saved for Chapter 8, "The Advanced Futures Trading Course (Or How to Analyze the Markets Technically)." I'll end this particular discussion of spreads with a caveat. Because the margins are generally much lower on spreads, there is a natural tendency to overtrade, or put on too many. Just because spreads are limited risk does not mean there isn't risk; on occasion, spreads can actually entail greater risk. A number of years ago, a friend of mine had the long July/short December cotton spread. One afternoon after the market's close, a change in some government policy was announced. Although I've forgotten the specifics, I do remember that the next day the market opened limit down in the July and limit up in the December—the result being he was hit to the max on both sides!

The "Voice from the Tomb"

At least two old-time grain traders I know swear by this, and you should check it out.

The story goes like this: There was a millionaire grain trader who had three children. After their mother died, he raised them by himself and dedicated his life to his children. But the children were lazy and thought they would inherit all the money. He thought his children wasteful, and believed they took him for granted. When he died, all the money went to charity. All he left them in his will were the following dates of when to buy and when to sell. The will indicated that if they strictly followed his advice (shown as follows), they would have the fortune they always thought was going to drop in their laps:

Wheat
Sell March wheat on January 10
Buy May and/or July wheat on February 22
Sell July wheat on May 10
Buy December wheat on July 1
Sell December wheat on September 10
Buy March wheat on November 28

Corn
Buy July corn on March 1
Sell July corn on May 20
Buy December corn on June 25
Sell December and March corn on August 10

This is the advice of the "Voice from the Tomb" (VFTT)

Practical experience using the "Voice"

When I first discovered VFTT, I was a bit skeptical because on the surface, it looks akin to voodoo. Then, when I thought more about it, I realized there was sound fundamental basis behind the advice. After all, discernable crop cycles revolve around planting and harvest. For example, the December wheat buy on July 1st coincides with the harvest in the Plains being about half finished. The market generally bottoms around harvest time because of the selling pressure of grain sold by farmers right out of the field. The futures market, being the anticipatory beast it is, anticipates the harvest bottom and, therefore, a buying date approximately midway through the harvest makes sense.

I've been collecting data for more than 35 years, and I have become to believe that there are pearls of wisdom buried within these dates. I have found that although both tend to put the odds in your favor, the wheat dates are more reliable than the corn. I have also found, in my practical experience, that the dates tend to be excellent signals when it comes to turning points, but one cannot just hold and reverse on the subsequent date. Instead, after initiation of a position, a trailing stop makes the most sense. A simple optimizing rule of my own is to use a 15¢ per bushel stop to make 15¢ per bushel. Using these parameters, there have been years where the "voice" had a perfect track record (see Charts 2.1 and 2.2). Actually, my data indicates (when using these parameters) a win ratio for wheat (somewhat lower for corn) of more than 70% during the past 30 plus years.

■ **Chart 2.1**   Voice from the tomb: 1999

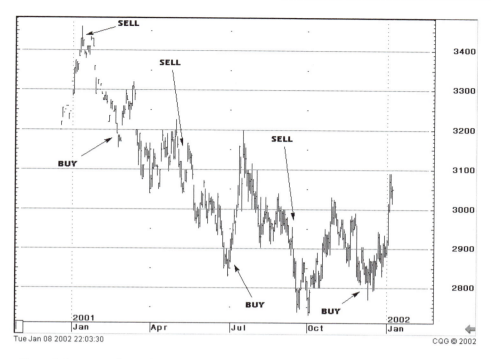

Chart 2.2 Voice from the tomb: 2001

Finally, here's a true story from the Chicago Mercantile Exchange. One day, before a major United States Department of Agriculture Cattle Report, a large trader in the cattle pit bought 100 contracts at steady money on the day to initiate a new long position. Several smaller traders in the pit also bought, figuring this guy knew something and that they could "coattail" him. Then the first wave of selling hit the pit. The market moved 50 points lower on the day. Instead of panicking, the large local bought more. So did the coattailers. Then the second wave of selling hit the pit. At 100 points lower, the big guy bought more. So did the "coattailers"—but at this point, their coattails were feeling a bit tight. Then the third wave of selling hit the pit. The market went limit down, or at that time 1.5¢ per pound under the previous day's close. If there had been more sellers than buyers, the market could have ended the day lock limit down, with traders conceivably being locked into a position until the next day. Still, the big guy bought even more. This time, however, the coattailers ran for exits; they just couldn't take it anymore. Just as they sold out, they thought they heard the big guy say, "Now we've got 'em right where we want 'em." Only one coattailer had the guts to hang on. As it turned out, that third wave of selling was the last wave of selling, and the market ended up closing higher on the day!

Perhaps this is where the following expression comes from: "I bought the first break; I bought the second break; I *was* the third break."

3

A diabolical story

The very same floor broker who told me the tale of the corn speculator and the fire chief told me this story also. He says he knows it's true because once upon a time (many years ago now), he hired one of the main characters as his clerk—which is how he got to hear the story in the first place. The clerk had an opportunity to join a college buddy of his in San Diego and become a commodity broker. He quickly packed, left Chicago, and moved to the west coast.

The San Diego office he joined produced some business, but nothing spectacular. Customers would come, many would lose and leave, and new ones would come to take their place. One afternoon, as these two characters were staring out of their office window (which looked out over the Pacific Ocean), they spawned an idea. They discussed how just about all of their customers would lose money; in fact, 80% of the trades would ultimately be liquidated as losers. With this thought in mind, the two characters placed an ad in the paper to hire rookie commodity trainees. After interviewing a number of applicants, they hired 10 average Joes. They told these newly hired gentlemen that they would perform the normal duties of a commodity broker, servicing customer accounts and the like, but in addition, they each were going to be given a rare opportunity. The 10 would each be given a no-strings-attached, $50,000 account with the firm to "manage" a portfolio of commodity trades. If they could show profitable performance, they would share in the profits and receive a bonus.

The trainees could each trade the 50K accounts as they saw fit, and there was just one procedure they had to follow. Unlike other trades for customers of the firm, if they were going to place a trade in their "managed" accounts, the order had to go through one of the two principals (either the owner or the guy from Chicago). You have to ask yourself why these two would trust 10 novices—we're talking 10 raw rookies here—with $500,000 of their money. Well, you see, this was all just a diabolical scheme the two hatched that one afternoon. What would happen is that 1 rookie broker would call to buy 10 cattle contracts, another would want to sell 7 soybeans, while yet another would buy 3 copper or short 5 silver. The two guys behind the scheme would call the various trading floors and *sell* 10 cattle, *buy* 7 soybeans, and *sell* 3 copper or *buy* 5 silver. In other words, they would do exactly the *opposite* of what their "traders" wanted them to do. You see, the money in the traders' account was fictitious. The firm's money was, in reality, going the other way, with opposite positions. The next day, fictitious position sheets would be distributed to the "traders," showing them what the rookies believed to be true. Eighty percent of the novices who trade lose money. Inevitably, the rookie who "bought" the cattle couldn't stand the market moving against him, so he would call one of the two to liquidate his "losing" position. This was the signal for the two to call the floor, buy back their shorts, and actually take the profits! The next day, the cattle "trader" would show a losing trade on his sheet—his $50,000 would be something less—but in reality the two were cashing in. This pattern continued with the guy in the beans, the guy in the copper, and so on.

In the very first week, one trader actually lost his entire $50,000. He was immediately summoned to the boss's office. Thinking he was about to be fired, before anything was said, he started to cry. He said he had been married for a year, just had twins, and really needed this job. He promised he would do better, he would learn from his mistakes, and he pleaded for another chance. Imagine his surprise when they gave him another chance. In fact, the boys couldn't wait to "recapitalize" his account with another "50K." They also couldn't wait for him to leave the office because they could hardly contain the laughter. By this fellow losing $50,000, they actually made $50,000 in the real markets. This was better than printing money.

The scheme proceeded much the same way for a while. One trader would blow out, then another. The only problem was that the two bosses were finding it increasingly difficult to supply the traders with the fictitious statements for every transaction. They couldn't keep up with the paperwork and started falling behind. Nevertheless, they continued on with the plan as best they could—until the silver trade, that is.

Now I should mention that this was all happening during the early 1980s, the same time the Hunt brothers tried to corner the silver market. Silver ran up to about $50 per ounce, and one day, one of the traders called to sell short five silver. Of course, our boys actually bought five silver. The silver market moved erratically sideways for a few days, and then it started to turn over.

During this time, the trader who sold the silver went to Kansas to visit his mom. While he was visiting, a tornado hit his town, a tree fell on the house, the roof collapsed, and he ended up unconscious in a hospital bed. He remained in a coma for two weeks.

Meanwhile, our masterminds back in San Diego were wondering where the hell he was, and when he was going to take his "profit" so they could take their loss. In New York, they raised the margin requirements and declared silver was for liquidation only, and the market started its famous collapse. The masterminds went belly up. The guy in the coma awakened, and the first words out of his mouth were "Get me a newspaper." He immediately turned to the commodity section, and when he saw how far silver had broken, he screamed in ecstasy. He quickly called San Diego, anticipating praise and looking forward to his big bonus. Instead he heard two words: You're fired!

4

The options primer

The commercials tout options as "the best of both worlds." *"Unlimited* profit potential with *limited* risk." Sounds wonderful, so why would anyone trade anything else?

The reality is that when trading options, as with every financial instrument, there are advantages, but certainly there is no free lunch. Actually, there are probably more ways to lose money when trading options than with any other financial instrument. You give something up for the limited-risk feature, but it just might be worth it to you to give this something up. I know people who trade *only* options and wouldn't think of touching futures. Many of these people do quite well. I know others who have told me options don't work for them; they despise the added costs, and most options expire worthless. Like anything else in the speculative world, options requires good judgment, a sound game plan, and at times a bit of luck.

This chapter is the "Options 101" course for beginners and those who want to brush up. In it you'll learn the basics: what options are, how they work, the jargon, and the various ways to play. In the next chapter, you'll delve into some of the more advanced strategies.

What is an option?

An **option** gives the buyer the right, but *no* obligation, to buy or sell a stated quantity of a commodity (some "asset") at a specified price on or before a specific date in the future.

Options are often compared to insurance. When you buy homeowner's insurance, for example, you pay a premium for certain rights. These rights are yours, but the policy can limit the payoff. To some extent, this analogy works for a hedger, but there are major differences when speculating. For example, the option buyer theoretically has unlimited profit potential. Insurance policies have a stated limit. Insurance is not transferable between parties and is usually specific to a person or property. Options are standardized and in most cases can be sold in the marketplace. Actually,

Exchange trade options are quite simple. There are just two types of options—the call and the put—the features are fairly straightforward, and they can be utilized effectively under certain situations by both the speculator and the hedger.

Like insurance, the cost of an option is called the **premium.** The premium is a one-time cost and represents the maximum exposure the buyer has. No matter how far the price of the underlying asset rises or falls, the option buyer knows what his maximum risk will be. However, the profit potential is not fixed. Just as in futures, potential profits are limited only by how far the market moves in the stated time period minus the initial cost. Options are available for just about every futures market, from orange juice (an old adage says to never sell call options during freeze season) to natural gas, to gold, copper, heating oil, Euros—you name it. The more liquid and active futures markets, as you might have guessed, generally have the most liquid option markets.

Just like futures, options trade in designated contract months. Know your expiration dates, because in many cases, the options expire in the month *preceding* the futures month they correspond to.

March grain options, for example, expire the third Friday of February. For most of the cash-settled futures contracts, such as the S&P 500 and Feeder Cattle, the options and futures expire the same day. You might have heard the term **triple witching hour**, which refers to the simultaneous expiration of index futures, stocks options, and futures options on the third Friday of March, June, September, and December. All this activity supposedly causes wild and crazy fluctuations, but in my experience, this has generally been a non-event. In many of the active markets, options are traded every month of the year. For example, the January, February, and March currency options all correspond to and are exercisable into the March contract. Consult the Exchange tables or your broker for the specifics on option months and expiration dates by market.

An option for what?

Options can be converted into the underlying futures contract at the discretion of the buyer, which is called the **right to exercise**. This is why the size of every option is the same as the contract it represents. By **exercising** an option, the buyer receives either a long or short position at the option's strike price. An owner of a **call** option who exercises his option receives a *long* futures position. An owner of a **put** option who chooses to exercise receives a *short* futures position.

Advantages and disadvantages

For option buyers, the primary advantage is definitely the limited-risk feature. Unlike futures, the most you can ever lose as an option *buyer* (not an option seller) is what you pay for the option. You could lose less by selling out prior to expiration, and you could even make a significant profit trading options, but you have a defined and maximum risk, and you will know to the penny the worst-case scenario at the outset. Additional margin calls are not a possibility, and you will not suffer sleepless nights because you know the worst-case scenario the day you initiate an option purchase. This statement cannot be made for futures.

For option buyers, the primary disadvantage is the premium. The premium must be paid up front, and this cost must be recovered in part or in whole through a favorable movement in price, or else you lose. You can even be right in your market assessment when buying options, but if the market doesn't move far enough in your favor, you still lose.

Consider this: If you buy a wheat option good for the current market price for a premium cost of, say, $1,000, and the market goes nowhere (it stays at the same price for the life of the option), you're out $1,000. The market moved nowhere, and whoever sold that option to you keeps your $1,000.

To profit, the option seller only needs a stationary market, a move in his direction, or a move that does not cover the premium in full. If you buy a futures contract and hold it for the same time period in a market that goes nowhere, you're out nothing except the commission costs. In this case, the "limited risk" option is definitely more costly than the "higher risk" futures contract. Of course, in this simplistic example, you do not know what transpired in the interim period. The market could have sold off wildly, resulting in a margin call or a stop loss being hit in the futures and subsequently recovered. The futures trader could have been knocked out, perhaps more than once, while the option trader (not subject to margin calls) could just sit it out. You see, there are no easy answers here, and we've only scratched the surface.

Types of options

Calls and puts are the two basic option types.

Call options are bought by bullish traders. A call option gives the buyer the right, but no obligation, to purchase the underlying asset at an agreed-upon price (known as the **strike price**) within a specified time.

Put options are the mirror image of calls. A put option gives the buyer the right, but no obligation, to sell the underlying asset at an agreed-upon price (the strike price) within a specified time. Bearish traders, those who anticipate a weaker market, would be the buyers of these options. What is the underlying asset? It is, for Exchange-traded options, the corresponding futures contract. Call buyers have the right to exercise into a long futures position and put buyers into a short futures option at the corresponding strike price.

Strike prices

Remember, the rules are set by the Exchange where the options are traded, and this also applies to the strike prices at which options trade. These prices are listed at set intervals.

For example, wheat options trade at every 10¢ per bushel: $3.50, $3.60, $3.70, and so on. Note that in this and the following chapter, I am referring to Exchange-traded options, because these are the options available to the general public. Some brokers and institutions also offer *over the counter (OTC) options*, which are dealt off the Exchange.

OTC options are completely flexible with the exact details, such as date and quantity, freely negotiable between the buyer and seller. OTC options are very common in the currency markets, for example, but generally available only to big players in lots of $1 million minimum.

Exchange-traded options (the ones you're most likely to be involved in) are standardized. The Exchange sets the strike prices, size, specifications, expiration date, and style (American or European). Most importantly, the Exchange eliminates the counterparty risk. If an Exchange member goes belly up, the clearinghouse (consisting of all clearing members) guarantees performance. If the bank on the other end of your OTC option has one rogue trader too many, there is no guarantee you will be able to collect even if you are profitable. Although the risk of non-performance by a large money center bank or multinational brokerage firm is slim, it is nevertheless a risk. (I have personally witnessed a number of rock-solid, old line firms go out of business during the past decade or so.)

Another major advantage of Exchange-traded options is quotations. This advantage may seem insignificant, because you are able to get a quote from the counterparty for your OTC option. However, with the OTCs, the quote comes directly from the other party (and whose interest do you think is foremost in their mind?). Quotes on Exchange-traded options are disseminated publicly by a third party—the Exchange—based on actual trades in an auction-like environment.

Styles of options

Two *styles* of options are available: **American** and **European**. The basic difference is in the rules of exercise. The buyer can exercise an American-style option at any time before it expires. The European-style option can be exercised only on the expiration date. All other factors being equal, the European option is generally slightly cheaper than the American option, because it can be exercised only on the one date and, therefore, involves less uncertainty for the seller. The vast majority of Exchange-traded options are American style, and the vast majority of OTC options are European style.

How are option prices quoted?

In terms of futures ticks, for example, a 102 Euro call might be quoted at 99 bid/102 offered. The settlement price is 101. These are ticks, and because a tick for the Euro contract (on the IMM) represents $12.50, at 101 the option is worth $1,262.50. A 390 wheat call at 22¢ goes for $1,100. (It is a 5,000-bushel contract, so each penny is worth $50.) One major exception—major because it is one of the most liquid of all futures options—is the U.S. Treasury Bond options. The futures have a minimum tick equal to $31.25. The options have a minimum tick equal to half the futures tick, or $15.62 (just like the T-Notes).

Buy 'em and sell 'em

Option buyers, puts or calls, pay a premium. Who gets it? The option *seller* receives the premium. In many cases, option sellers (also called option writers) are professional traders, because the public generally prefers buying options. However, anyone, including you, can be an option seller. Why would you want to be an option seller? It places the odds in your favor. You receive the premium; it is credited to your account and becomes a cushion against an adverse market move.

Call options are sold by bearish traders. Call options are also sold by traders who expect a market to go nowhere over the specified time period. Call options are also sold, at times, by bullish traders who wish to receive protection, or **cover**, a long position or gain additional income from a long position.

Put options are sold by bullish traders. If the market moves up and remains above the strike price within the specified period, the put seller keeps the premium with no penalty. Put options may also be sold by traders who feel the market is not going anywhere. Bearish traders who are looking for protection to cover a short position or to gain incremental income for a short position sometimes sell puts.

Advantages and disadvantages of selling

The primary advantage of selling options is that the seller receives the premium income paid by the buyer immediately. All he needs to make money is for either a quiet or stable market, or a market move away from the buyer, or the market must move in favor of the buyer less than the premium received. In other words, there is a wider range of price movement versus the option buyer, in which the option seller profits. The odds are in the seller's favor, and this is why professionals like to sell them.

The disadvantage of selling options is the unlimited risk. Selling is the mirror image of buying options. Because the market can, theoretically, move an unlimited amount away from the strike price, the risk cannot be predetermined. You can think of it like a Las Vegas casino, with the option seller as the house. You know the house has the advantage, but this doesn't mean any individual on any particular evening couldn't make a major hit against the house.

How options work

Let's look at a typical example.

eg **You're bullish gold and want to play this market using options. It is January, and the price of gold is $400 per ounce. You're a bull, remember, so you can employ two basic strategies: You can either buy a call option or sell a put option. However, other decisions need to be made. It's like the kid who goes in to buy his first pack of cigarettes. The clerk asks him which brand he wants. The kid asks for Marlboro. Standard or Menthol? Standard. 100s or shorts? Shorts. Box or soft pack? Box. Lights or Regulars? With his head spinning, the kid runs out of the store rationalizing that cigarettes aren't good for you anyway, and this just isn't worth it.**

Similarly, options come in a variety of flavors. The simplest way to participate is to buy a call (if you think the price will rise) or buy a put (if you're bearish). Suppose it's December, and the price of gold is $399 per ounce. You can buy an April 400 call for, say, $6 per ounce. The option is exercisable into a standard futures contract, and this option has a size of 100 ounces, so $6 is equal to a cost of $600 per option. This option gives you the right, but not the obligation, to receive an April futures contract at a price of $400 at any time at your discretion, prior to the expiration date (which in this case is mid March). You can pay less for an April 420 call, or more for an April 380 call. You can pay more for a June 400 call, or less for a February 400 call. You can pay much less for an April 500 call, or a lot more for a February 340 call. The permutations are just about endless. Of course, you can sell any of these as well. Clients who have a market opinion often ask me, "Which is the best option for me to buy?" How do you determine this? It depends not only on your outlook, but also your outlook for your outlook. There are a few other issues you will need to understand before you make your first option trade.

Time

The first issue is time. You have to decide how much time you wish to pay for. A basic rule of thumb is—and this should be no surprise—the more time you want the option to have before it expires, the higher the premium. You can go far out in time, receive a lot more time for your position to work, but this is generally a bad idea. Remember, there is no free lunch. Long-dated options are more expensive, and you tie up more money for a longer period of time. Instead, you could have used this money for alternative transactions. Plus, the further out you go, the less liquid the options become. When trading in long-dated options, you are generally dealing with a market professional who will quote a wide bid-to-offer spread. If you want to liquidate the option in the options market (as opposed to exercising the option), you will have to deal with this spread once again. In other words, the slippage is high, and these are additional hidden costs. The cheapest options are the nearest options time-wise. The problem with a short-dated option is, and I think this is obvious as well, you have a much shorter time for the market to move your way. Unlike futures, it not only has to move your way, but it needs to do so more quickly. This works at times, but the market doesn't always know *your* option's expiration date. I should also point out that no simple formulas can tell you how much is a fair price to pay for time at any particular point. A six-month option might or might not cost twice as much as a three-month option. You are dealing with the spreads of the underlying commodity, which, of course, can change. Many times the near month moves faster than the back months, and this is reflected in the option's cost.

Time decay

All else being equal, the time value of an option decreases slightly each day (providing there is still a reasonable amount of time left before expiration). The rate of this decrease becomes more rapid as the option gets closer to expiration. This is termed the **normal time decay**, which works to the detriment of the buyer and the benefit of the seller. As an option gets close to expiration, **time value** becomes less and less. What matters is the relationship between the strike and the underlying commodity. This is because at expiration, the option can only be worth something or alternatively nothing, and that's it. Remember, you might buy a call because you think a particular commodity will increase in price, but you could show a loss even if you are correct. This happens when the extent of the rise is insufficient to compensate for the time it takes to occur.

In, at, and out of the money

If you look at an options price table, you will notice that it is separated into two major categories: puts and calls. Then you will see listings for different months into the future. Under each month, you will see a variety of different strike prices. These are the prices at which the options can be **exercised,** an important feature of options that makes them more complicated than futures.

eg **Let's look at the gold example. You are bullish gold and decide to purchase the April $400 call when April gold is trading at $399. April gold futures subsequently rise to $425 per ounce. At this point, the option has *intrinsic value*, because the price of the underlying asset (in this case, April gold futures) is above the strike price. At $425 per ounce, the 400 call has $25 of intrinsic value. This is now an *in-the-money* call option, in the money by $25. Because a gold option is for 100 ounces, and every $1 is worth $100 per option, the value of this option is at least $2,500 ($25 times $100 per ounce). Another way to look at this is that the right to buy at 400, when the current price is 425, must be worth *at least* 25 because it is already profitable by this amount. It could be worth more, of course, if there were still *time value.***

- Time value is that portion of the premium price outside of the intrinsic value. An option's price is dependent on time, but there are other factors as well that determine an option's value.

- By definition, a call option is "in the money" when the market price of the futures is above the strike price of the option. A cocoa 1400 call is in the money when the futures are trading at 1458. A call option is out of the money when the futures price is below the strike. The same call is out of the money when the futures are at 1361. Because puts are always the mirror image of the calls, a put option is "in the money" when the market price of the futures is below the strike price of the option. A 1400 cocoa put is in the money at a 1361 futures price but out of the money at 1458. Out-of-the-money options have time value only.

How are option prices determined?

Like futures, options are traded in an auction-like environment either in a pit on the floor of the Exchange with open outcry or electronically. In many cases, the option pit is adjacent to, or sometimes right in the middle of, the futures pit for the same commodity. The futures traders are looking at whatever technical or fundamental factors they use to determine the value of the particular commodity they are trading, whereas the option traders are also looking at the futures. It goes without saying that the underlying asset determines an option's premium price. Dissecting this a bit deeper, you see that any particular option's premium has two basic parts: time value and intrinsic value. Options that are out of the money have only time value. That is, these options have no value other than potential value.

For example, in the earlier scenario, the April $400 gold call was trading for $6 per ounce in December and would have cost the buyer $600. The price of April gold at that time was $399, so the option could not have been exercised at a profit. Nobody in his right mind would exercise an option to receive April futures at $400 when he could go immediately into the marketplace and buy it $1 per ounce cheaper.

So why, then, would anyone in his right mind pay $600 for this right? The reason is that this option has *potential*. To buy futures, the risk is potentially greater than $600. Yes, you could buy April futures at $399 and place a $6 stop. Although this would essentially provide the same risk without having to fork over the $600, some major differences exist. For one thing, when you buy an option for $600, you know what your maximum risk is guaranteed. If you purchase futures, with a $600 stop loss, the stop could be filled better at times, but more times it would be a bit worse than your stop loss point. It is entirely possible that April gold could close one afternoon at $394.10, not elect your $394 stop, and then open the next day at $390, thereby stopping you out at a $900 loss when you thought you were risking only $600. Let's say the overseas market fell due to sales by the Belgium Central Bank, London gold fell $4.10 per ounce, and New York (where you bought your contract) opened in line with London due to arbitrage selling. Now your projected risk of $600 per contract turns into a $900 loss, which is 50% more than projected. This cannot happen with options, which brings us back to the main advantage.

Another possibility is that the market could trade in a range. The market could fall $6 or more, stop you out of your futures, and then eventually trade back up to profitable levels. This underscores another main advantage of option purchases, which is **staying power**. The other side of the coin has to do with the cost. If you analyze correctly and are willing to take the risk of the futures, you are guaranteed to make more than buying options. If the price of gold rises to $425, and you bought your contract at $399, you have the ability to cash in with a $2,600 profit per contract ($26 times $100 per ounce) minus fees. You have the right to sell your option, and/or exercise it, but your profit has to be less than the $2,600. Remember, you paid $600 for time, or $600 for the potential to make a score. Some time has passed, and some time value will have disappeared. You will not get back that full $600, only a portion of it.

Let's review these concepts and clear up any confusion that remains.

Calls that have a strike price above the market (for example, a $400 gold call with the market at $399) and puts that have a strike price below the market (a $390 put with the market at $399) have premiums composed of time value only. In-the-money options ($400 call with the market price at $425, or $440 put with the market at $425) have both time and intrinsic value. The more an option is in the money, the more valuable it becomes, so by definition, it becomes more expensive.

Another way of looking at this is with a simple formula: Time Value = Premium–Intrinsic Value. Time value increases for options with greater time to expiration. It makes sense, of course, because the more time an option has until expiration, the more potential the option buyer has for something to happen that increases the value of the option. The seller is taking additional risk (there's more time for something to go awry from his standpoint), and he demands additional compensation for this additional risk.

We now know in-the-money options have intrinsic value and time value. Out-of-the-money options have time value only. You'll hear the term **at the money** as well, which refers to an option for which the strike price is equivalent to the underlying futures price. In practice, at the moneys are those options for which strike prices are close to the price of the futures.

In the example, with April gold at $399, the 400s are "at the money." The 410s are definitely out of the money, and the 390s are certainly in the money. The 360s are *deep in the money*. What would you call the 500s? You could call them *deep out of the money*, what I might refer to as a long shot.

Long shots are generally cheap. You can buy quite a few out-of-the-money options for relatively little money, which means that if something extraordinary occurs, you stand to make a killing. A good analogy would be the Megabucks slot machines in Nevada. The state's casinos link up for the Megabucks jackpot, where $3 can win $20 million or more. People do win these, but how many do you know? Of course, the jack does pop out of the box every blue moon. I once had a client with way-out-of-the-money wheat calls (worth less than a penny each if I remember correctly) and only three days to go. It looked hopeless, and I felt he should have salvaged a few pennies so he could at least cover commissions. Then something called Chernobyl happened. We had never traded a nuclear accident before, and the rumors started to fly. The first rumor was that the entire Soviet wheat crop was wiped out. Wheat went limit up the next day and the day after. The options came back from the dead, and my client eventually cashed out each option on expiration day for 39¢ per bushel. In other words, options were selling for less than $50 each just days before and blossomed to $1,950 on expiration day. It was a good thing he had to sell that day (and that he didn't decide to exercise), because after the real facts became known and the extent of the radiation damage was deemed not as severe as first feared, wheat prices came all the way back down a few days later.

You do hear rags-to-riches stories at times as cheap options come to life. I personally owned some Euro puts that were just essentially worthless, and then the day of the Soviet coup, they blossomed to 50 points, or $625. When Yeltsin stood on the tank, and the coup failed the next day, they became virtually worthless again. Sometimes you need to be nimble. The point is, deep out-of-the-money options can hit at times, but they are long shots and generally a loser's game. I prefer both buying and selling at the moneys in most normal situations. With deep in-the-money options, you tie up capital that otherwise could be used for diversification. Deep out of the moneys generally expire worthless. Given the choice, I also prefer to pay more for time.

To review, we have discussed how an option's value is determined—time and the relationship of the strike price to the underlying futures price. Oh, and I almost forgot, there is another component: **volatility.** Very simply, as the volatility of a market increases, so do option premiums. This is an important determinant in pricing options. Sleepy markets supposedly have lower potential price movements, and option buyers bid less. However, some of my best option purchases have been "cheap" buys. When everyone is buying, the smart money is selling. The reason premiums increase with higher volatility is very simple: Option sellers demand higher premiums to offset the higher risks their options entail in a more volatile environment.

Many of the option pricing models place a great deal of emphasis on **historic volatility**. In determining "fair value," you are asked to input this number. For example, if the market is moving at a rate that equals 20% of the price annualized, this is your historic volatility. I have found this to be an academic exercise of limited value. It is only a prediction, and the past is not necessarily a good predictor of the future. My experience has shown the opposite: Quiet markets lead to more volatile markets and vice versa. When volatility is high, option prices are expensive, and although it takes guts, this is generally the time to sell. On the other hand, an old-timer once gave me some sage advice: "Never sell a quiet market." Let me sum this up another way. In general, the premiums reflect recent market conditions. In explosive markets, the premiums are larger than quiet markets. The risk equals the reward; however, in some situations, the majority does not see the change coming. Premiums could be tiny just before a major move comes; options are their cheapest when they are the best buys. Conversely, at the pinnacle of expectation, decent opportunities to sell arise because premiums are at their highest.

One last point about volatility: on a percentage basis, volatility affects at- and out-of-the-money options to a greater extent than in-the-money options. Here's the reason: In the moneys have both intrinsic and extrinsic (anything other than intrinsic, mostly time) value. Intrinsic value is not affected directly by changes in volatility. Therefore, a change of 10% in volatility might change the in-the-money option's value by 2%, whereas it would change an at-the-money's value by 10%. Out of the moneys are affected most by changes in volatility, because they can become profitable only when the market moves to them. A change of 10% in volatility could result in the option price moving by up to 50% or more. This percentage move is also easier to accomplish for out of the moneys, because they are cheaper.

One final factor that determines option premiums is the cost of money or interest rates. I won't dwell on interest rates here or discuss the various models for fair option pricing, because I have found these variables to be more theoretical than practical. In most cases, the professionals on the floor are able to exploit minor degrees in option mispricing, but this is not what we are playing for here. We are in this for bigger moves that can be exploited (or, for a hedger, options as a tool for price protection).

How changes in the price of the underlying commodity change the option's premium

The basic rule of thumb, all other things being equal, for how changes in price of the underlying commodity change an options' premium are as follows:

- At-the-money options move at a 50% rate of change. For example, if the S&P moves 200 points, an at-the-money option will increase or decrease by about 100 points.

- In-the-money options move at a 50 to 100% rate of change, depending on how deep in the money they are.

- Out-of-the-money options move at 0 to –50% rate of change, depending on how deep out of the money they are.

Again, these are rules of thumb. I have seen days in quiet markets when both puts and calls lose premium regardless of the move of the market. Then again, in times of wild fluctuations or greater than normal expectations, both puts and calls can gain premium in the same day. However, in normal markets, these rules work fairly well. An at-the-money option moves at about half the speed of the futures. The next strike price below might move 45% of the futures if a call and an up day, the next strike up 40% of the futures move and so on.

If you trade options, you hear the term **delta,** which is what we are referring to here. Delta values range from 0 (for very deep out-of-the-money options) to 1 (or 100% for options so deeply in the money that they move just like the underlying futures). At-the-money options have a delta value of 50% (or .5). Calls have a **positive delta**, whereas puts have a **negative delta**. If, for example, a 100 copper call trading for 250 points (or 2 1/2¢) has a delta of .6, a 1¢ (or 100 point) move in the copper price results in a move of 60 points in the value of the call to 310.

You might also hear the term **delta hedging**. On the floor, many professionals who specialize in selling options to the public strive to manipulate their position to always be neutral delta hedged. In this way, they look to maximize the benefits of time decay. You can understand this best with a simple example.

Say you buy 10 March 600 silver calls for 23¢. They are in the money and have a delta of 70% (or + .7). You are bullish silver longer term, but you do not like the way the charts look temporarily, and instead of selling out the position, you wish to hedge it. You would sell short 7 March futures to hedge your 10 calls. For normal moves in price over relatively short periods of time, the 7 futures would offset the change in value of the 10 options. You still risk loss of time value, but that's essentially it. If volatility increases, you could possibly gain a bit. On balance, however, to be delta neutral is a no-win no-lose situation, which should be used for short-term protection only.

Gamma is an interesting concept in theory, but I have found it of limited use in practice. The average trader needn't monitor gamma, but because you might hear the term, you need to know what it is. Gamma is the extent to which the delta itself is changing in relation to the underlying price move, or the change in volatility. For those who wish to achieve delta neutrality constantly, it is something to keep an eye on, but a more detailed explanation is beyond the scope of this discussion.

Exercising profitable options

When you exercise an option, you receive the underlying asset. In the case of a put option, you receive a short futures contract. (The seller or option writer receives the other side of the transaction, which is the long position.)

eg **For example, let's say it is March. You feel soybean prices are overvalued and purchase May $7.00 put options when the May futures are $7.02 for 10¢ per bushel. Then the futures fall to $6.85. The puts reflect the increased intrinsic value, in this case. They trade for at least 15¢, the difference between the strike price and the intrinsic value, or the amount the option is in the money. The put buyer could exercise his option, receive a short futures at $7, and if desired, could cover the short futures at $6.85 in the futures market to realize the 15¢. He makes an automatic profit of 5¢ per bushel, or $250 per contract, which is the difference between the purchase price of the option and the futures profit.**

Of course, this example does not include commissions, one of the basic reasons more options are not exercised. Instead of paying the commission to receive the futures and an additional commission when you offset the futures, it is much simpler and easier to sell the option back in the options market.

Most option transactions take place entirely in the options market. When you are in the futures (which is what happens when you exercise), you assume the additional risks of futures. You can still lose more than your initial investment if you're not careful, and you must post margins required for futures. In fact, option buyers never have to get involved in the futures at all. Option premiums reflect the change in value of the underlying futures. In addition, there is another good reason not to exercise options in normal markets. You are giving up, in most cases, some additional money, which represents any time value remaining.

eg **Let's look again at the soybean put option. The put value always includes any cash value, or intrinsic value, which is determined by the underlying futures. When the market is trading at $6.85, the $7 put is 15¢ in the money and has 15¢ in intrinsic value. Depending on how much time is left until expiration, this put also has some time value associated with it. It may be trading for 20¢ or more if a lot of time is left or perhaps 16¢ if just a few days are left. This is an *in-the-money put* in this example. The $6.80 also has a quoted value. With months left, it could be 10¢ or more, or with days left, only a few pennies. This is an *out-of-the-money option* with no intrinsic value. Its total price consists of time value, or the potential to become profitable based on time, market outlook, and volatility.**

In conclusion, the most profitable, least costly, and easiest way to liquidate an option is to sell the option back into the options market instead of exercising it.

Should you ever exercise an option?

In only one instance would I consider exercising a long put or call. On the last day, no time value is left, generally speaking. Options are priced according to their cash value. This also happens, at times, to deep in-the-money options prior to expiration. You might think you could always sell an option for at least its cash or intrinsic value, but this is not always the case. At the very end, you are most likely dealing with a local or professional trader. The public is not interested in selling in-the-money options on the last day. The locals require a sweetener to take the other side of your transaction if you are looking to sell an option like this, and you may need to give up a small piece of the premium you earned to liquidate in the options market at an illiquid time.

eg **Looking at the soybean put example once more, let's say the market is at 660, and you try to sell your 700 put for 40¢ with very little time remaining. You might not get the order filled. You might need to price it at 39¢, which would guarantee the local a modest 1¢ ($50 per contract) profit. He just offsets the transaction in the futures market, and this guarantees him a profit. Another option is to buy the futures at 660, exercise the 700 put, and be assigned a short futures at 700, which offsets with your long from 660 and results in a 40¢ futures profit. Your net profit in this example is the 40¢ minus your original option cost minus commissions. You need to consider whether this makes more sense than letting the local take the sweetener. Or, if you still feel the market is going to move in the direction of your option, consider exercising a profitable option on the last day. You don't need to even consider this prior to the last day, but on the day of expiration, you do.**

Remember, you are subject to the margining requirements of futures. In many cases, however, for a deep in-the-money option, you have this covered by the value of the option—at least temporarily. A greater concern is that you are now in the futures, something option buyers have been trying to avoid. The risk is no longer limited, and an unfavorable move in the underlying futures can now wipe out your profit, so use a stop loss to prevent losing what you made.

If selling options puts the odds in my favor, why not do it?

Professional traders sell more options than the public. Traders like getting the head start that selling (also called option *writing*) entails. Anyone can take the other side of an option purchase; however, the field is wide open. It is something to consider, but first think about the following.

The primary advantage of buying options is the option writer's disadvantage

When you sell an option, you agree to provide the option buyer with either a long position (when writing a call) or a short position (when writing a put). You receive the premium, but because the market could move an unlimited amount away from the strike price, the associated risk is also unlimited. The greater the premium received, the lower the risk to the option writer. The lower the volatility (not always an easy thing to predict), the lower the risk to the option writer. As a general rule of thumb, the less time that exists until expiration, the lower the risk to the option writer. The option writer is also subject to the risk of exercise. This is a right specifically granted to the option buyer, over which the seller has no control. When the buyer exercises a call option, he is credited with a long futures position at the strike price; the seller receives the short side of the transaction (at the strike price). When a put is exercised, the buyer is credited with the short, and the seller with the long. An option is exercised by the buyer only when it is profitable for him to do so. Because profitability is the main reason the buyer is in options, there is no other reason to exercise the option. The buyer would just walk away from an unprofitable option, either by letting it expire worthless or by selling it back to the option market if there is time value left. By definition, when an option is exercised against the seller, it is unprofitable to the seller. The only time it would not be unprofitable is if the seller sold the option in the aftermarket when it was already unprofitable to a previous seller.

The risk of exercise and the unlimited potential risk are the risks all option sellers must, by contract, accept. So why take these risks? The option seller has a head start; he receives the premium. This insulates his risk to some extent, and he makes money in more situations than the buyer. The buyer needs a move in his favor. If he holds the option until expiration to realize a profit, the buyer needs not only a favorable move but also a move that exceeds the premium he paid. The seller can make money if there is a move favorable to his position (up when selling puts or down when selling calls). He also makes money in a quiet or stationary market, something the option buyer cannot do. Finally, he can profit even if the market moves against him, as long as it moves to a lesser degree than the premium received.

You no doubt will hear the warnings against "naked" option writing. But just how risky is it to sell options? Well, it can be risky, certainly more so than buying, but actually less so than futures. It's risky because you receive a premium, and in the case of writing out-of-the-money options, you have the additional cushion of the gap between the market and the strike price. Furthermore, the option writer can employ defensive strategies to protect himself. The writer can always buy back his short position, just as a short futures trader can buy back his. He can use a stop loss in the option market, just as in futures. Some options are not all that liquid, and you need to take this into account, but many of them trade actively and are as liquid, in some cases more so, than many futures markets. Finally, the option writer can buy (in the case of selling a call) or sell (for a put) a futures against his option if he gets into trouble. In many cases, professionals use this strategy to become more neutral.

eg **For example, assume you're bullish corn, and you are looking for an up move but not necessarily a major move. You can buy futures, buy calls, or sell puts. It is late September, and December corn is trading at $3 per bushel. You can buy the futures at $3, have unlimited upside, and (theoretically) unlimited risk. You can buy the December 300 calls for 10¢ per bushel, or sell the December 300 puts for 10¢. You project the market will make a move to the $3.10 level, so you decide to sell the puts. If the market closes anywhere above $3 at expiration, you keep the entire premium, which in this case is 10¢, or $500 per option (minus the**

inevitable commission). If the market does close at $3.10, you keep the premium (because the 300 put expires worthless and is abandoned by the buyer). This is a profit, the same as the futures buyer who buys at $3 and sells at $3.10. However, the put seller realizes the same profit—at a corn price of $3 at expiration, whereas the futures buyer only breaks even.

You can even be wrong and not lose. At expiration, if the market drops to $2.90, while the futures buyer is sitting with a 10¢ loss, the seller can still get out of his obligation in the options market at about 10¢, or no worse than a break even—wrong, and no loss. The beauty of selling options is that you can also be wrong and still profit. In this example, if the market falls to $2.95 by expiration, the option can be covered at 5¢ for a 5¢ profit. You can be wrong and still make a profit, which is an impossibility with futures or any other investment I can think of. The odds are in the option seller's favor, because the majority of options do expire worthless and are never exercised. However, the payoffs are not as potentially high. Here's the rub: The most the option seller ever receives is the premium, never a penny more. The risks are greater than buying, and for some traders the risks are just too high for the potential gain. This is the trade-off. Sellers have the odds in their favor, but buyers have the greater potential. This is not to say that sellers are stuck with the position. Just as in futures, the risks can be managed. Just like a short seller in the futures, the short option seller can get out by covering his position in the option market. Stop-loss orders are accepted in options and should be used. Should *you* write options? Nothing is wrong with it for those who understand the risks and how to manage them. Some traders, however, just cannot find it in themselves to cut the losses (one of the most important lessons I am trying to teach in this book), and they should buy only options—nothing else. You know who you are.

Options, a prime hedging tool

Hedging is the offsetting of risks from other positions. Although I personally prefer futures to options as a speculator, I also believe hedgers should strongly consider options versus futures. Options truly can offer the best of both worlds.

eg **For example, a cattle feeder should know what his break-even cost is. He knows what he paid for the calf, and he knows his feed costs. (He hedged his corn, of course.) He knows his vet costs and labor, he has an allowance for death loss, and he can to the penny calculate his cost to finance the entire operation. Therefore, he would know that his break even is 70¢ per pound for the finished product (a market-ready animal 120 days hence).**

What he doesn't know is what his ultimate selling price will be on that date. After all, he is dealing with the unknown to some extent here. The futures 120 days out could be trading at 73¢, and by selling the futures today, he can guarantee himself a 3¢ profit. This isn't all bad, except that cattle feeding is a risky business. In periods of windfall profits, 20¢ per pound or more can be had. In other periods, 120 days of work and risk result in a net loss. If a 3¢ profit could always be locked in, a lot of the risk and uncertainty would be taken out of the equation, but in the real world, it's not always possible to lock in a profit.

The bottom line? You need the windfall profits at times to offset the marginal profits and losing periods that also occur. Futures hedges lock out the windfall profits. If you sell futures at 73, and the price at finish is 80, you have a futures loss of 7, which offsets the windfall cash gain of 10. The net result gets you back to your 3¢ profit. Today, most cattle feeders just accept the risk of the marketplace. They feed cattle and hope for a decent price in four or five months to reward them for their efforts. Sometimes it is, but there are also many *former* cattle feeders out there. On the other hand, the big, profitable corporate cattle feeders use options. This should tell you something.

Here's how it might work.

The feeder, in this case, could buy a 120-day live cattle put at, say, a 73 strike price for 2¢ per pound. In effect, he is "locking in" a 71¢ selling price (73 minus 2). If the price falls to, for example, 66 at expiration when his cattle are ready, he will take a 4¢ bath in the cash market. His break even is 70, so a sale at 66 is a 4¢ loss. However, to offset this loss, his option will be worth 7¢, for a net profit of 5¢ before commissions (recall he paid 2¢). Add the 5 back to the 66, and he, in effect, gets back to his 71¢ in the worst-case scenario. So the feeder is giving up 2¢ of potential profit for the ability to avoid catastrophic loss. The real beauty of the options, unlike futures and unlike forward contracting in the cash market, is that his upside is totally unlimited. If prices rise to 80, he reaps a 10¢ profit in the cash market. This is reduced by the cost of the option, in this case 2¢ down to 8¢, but his upside is unlimited. The bottom line is that the farmer has a tool in which he can guarantee himself a price floor, a worst-case scenario, while not constructing a ceiling (which is what he is doing with futures hedges).

Precious few opportunities exist for the farmer to reap windfall profits, and he needs them to offset the mediocre or worse-than-mediocre years. Options are a powerful tool that, when used properly, achieve this goal.

This concept works just as well in financial futures. A U.S. company receives an order from Germany for equipment not yet built, with the U.S. company receiving Euros on delivery in six months. The Euro is trading today at 95¢ to the dollar. The profit margin is good, but it could be wiped out by exchange-rate fluctuations. Also, a windfall gain could be possible if the currency moves up in relation to the dollar within the time period. The company is not in the business of currency speculation; its business is building equipment. The common practice is to hedge in the currency forward by using the Interbank market (the electronic market between banks for foreign exchange trading). This might be prudent, and it certainly makes more sense to a manufacturing business than floating in the wind. Options can be just as prudent, and they offer something else, a sweetener—the possibility of *improving* on a position while limiting the risk for a predetermined cost.

The company can purchase an option, giving it the right to sell Euros at, say, 95¢ to the dollar in six months for 250 basis points, a 95 put. A standard contract traded at the IMM (a division of the CME) is for 125,000 Euros. The minimum tick is for $12.50 per contract, so a quote of 250 points would cost the company $3,125. If the order is for $1 million worth of equipment (today's exchange rate), the company might buy about eight of these puts—profit insurance, so to speak. If the Euro rises, the company loses the premiums, but it can reap an additional currency profit theoretically unlimited. If the Euro falls, the company sells the put for a profit, and this offsets the cheaper currency. Ultimately, the company is willing to pay the $25,000, which reduces its bottom line profit to ensure a profit.

Finally, let's look at this from the other side. If a company places an order for merchandise or equipment and is required to pay for it on receipt sometime in the future, this firm also has a currency exposure. A rise in the value of the Euro, or Yen, or whatever currency means higher costs. A fall cheapens the purchase and adds to line profits. Unless the firm's purchasing people are gamblers, which translates into being a hero or a bum (and bums don't keep their jobs), they will hedge this risk. The traditional method is to forward contract in the Interbank market or buy futures. Both methods lock-in a price or cost of the currency. However, buying calls might be a better way to go, establishing a ceiling price on costs while allowing for windfall profits if the currency falls by more than the option price in the time period.

Stock index options

How many times have you been right about the direction of the stock market but *your* stocks went nowhere? Well, you guessed it, there's a simple way to gamble on the stock market without having to be a stock picker. A trader who is bullish can buy S&P 500 (or any of the other) stock index call options. The bear would, of course, buy the puts. Or, when the premiums are high, a sale might be warranted. Much of the volume in the S&P is institutional, where a portfolio manager uses the futures or options for protection, but any individual can use S&P at-the-money puts for price protection. They allow the buyer to sell the S&P 500 index (500 biggest stocks representing more than 80% of the U.S. market) at today's market price. One put protects 250 times the index. In other words, if the index is at 1300, one at-the-money put will "protect" a $325,000 stock portfolio (250 times 1300) for a specified period. The option gives the buyer the right, but no obligation, to sell the S&P 500. It increases in value by at least $250 (minus the purchase price) for every point the S&P falls (a point is a move from, say, 1300 to 1299). It can be sold prior to expiration. If prices rise by expiration, the purchase price and commissions are lost, but no additional funds are required. This is a hedge, however, and if you lose on the put, hopefully your stock portfolio rose. If the market falls by the same amount as the premium, you'll get your purchase price back. In other words, you're protecting your portfolio from a fall of *greater* than the premium paid. If the market falls by a greater percentage, you lose on your portfolio but gain on the put option. Why wouldn't a bear just sell his stocks? For long-term investors wary of a market dip, this is cheaper and easier. Selling $325,000 worth of stocks would involve numerous and costly commissions. The commission on one S&P option generally costs less than $100. Plus, you need not forego dividend income on your stocks, worry about long-term capital gains taxes, and if your stocks outperform the market in general, you have a relationship gain. If the market declines, the investor/hedger can sell his put at a profit and hold onto the stocks. If the market rises, the stocks will be worth more, and the put has to be considered insurance that just didn't need to be used.

This chapter covered the options basics. If at this point you feel options are not for you (they're not for everyone), skip ahead to Chapter 7, "How to Analyze the Markets Fundamentally." Options can be quite useful, however, even to the futures trader. Trust me on this. If you are intrigued and are starting to see some new ways to make money, you're ready for the more sophisticated techniques covered in Chapters 5, "Advanced Options Strategies," and 6, "Eight Winning Option Trading Rules."

5

Advanced option strategies

Entire books have been written about options. Many of them get too precise for practical real-world trading, covering such academics as complex butterfly spreads and other strategies that might look good on paper but in practice are seldom useful. Here, and in the following chapter, I cover the basic strategies I feel are worth your consideration.

Buying options to protect futures

Buying options to protect futures involves buying a put with long futures or buying a call with short futures. This strategy is also known as creating **synthetic** options, because a put combined with a long futures is similar to a call, and the call in conjunction with the short futures is similar to a put. You can make a case that if you buy an at-the-money call option while simultaneously holding a short futures position (synthetic put), or you buy a put option while simultaneously holding a long futures position (synthetic call) that the overall position will act just like a put or a call (so why bother?). However, this can be a better strategy, because it gives you added flexibility, and I use it quite a bit.

eg For example, you are fundamentally bullish about the hog market, but you are concerned that the upcoming Hogs and Pigs Report could move the market substantially (hopefully in your direction, but there are no guarantees). In fact, the Hogs and Pigs Report, released quarterly by the USDA, has a reputation for moving the market's locked limit, at times consecutive multiple limit days in a row. Lock-limit moves (or abnormal moves in markets without limits) is a risk every futures trader has to accept. If the Report is a bearish surprise, you could lose many times your initial margin because you might not be able to liquidate the first day or even the second. This can become a real nightmare when you're caught on the wrong side of a three-day lock-limit report, and it does happen.

Of course, the Report could confirm your fundamental bias. If you are not in a position, and the market starts moving limit in your intended direction, you might be unable to enter at a reasonable price. You could buy a call, of course, but here's a more flexible approach using hypothetical prices.

You buy the hogs at 72 and simultaneously purchase a 72 put for a premium of 180 points, or $720. If the Report is bullish, you can abandon your put for whatever the market will offer and reap your profit on the futures. If the Report is bearish, you are protected, and regardless of how many limit moves the market makes, you know your worst-case scenario—in this case, a $720 maximum risk plus fees. If worse comes to worst, you can exercise the put, and you will be assigned a short futures position that automatically offsets your long futures. You always have the right to sell your 72 purchase for 72–in other words, a wash in the futures. You are out, at most, the cost of the put.

This is the point where flexibility comes in. These reports are unpredictable, and I've seen markets open limit in the direction of the report and close totally opposite by day's end. The markets trade off the reports initially; however, the reports are not always right, and the smart money uses the news as an opportunity. It is almost always a bullish sign when a market closes opposite the direction a report indicates it should. Let's say, in this case, the consensus was looking for 3% more hogs, and the Report indicates there are 7% more–in other words bearish.

You're glad you had the foresight to buy the put, because the newswires are talking two, maybe three, limit days down. The market opens limit down at 69. The put increases in value from 180, to 450 at the open. The market should theoretically remain limit down, and if two days down, the put should theoretically trade up to 550 or higher. You place a sell stop on the put at 320. Remember, if the market rises, the put loses value. The only way for the stop to be hit is for a rally to happen sometime during the day. If the market remains weak, your plan is to leave the put in place, but if the market starts to rally, you're stopped out of your put at a profit of 140 points, and you still own the long futures.

You are long the futures in an environment where the market is trading; in effect, the abnormal situation is more normal and, therefore, more manageable. You now can place a stop loss under your futures. If the market keeps rallying, you have a good position. The Hogs and Pigs Reports have been proven to be inaccurate 40% of the time, but nobody knows for sure until six months down the road when the pigs actually materialize, or not.

In this scenario, you have protection if the Report proves unmanageable. In effect, if it is a good Report, this protection becomes a "mistake" you are happy to make, because the futures would rise more than the put would deteriorate. Bottom line, you have a lot more flexibility than just buying a call or being naked long futures.

This example represents only one of the many variations and permutations of using options in conjunction with futures. They can give you staying power while allowing you the choice of lifting one side or another at any time. If your technical or fundamental bias changes, you can always lift one side and keep the other. If you reach your profit objective on the futures, you can liquidate and hold the option. At times, "dead" options return from the dead and earn you a double profit.

Another variation on this theme involves buying options to protect profits for a position that has already moved your way. You'll see later that I'm a big fan of riding a trend for all it's worth. In a big move, a market always seems to go further than reason alone might warrant. However, at the end of a move, a market can get overheated, and when you know the top is in, it could be too late. When you feel the end is near, but there is no reason fundamentally or technically to liquidate, why not just buy an option to protect profits? It could be money well spent, and if you are too early, this is the kind of mistake you like to make, because you will make more on the futures than you spend on the option.

Writing options as a hedging strategy

In the previous chapter, you learned how a company with foreign currency risk could purchase options to hedge this risk. A more sophisticated strategy, however, involves the selling of options to generate additional income.

For example, what if a company needs to buy Japanese Yen and is happy with today's rate of exchange? To generate additional income, the manager could sell at-the-money put options. Let's say the Yen was trading at 88, and the 88 puts for 90 days were priced at 200 points. By selling the puts, the company's account is credited with the premium—in this case $2,500 per option. In effect, the company is saying it is willing to buy Yen from the option buyer at 88. If the value of the Yen rises, the puts remain unexercised at expiration, and the company keeps the entire premium. This is a hedge, in that the money can be used to offset the higher Yen.

If the Yen rises by less than 200 points, the company is money ahead. If it rises by more, the company can buy calls or futures, or forward contract at an appropriate spot (if it is unwilling to accept additional risk in the marketplace). If the Yen falls, the company simply honors its commitment to purchase Yen at the higher price. (It will be assigned long futures at 88, a price it was willing to live with.) But the company still keeps the 200 points that effectively lowers the purchase price to 86 points.

This strategy works best if the outlook is for a stable, slightly rising, or slightly falling market. By receiving the premium, the traditional costs of hedging are not only reduced, but at times they can be totally paid for plus a bonus.

Covered option writing

The advantage and attraction of *buying* options is that your risk is limited and predetermined, with the profit potential unlimited. Be aware, however, that most options expire worthless, and the premiums eventually disappear. Therefore, buying options is generally a losing proposition. This is not to say you cannot make good money in a major bull or major bear market, but be advised that most professionals primarily sell options (generally to the public). They might hedge these sales with a ratio of long or short futures, but the public generally likes to purchase premium. The advantage of *selling* options is that you can capitalize on the time decay of options. Because the premiums that people pay for options eventually rise to option heaven, the option seller gains these premiums. Writing options is generally a winning strategy; however, the big disadvantage is that the risk is unlimited, while the profit potential is limited to the premiums received. When option premiums are high, the general rule of thumb is that it is better to sell options than to buy them.

The advantage of futures is the unlimited profit potential, but the risk is theoretically unlimited also. You should, therefore, use risk-management techniques (stops). Stops are not foolproof, but they generally work efficiently. The main problems with stops is that they can be filled away from your intended risk level at times, and in a volatile market, you can be stopped out only to have the market eventually go back your way. On the other hand, if you do not have stops, you cannot predetermine what your risk is.

Covered option writing can allow you to take advantage of the high option premiums just like the professional sellers, but it is less risky in a volatile market. This basically involves selling call options and buying futures, or selling puts and shorting futures. For example, in a recent bull soybean market, I bought the November beans at 800 and sold the 800 calls for 45¢. This gave me 45¢ in downside protection. At expiration, if the market was anywhere above 755, I still would profit on this trade. If the market was anywhere above 800 at expiration, I would keep the 45¢, or $2,250 gross per covered contract position—not a bad profit.

The disadvantage of this strategy is that the most I could make on each transaction was 45¢. So if "beans in the teens" became a reality, the covered positions would allow only a limited profit. Here is how I overcame this disadvantage: My plan was to pyramid the position approximately every 25¢ up. So if the market moved to, say, 825 (this number is not written in stone, because it depends on circumstances), I would look to buy more futures at 825 and sell the 825 calls for approximately 45¢. At this point, my lower buys are safer. I could theoretically ride these 800 covered writes back down to 755, so the market would have to fall 70¢ before major trouble. If I happened to have the 750s on at this point, they would look even safer, and so on.

Now, if the market appreciated rapidly and we added every 25¢ up taking in an average of 40¢ each time, we make $1.60 for every $1 move up if the market remains strong. With a call option, if you pay 40¢ and the market moves up one dollar you will make only 60¢ at expiration. So, this pyramiding technique is actually a more profitable strategy than just buying calls in a major bull move.

In corrections to the major up-trend, you are better able to ride out the fluctuations than you would be with uncovered futures. In a sideways market, you would make money with this strategy also, whereas you would lose when just buying calls. Of course, with this strategy, there is no predetermined risk if the market goes down more than the short premium, whereas with option purchases, the risk is limited. With the covered position, the risk is less than futures, but you'll need to monitor the position and use a risk point on the futures/option combinations if the market looks too weak.

Option spreads

Futures can be spread in many different ways, and options can be spread in even more. Only with options can you spread two different contracts of the same month. Option spreads can be constructed in a variety of ways to fine tune market outlooks. Although I rarely spread options, some of these strategies are very popular, and they fit in nicely with some trading styles.

Vertical call spreads

A **vertical call spread** is where you have two options of the same month but with different strike prices that are spread against each other. The vertical call spread is bullish, and the vertical put spread is bearish. For example, you're bullish wheat, it's March, and May wheat is trading at $4.20. You buy the May 420 call, pay 22¢, simultaneously sell the May 450 call, and take in 7¢. Your cost (excluding commissions) is the difference between the two premiums–in this case 15¢, or $750. The difference (always a debit) is your maximum risk. If the market at expiration closes below 420, you lose the 22¢ and keep the 7¢, a maximum risk of 15. Your maximum profit is the difference between the strike prices minus the debit. In this case, 450 − 420 = 30 and 30 − 15 = 15. At expiration, above 450 you lose penny for penny on the 450 what you make on the 420. So your maximum profit is at or above 450. Returning 30 for your 22 investment is the lower-priced call, but you keep the 7¢ for a total of 15¢.

Why do this? In one respect, bull-spreading calls offer the best of both worlds. The risk, as in buying options, is strictly limited. You lower your overall cost by benefiting from the time decay of selling premium. You are selling premium on the greater out-of-the-money option, which is more likely to expire worthless than the lower-priced option. The main disadvantage is that the profit is absolutely limited, which eliminates one of the main advantages of buying options. There is still a premium cost, one of the main disadvantages of buying options, and you incur double commissions.

Vertical put spreads

This is the mirror image of the call spread. For example, you are mildly bearish in the stock market. It is July, and the September S&P is trading at 750. You buy the August 740 put (which keys off the September contract and expires the third Friday in August) for 1800 points and sell the 710 for 450 points. Your maximum risk is 1800 points minus 450 (1350 points), or $3,375. You lowered your maximum risk by $1,125 instead of just buying the 740 put. Your maximum profit takes place under 710 and is the difference between the strike prices (in this case 30 points, or $7,500 minus the debit of $3,375, which is $4,125 excluding commissions). By writing a lower-priced put against a higher-priced put, you take on less risk for a lowered potential profit. For call spreads, by writing a higher-priced call against a lower-priced call, you do the same thing. There are quite a few variations, but in practice, if you use a call that is priced too high or a put priced too low, you will not receive enough premiums to lower the cost sufficiently.

Calendar spreads

Also known as time spreads, **calendar spreads** take advantage of the tendency of nearby options to decay faster than distant options. This strategy involves the sale of an option in one month and the simultaneous purchase of an option (usually, but not necessarily, the same strike price) in a later month. For example, you might sell a September 1500 cocoa call and buy a December 1500 cocoa call for a net debit. If the market remains fairly stable, you eventually gain the premium in the nearby to cheapen the ultimate cost of the distant, or there will be a net gain on the entire position after some time passes. (You can, of course, liquidate both sides or just one side at any time.) One of the potential pitfalls in this strategy is that the spread values of the underlying commodity can change, perhaps favorably, but contrary to expectations as well. Many times, the nearby month, which affects the short side of the spread, moves more dramatically because of higher open interest and greater speculative play. The risk cannot always be predetermined to an exact level like the vertical spreads; however, there is merit in this strategy if it is monitored and used correctly.

Straddles and strangles

Straddles and **strangles** are option spreads that involve both puts and calls. The straddle involves buying or selling puts and calls at the same strike price. During the life of a straddle, it is almost a certainty that one or both of the options will be in the money at any point in time. The strangle involves different strike prices, so it is less likely that both, or even one of the strangle legs, will be in the money at any point in time. However, it is certainly quite possible. There are two sides to each of these market plays, so let's examine the four possibilities.

Buying a straddle

 It is late September, and the December T-Bonds are trading at 10503. You buy the December 105 call and the 105 put. The call is trading for two full points and 1/32. The put is trading for 1 and 31/32. Your cost is the sum of both premiums, or in this case, four full points or $4,000 (plus commissions). So that you can be profitable at expiration, bonds must move more than four points, above 109 or below 101.

The advantage of this strategy is that you know, to the penny, your maximum risk on the trade. The disadvantage is that you must overcome double premiums to be profitable. Why do this? The only situation in which this makes any sense is when you anticipate a volatile market but do not have any idea which direction the market will move. Suppose there's a big unemployment report coming out that will determine Federal policy. You know this report will move the market, but you have no clue as to how it will come out or how it will be received. After the report, you can decide whether you want to cut the losses on the bad option and let the good one roll, or whether the move is dramatic enough for the good one to cover both premiums. In practice, I've found this strategy works only if you are willing to manage it.

To overcome the time decay of two options, you need to be very right over time. At times, after a move of significance, it could make sense to take a profit on the good side and hope the other returns from the dead, or to cut the loss on the unprofitable side and look to maximize the good side. There are no hard and fast rules here. It takes management and smarts. Back to the example, the report is released, and unemployment is up dramatically. Because this indicates a weakening economy, the thought is that the Fed could lower rates, which means bullish bond prices.

Next, you observe how the market reacts to the report. Remember, it is not the news, but how the market reacts to the news, that is important. In this case, bond prices move up dramatically, rallying more than 2 1/2 full points to close at 10718. The call gains about a point and a quarter, and the put loses one point. Because of the delta pricing of options, the first leg of the move is the least profitable for this strategy. As your profitable option moves deeper into the money, it acts more and more like a futures contract, and this strategy becomes increasingly profitable. The out of the money loses comparatively less, because it has less to lose. Of course, at any time you have the choice of selling out one leg of the straddle or both. If at some point your indicators tell you the move is over, you might wish to take profits on the call and hold on to the put, hoping the move reverses to the downside. You could, if you are looking for a major bull to unfold, cut your loss on the put and hold on to the call. In this case, you would realize a loss of about one point, and you would most likely be out about $1,000 or so on the realized side of the equation.

If, at expiration, the market falls back under 105, you would lose your entire call premium, and this "limited risk" trade would cost you more than $3,500 per straddle. For this reason, it is important to protect profits on the good side of the spread. You could place a stop on the call at break even (for the call), and this action would limit your risk on the entire position to approximately the put loss while leaving your upside open. After you are out of the put, you need a move (at expiration) to more than 108 to show a net profit. Every point move above this level results in a $1,000 profit per point per straddle. The important thing to remember is to use sound judgment and good money management when employing a strategy like this. At expiration, one side of the straddle expires worthless, so you need to make this up.

Selling the straddle

In the previous example, there was someone on the other side of either or both options. Most likely, the buyer of the straddle bought from two different sellers, but you could be a seller of the straddle, too. This is a strategy that places the odds in your favor but raises the risk level. In the previous example, the seller of the December T-Bond 105 straddle receives both premiums, or in this case, about four points. If the market doesn't move, and at the expiration date closes exactly at 105, the seller gets to keep *both* premiums. The odds of this outcome are small, but as long as the market remains within a range, the seller makes something. In this example, he has four points to work with. If the market stays within the relatively wide range of 101 to 109, some profit is possible. The market must move outside of the range for the straddle writer to lose. The problem with this strategy, in many cases, comes in the timing of the move. If the market moves fast (either direction) and volatility increases, the seller could get in trouble. Just as with any limited profit strategy (in this example, the profit is limited to an absolute maximum of $4,000), unlimited risk strategy needs to be managed. If the unemployment report results in a ho-hum reaction, you might want to stay with the entire position. If there is a dramatic move, it certainly could make sense to cut the loss on the unprofitable side but then look to lock in a profit by using some form of risk-control measure (a stop comes to mind) on the profitable side.

Buying the strangle

The strangle is similar to the straddle but with an important difference. The strangle player uses different strikes, usually at either side of the market price. As a buyer, your risk is limited. Your leverage increases, because a major move results in a greater profit on funds at risk. Let's go back to the T-Bond example. In the straddle, you purchased the 105 call *and* a 105 put with the market trading about 105. The strangle buyer might buy, as one of numerous examples, the 108 call for one point *and* the 102 put for just under one point. Therefore, your cost is perhaps $2,000 instead of $4,000, and your risk is cut in half. Your outlook is most likely the same as the straddle buyer; that is, you are looking for a substantial move in a volatile market but don't have a clue as to direction. The disadvantage is that the market must move substantially for you to show a profit. In the straddle example, at expiration the profit zone is outside of 109 or 101. For this strangle, the range has widened to 110 on the upside (108 plus the two points in premium paid) and 100 on the downside. However, if bonds soar to 118 at expiration, this strategy results in a gross profit of $8,000. The 102 put expires worthless. The 108 call would be worth $10,000. The cost was $2,000, resulting in a gross profit of $8,000, or 400%. In the straddle example, the gross profit would be $9,000 at 118. The 105 call would be worth $13,000 minus the $4,000 cost, which equals $9,000. Although the gross profit is higher, the leverage is lower. On a $4,000 risk, the net profit was 225%. For the same risk, you could have purchased two strangles, resulting in a gross profit of $16,000. Don't forget, I am hypothetically assuming a major move here. They do happen, but don't count on them coming all that often.

Selling the strangle

This strategy, which would involve taking the opposite side of the previous example, is profitable most of the time because most out-of-the-money calls expire worthless—or at least they do not totally overcome the premiums paid. In this case, you are writing two out-of-the-money calls, but this does not necessarily put the odds doubly in your favor. If a major bull or bear move takes place, the strangle seller could find himself in big trouble. I cannot stress enough how important it is to manage these option spread strategies, especially when you are a strangle writer. The risks are less, but they are still there, and they are very real. Strangle writing has a lower potential profit than many other plays.

In conclusion, the strangle buyer pays less than the straddle buyer, but his profit potential is lower. The strangle seller has better odds of a profit, but his risks are higher. The strangle and straddle sellers can do quite well in quiet, trading-range type markets. The buyer does well during major bull or bear moves and particularly well in runaway moves. Your market outlook is not as important using these strategies as the *degree* of the move is. Premiums vary by market conditions, so you need to vary your strategy based on these conditions and your outlook. The one rule that always holds true is that the rewards are higher with the risks!

Butterfly spreads

In an effort to be complete, because you will hear this term if you trade long enough, I will tell you what a butterfly spread is, but with a word of advice. A **butterfly spread** is a combination of both a bull spread and a bear spread. It involves three strike prices, for example, buying a May 290 corn call, selling two May 300 corn calls, and buying a May 310 corn call. These are limited risk, but the profit potential generally does not justify the costs involved. Remember, you have the commission costs (in this most simple case, there are four of them), and then you have to overcome the bid to offer spreads on three positions for both the in and the out. Your broker might like the butterfly, but I suggest you fly away from it.

Ratios

Ratios involve buying or selling a greater number of calls or puts on one side of the transaction than the other. They are basically a combination of strategies already discussed and are useful in certain situations.

Ratio writes

Simply stated, a ratio write involves selling a greater number of options than the underlying futures position, with the most common being 2.

eg **For example, it's September 15 and you buy December cotton at 8055, and you simultaneously sell two December 86 calls for a premium of 130 each. You are taking in 260 points in premium. (For cotton, one point is worth $5.) Therefore, this strategy gives you $1,300 in downside protection. The downside risk still exists here, but it is less than an outright futures position. The market at expiration must move below 7795 for this strategy to produce a loss (not including commissions). With the futures, any move under 8055 results in a loss. Profits are also higher on a normal bull move compared to an outright futures position. If the market on option expiration date closes at 8305, a single futures position shows a gross profit of 250 points, or $1,250. The ratio write shows a much more impressive profit of $2,550, because the 86 calls expire worthless, and these premiums are kept in full. It should be noted that this profit is also greater than naked call writing. In this example, the naked call seller receives the $1,300, not the $2,550.**

The rub? This ratio write has a two-sided risk, which is not seen in either covered or naked writes. If the market falls substantially, the risk on the futures is not limited. If the market rallies substantially, the upside risk is unlimited as well, because there is an extra naked call to contend with. A ratio call writer has a neutral to slightly bullish outlook. A ratio put writer (short December cotton and also selling two December puts) has a neutral to slightly bearish outlook. I've stressed this before, and I'll do so again: This is a strategy that can be quite profitable but must be managed. The ratio writer should know his break-even point, both above and below the market, and he should manage the position when it appears threatened. The best positions are those that have a wide enough profit range to allow for defensive action should it become necessary.

Ratio spreads

A 2:1 ratio call spread involves buying one lower-priced call and selling two higher-priced calls.

eg **For example, with May beans trading at 689, you might buy a May 700 call for 14¢ and sell two 725 calls for 7¢ each. Under $7, there is no real risk other than costs on this one. In fact, if you can establish the spread at a credit initially, there is no downside risk. The maximum profit occurs at the upper strike price at expiration. If the market expires exactly at 725, you keep the 14¢ plus show a gross profit of 11¢ (25 minus 14) on the 700. The 25¢, in this case, is the maximum profit.**

The profit potential is reduced above the upper strike price, because the loss is theoretically unlimited for the naked portion of the spread. The greatest risk for ratio call spreads always lies above the market. Ratio put spreads, as you might have guessed, have their greatest risk below the market. Ratio spreads and ratio writes are similar in that they both involve uncovered writes, and both have predetermined profit ranges. The difference is the downside risk (for ratio call spreads) or upside risk (for puts) is small and in some cases nonexistent. Again, you would use this strategy in a neutral or mildly bullish or bearish environment. Virtually unlimited permutations of ratios and strike prices can be used; just remember to use good judgment.

Reverse ratio spreads

As the name implies, this is a strategy opposite to the more commonly utilized ones; therefore, you don't hear much about it. Nevertheless, I like it. It involves selling a call or put at one strike price and then buying a greater number of calls at a higher strike price or buying a greater number of puts at a lower strike price. This is also commonly called a **backspread**. You want to look for backspreads that you can establish for a *credit* and in a market where you anticipate a relatively substantial move for the best profits.

eg **For example, it is February, and May sugar is trading at 1112. You sell an 1100 call for 65 points and you buy two 1200 calls for 23 points each. The spread is established at a credit of 19 points (plus 65 minus [23 times 2]). If May sugar expires under 1100, then all the calls will expire worthless, and the credit of 19 points will be the profit. In fact, this is your maximum downside potential.**

You don't put on a bull backspread anticipating a down move, but if you are total-ly wrong and the market falls, you can still earn a slight profit. This strategy has lim-ited risk. The maximum loss comes at expiration at the purchased calls. In this case, at 1200, the 1100 call sold will show a loss of 35 points (100 points of intrinsic value minus the 65 received) and the 1200 calls will expire worthless. Therefore, the total risk on this one is 35 plus 46, or 81 points. The risk is never more than this.

The real profit potential comes when the market moves above 1200, with no lim-its on the maximum profit potential. If the market expires at 1300, the short call will show a loss of 135 points. However, each of the 1200 calls will show a profit of 76, (76 times 2 minus 135, or 17), a relatively small profit, but at this level the profit potential is now unlimited should the market continue to move in the anticipated direction. One short and one long call offset each other, but the added call gains with the futures market. At 1400 in this example, this strategy results in a 117 point prof-it, at 1500, 217, and so on. The profit range (without fees) is anywhere below 1119, anywhere above 1283, but not in the middle. Very simply, this is a bullish strategy, one that is hedged to an extent by the short sale. The profit is unlimited on a major upside move, and yet there is a wider range of potentially profitable outcomes because the trader can also profit to an extent when totally wrong. As with all these plays, this one can be performed with puts when bearish. It should be used when the outlook is for a relatively large move in a volatile market. It generally makes more sense with more time, and it ties up less money than just buying options. The drawback comes with a relatively normal move in the direction anticipated. If the move is not large enough, a loss will result.

This chapter covered the basic ways to trade options, as well as some more sophisticated strategies. In the next chapter, I'll pull this together by sharing some of my observations on how to use options to your advantage.

6

Eight winning option trading rules

1. Stay away from deep in-the-money options.

The key advantages to buying options are the high leverage and the limited risk. If an option is deep in the money, it cuts down on your leverage and adds to your risk. Even though the risk is still limited, you're paying more and therefore have more to lose. You cut down on your leverage, because you need a bigger move in the underlying asset to generate a significant profit. The whole idea of leverage is to take a small amount of money and have the option to exercise into an asset worth many times as much. When buying deep in-the-money options, you tie up a lot more money that can be used for other opportunities. I don't like selling deep in-the-money options either. You tie up a considerable amount of capital this way (since you need to margin the position). The biggest advantage to the option seller is time decay, and deep in-the-money options have less time value; therefore, you have less to gain the easy way and more risk with the intrinsic value component. Bottom line, I stay away from deep in-the-money options when buying or selling. Of course, when buying options, your objective is to turn an out-of-the-money, at-the-money, or slightly in-the-money option into a deep in-the-money option. Your objective when selling options is to avoid turning your sale into a deep in-the-money. This is an effective way for your wallet to go deep out of money!

2. Stay away from deep out-of-the-money options.

The illusion is that deep out-of-the-money purchases give you a lot of leverage. In reality, they give you a lot of hope, encourage over-commitments, and generally offer little profit opportunity. Yes, they hit at times, but this is a game of probabilities, and the odds are certainly against you when buying deep out of the moneys. You have to be realistic. If the premium appears cheap, there's usually a reason. Of course, you could buy an August 900 soybean call in July when the beans are at 600 and hope for a crop failure. You could probably buy a lot of them because they'd be cheap, maybe just a few pennies or $100 each. Yet, it would be unlikely for beans to rise $3.00 per bushel in just three weeks. It may make more sense to purchase a deep out-of-the-money option if you have sufficient time, but then again you lose some leverage because you are paying for time. The odds are greatly in your favor when you sell deep out-of-the-money options, but the expected reward is minuscule in relation to the risk. You could be profitable 99 out of 100 times when selling deep out-of-the-money put options on the stock market, but that crash will inevitably come on some unexpected event when you least expect it. Unless you wish to be "the house," the one who is capitalized enough to cover its lottery or slot machine jackpot, stay away from deep out of the moneys.

3. Trade slightly out-of-the-money, at-the-money, or slightly in-the-money options.

The reasons here are the opposite of the reasons I prefer to stay away from the deep options. These options have a reasonable chance of proving profitable when buying; you gain from the maximum possible time decay when selling; and they are generally the most liquid of the bunch, resulting in a tighter bid/asked spread, which in turn saves on transaction costs. The one variation on this theme has to do with selling options; in this case, it is certainly fine, and even advantageous, to sell out-of-the-money options with this one caveat—the premium received must warrant the risk. What price might this be? There are no hard and fast rules; you just need to use good judgment. It is also advisable to use good judgment when cutting losses. This involves taking a reasonable or small loss when covering short options that are not working. It is important, as well, to cut losses in long options that aren't making you money. Human nature makes it all too easy to become complacent when buying options. I've seen too many people play them out all the way to expiration when all the indications say the play isn't working. This is just another form of hope, and hope is not a recipe for success. The fact that most options expire worthless should be a strong clue to the buyer to sell out prior to the end in cases of nonperformance. This is easy to do—just pick up the phone (or click the mouse) and "sell"!

4. There is a time for all seasons.

This means you need to have a feel for market conditions prior to implementing any option strategy. I've known traders who have initial success with one or another strategy and think they've found the Holy Grail. I met a doctor who was lucky enough to turn $5,000 into six figures during the bull corn market of 1996. His first trade was a long shot that worked—the purchase of deep out-of-the-money calls for March that turned deeply in the money by expiration. He took his profits and rolled them into at-the-money Mays that also eventually went deeply into the money, then once again into Julys, and that worked, too. He caught the best kind of market for this strategy and then proceeded to give all his profits back in a dull period in a variety of flat markets. I've also seen people win 9 of out 10 times when selling out-of-the-money calls only to fall flat on their faces later. In the early 1980s, a firm called Volume Investors became one of the largest option players in the gold pit by continually selling premium. It worked beautifully for years, but it took just one unexpected, yet volatile spike to wipe them out—to the tune of $6 million. The lesson: Know your market. Option writing can be extremely profitable in dull, flat markets. If the tone changes, cover fast before that catastrophic loss. If option premiums feel too low to give you an adequate cushion of income, they probably are. The common wisdom is to "sell flat markets," but I suggest this is just the time to start thinking about buying. Avoid selling in periods of rising volatility. Option purchases will start to become more expensive, but then the rising volatility will work in the buyer's favor. Only when volatility reaches wild proportions should you think about selling—just make sure you're adequately margined to take the heat.

5. Covered call writing is a good strategy for what appears to be a bullish environment, and covered put writing is generally good for what looks like the bear.

This is one of the few strategies where you use futures and options together and have the ability to profit on both legs. The strategy works well in a modestly bullish or bearish environment as well. It is not risk free, but it is less risky than the outright purchase or sale of futures. Furthermore, by using my limited pyramid strategy discussed in the previous chapter, you have the additional flexibility to capitalize on a major move when using covered positions.

6. In "normal" markets, write straddles and strangles.

Selling puts and calls works in most market environments. It is a good strategy, as long as it is managed properly. "Normal" is a term I am unable to define specifically for you; it's a feeling you will develop after trading for a while. In most cases, the premiums received when writing straddles and strangles give an adequate cushion to weather most storms. However, when the typhoon hits and your margin starts to feel impaired, run for the exit door.

7. Look for opportunities to backspread.

Backspreading is a seldom-used strategy, but when used consistently, it has the potential to make you rich. Recall, this involves selling a call or put at one strike price and buying a greater number of calls at a higher strike price, or buying a greater number of puts at a lower strike price. Look to establish backspreads for a credit to benefit from time decay, and only consider markets with the potential to move big. This strategy always has a predetermined and limited risk and is one of the few that can still prove mildly profitable (or at least keep your equity together) when you're dead wrong. The profit is unlimited on a major upside move. It is not the Holy Grail, and there certainly is risk here as well, but I know of one S&P option trader who traded backspreads only. He held his equity together quite well over a number of years and was always positioned for a major move in either direction. During the stock market crash of 1987, his bear backspreads worked so well he was able to retire as a young man!

8. Use options to hedge a profitable futures position.

If you are a trend-following trader, like I am, and you are lucky enough to catch a major move that is showing massive unrealized profits, the great dilemma is when to cash in. You know you inevitably will have to give up a large portion of your paper gains if you wait for confirmation of a trend change. Yet, top and bottom picking are very hard things to do. There is only one top, and there is only one bottom in major moves of importance, which could develop over hundreds of trading sessions. Many times, the most important leg of a major move takes place in the past 48 hours. Why not use put options to lock in bull-move profits and calls for the bear-move profits? Commercial hedgers use options all the time. Trading is a business, and options are a prime tool as an individual trader to hedge your profit while still allowing for additional profits. For example, you own soybeans in a major drought. You're in at $7 and the market is now $9. There is no rain in the forecast, it's mid-July, and with another two weeks of this, the old rallying call of "beans in the teens" will become a reality. Options aren't cheap, but this is a situation in which I would buy premium anyway. The $9 August puts are running 40¢. Buy them. This is a no lose situation. It's cheap insurance at 40¢, yet you assure yourself a $1.60 profit per contract, $8,000 per contract, and that's not bad. In addition, this is insurance you hope you never need to use. Let the good times roll if the forecasts prove correct! They're not always correct, as I've found out. During the drought of 1988, no weather service that I know of called the end. It was a long holiday weekend, and when we went home on Friday, it was more than 100 degrees with "no chance of meaningful precipitation for at least two weeks." Soybeans were approaching $11 with "beans in the teens" a virtual certainty. It remained hot and dry Saturday and Sunday with not a cloud in the sky. Then, seemingly out of nowhere on Monday afternoon, with the markets closed, the skies opened. It poured rain over a wide area, and we were greeted with a multiple limit down situation beginning with our return Tuesday at the open. If I had only used puts to lock in the significant paper profits, and it turned out to be a mistake, it would have been the kind of mistake we like to make. On the other hand, buying options to lock in profits on futures is the best way I know of to avoid premature "profit-taking-itis." This affects us all at one time of another.

These options are wonderful tools. They're not a panacea, but to an extent, the options can offer you the best of both worlds. Constantly be on the alert for ways to use them to your benefit!

How to analyze the markets fundamentally

There are basically two methods used to analyze the markets: fundamental analysis and technical analysis. Both the fundamental analyst and the technician are trying to solve the same problem: to predict future price movement. However, they approach this problem in different ways.

Fundamental analysis

Fundamental analysis basically is the study of supply and demand. The fundamentalist says that the cause and effect of price movement is explained by supply and demand.

eg **For example, if new copper mine-production is 300,000 tons, manufacturing demand is projected to be 400,000 tons, and "above-ground" supplies available to the market are 50,000 tons, the fundamentalist projects a coming supply** *deficit* **of 50,000 tons.**

Therefore, the conclusion is that price must rise to **ration** or diminish this impossible level of demand. Fundamental analysis appeals to our logic. After all, if Brazil is suffering through a drought during the flowering phase of the soybean plant, you can rationally explain why bean prices are rising. A good fundamentalist is able to forecast a major price move well in advance of the technician. Some fundamentalists have what amounts to "inside information" (and this is perfectly legal in the futures markets). If Cargill has a scout in Africa who identifies a cocoa-killing fungus that is devastating the crop, odds are Cargill will act on this information long before you or I hear about it.

Fundamentalists are able to trade the courage of their convictions and are not shaken out as easily during false market movements. They are better able emotionally to maximize positions, because fundamentals can take a long time to change.

In late 1995, with corn trading in the mid-two-dollar per bushel range, I read that China (formerly the third largest corn exporter, and the largest exporter in Asia) had turned into a corn importer. Apparently, its livestock production had grown to a rate that could not keep pace with its reduced crop production of that year. In my mind, this was a significant fundamental, which was a major reason corn prices were able to hit all-time record highs within a six-month period. No doubt, fundamentals can be powerful and allow a trader to stay with a position longer than he otherwise might stay. However, they also can prompt a trader to stay with a position longer than he should stay.

Technical analysis

On the other hand, a technician is concerned with market action only. The basic issue here is not that fundamentals are what ultimately moves price—the technician concedes this point. The technician believes it is virtually impossible for most of us to know all the fundamentals that affect price at any given time. By the time the news reaches most of us, it has been disseminated so widely that it has been discounted in price. Because a trader makes or loses money via price movements, the technician believes this is what should be studied. In other words, the technician believes price is the ultimate fundamental.

In early 1997, corn had retreated back to the 1995 lows—in the mid-two-dollar-and-fifty-cent per bushel range. The price was that low because the fundamentals were decidedly bearish. Supply was dramatically up, with an excess of a 1-billion bushel carryover supply projected. The livestock numbers were way down. Exports were falling, and China had once again turned into a corn exporter. However, the market traced out a technical "bottom formation," and the commodity funds bought and then bought more. One day in February, they bought 100 million bushels. Many of the commodity funds trade technically. It seemed they all saw the same price action at the same time, and they acted on it. The 100-million bushel purchase pushed prices higher, despite the bearish fundamentals. The higher prices attracted more technical buying, and this new buying hit price stops above the market. Undercapitalized shorts could not meet margin calls and had to cover their positions, and this meant more buying. The commercials were selling into the market, but the funds bought more as additional price objectives were hit. In a four-day period, the funds added another 150 million bushels to their initial purchases. Prices soared by 50¢ per bushel, more than 20%. Farmers started to notice prices were rising and started to hold back on their cash corn sales as they became bullish and waited for higher prices. In this case, a technical move actually resulted in the fundamentals changing (that is, a restriction of supply due to less farmer selling). Eventually, the market fell of its own weight, but there is no denying you could have made a nice profit in a case like this by ignoring the fundamentals and just listening to the sounds of the market.

In some ways, technical analysis can be said to include fundamentals. However, the reverse is not true—a pure fundamentalist does not look at charts. The best fundamentalist tends to make the most money, but he also tends to lose the most when he misses something. In the 1970s, there was a phenomenal pork belly trader who had amassed a fortune amounting to several hundred million dollars. When short-term interest rates started their rise from 4% to 10%, he began to short T-bill futures under the fundamental belief that rates at this level were unsustainable. By the time they reached 18%, he was broke. He was ultimately right in his analysis as rates eventually plummeted, but not before he lost all his money.

Which is the best way to go?

Correct fundamental analysis can make you money, and so can a good technical plan. In either case, a good forecaster can go broke if he is not a good trader. A good trader can make money regardless of whether he can ascertain the correct funda-mentals or technical tone of the market. I believe that a marriage of the two, com-bined with a sensible money management plan, produces the best results over time. In my experience, the best trades come when solid fundamentals (as we see them) agree with the technical action of the marketplace. The subsequent two chapters explore the idiosyncrasies of the technical world. However, because you need to know what it is you're trading (although I know a soybean trader who had not even seen what a soybean looked like until after he had spent his third successful year in the pit), we'll first delve into a brief overview of the fundamentals inherent in the major markets we will be trading. Although this brief introduction will not auto-matically make a good fundamental trader of anyone, it will give the potential spec-ulator background information about the relevant industries as a starting point. As the next step, I suggest you consult the Web sites of the Exchange for the market you are most interested in trading. They all provide detailed fundamental information on the markets they list.

There are hundreds of Exchange-listed futures contracts globally, and most of them have liquid options markets. (Unfortunately, this book does not have enough space to cover them all.) Some do not trade very actively, and some are so specialized that they should be left to those who know. So this book, for example, doesn't cover raw silk or dried cocoon (which is listed on the Manila International Futures Exchange). Instead, I've arranged the major futures markets into four groupings:

- Financial futures

- Energy

- Agricultural markets

- Metals

Financial futures include three major subsets: the interest rate futures, the stock indices, and the currencies. The agricultural markets include the grains, the meats, and the softs. The metals are classified as either industrial or precious. For any of the markets you have an interest in trading, I encourage you to contact a commodity bro-ker or the Exchange where that particular market is traded and ask for additional information.

Financial futures

The highest volume futures and options contracts are not the traditional physical commodities; they are financial futures. After all, money is the ultimate commodity.

Financial futures can be broken down into three basic sections: interest rates, stock indices, and currencies. Many of the fundamentals that affect one group affect the others. Obviously, interest rates affect stock prices and currency valuations. In fact, interest rates are perhaps the most important fundamental capable of moving stock markets and currencies.

Interest rates

Governments allow interest rate futures to exist so that hedgers can neutralize or shift some of their price risks. A mortgage banker can transfer his price risk to a speculator, just as a corporate comptroller can lock in his cost of borrowing funds. The best way to think of any hedge is as a temporary substitute for a transaction that will occur at a later time in another market. When talking about interest rates, some hedgers are interested in protecting against higher rates in the future, and some lower. Speculators are trying to profit from the inherent risks in changes in the cost of money. Of course, in a global economy, rates can be moving in one direction in Japan and another in the United Kingdom. The fundamentals that move interest rates and, therefore, interest rate futures, are varied and dynamic. Human emotion is just as important a fundamental as credit flows. The following sections cover the major interest rate contracts traded in the world today and include a brief summary of some of the major fundamentals that traders should be aware of. Be aware that entire books have been written on how fundamental factors affect the economy and interest rates. I am not trying to imply that my list is all-inclusive, and I do not believe any mortal can factor in all the variables that affect interest rates. Instead, I want to give you a taste for what I have found to be the most important factors. If you feel you want to use fundamental analysis to forecast interest rates, you will have a basis from which to delve further.

There are more than 60 interest rate contracts traded around the world. You can speculate or hedge interest rates in numerous currencies, lengths of maturities, and varieties. The following sections cover the largest and most active of the interest rate futures contracts. All of these contracts have active and liquid options.

Eurodollars

Futures have been traded on commodity exchanges for more than 100 years. The first interest rate futures contract was introduced in 1975. Today, the highest volume futures contract in the world is a short-term interest rate contract traded on the Chicago Mercantile Exchange. Eurodollars also are traded actively on London's Euronext exchange. Yields reflect interest rates in various money market investments. It goes without saying that the yield on a short-term instrument is, in most cases, dramatically different from longer term "paper." You will sooner or later hear the term **yield curve**, which measures the relationship of the yields of various securities against their maturities. The Eurodollar is based on a short-term, 90-day debt issue. Technically, a Eurodollar is defined as any U.S. dollar on deposit outside of the

United States (generally dollar deposits at London branches of major world banks) that, therefore, fall outside the reserve requirements of the Federal Reserve. Actual Eurodollar time deposits are securities available in a short-term maturity time frame for either taking or placing deposits. In reality, this market has become the benchmark for short-term interest rate price discovery for shorter-term U.S. rates. The Eurodollar prices are quoted in terms of an Index. The Index is based on the difference between the actual Eurodollar yield. There is no $ sign here, just the number 100.

eg **For example, a yield of 5.00% is quoted as 9500. If yields rise to 5.50%, the Index falls to 9450 (the difference between 100 and 95.50). The contract size is $1 million, but because this is a 90-day instrument, one basis point is worth $25 per contract (.01 of 1%). So, if yields rise by 1%, the price falls by 100 basis points or $2,500 per contract (100 points times $25 per point).**

U.S. Treasury bonds and notes

The 10-year, 5-year, and 2-year T-Note futures and options consistently rank in the top 10 in terms of volume. Treasury Bonds futures are designed to reflect prices of longer-term interest rates (such as mortgage rates) and are based on a hypothetical 6% bond of at least 15 years in length. These contracts are traded at the Chicago Board of Trade and are based on a security with a face value (par amount) of $100,000. Bond and note prices are a mirror image of interest rates. When interest rates rise, bond and note prices fall (and vice versa). Prices are quoted in thirty-seconds of 100% for bonds and in sixteenths for notes. For example, for the long-term bond, a minimum fluctuation is 1/32, with a full-point move (32/32) having a value of $1,000. Do not confuse a full-point move in the T-Bond price with a full-point interest rate move. It takes roughly an eight- to nine-point futures move (depending on price) to equal a full percentage point move in the yield of U.S. Treasury Bonds.

Commercial borrowers have various financing needs that dictate the market they use for hedging purposes. Investors have different objectives that determine the maturity they wish to be involved in. If interest rates are rising, the investor wishes to keep his cash in shorter-term issues, because the value (or price) of the shorter-term instruments falls less than the longer. When interest rates are falling, cash values grow to a greater degree in the longer-term issues, because the price of these grows more than the shorter. Yields are only half the story; the other half is currency values. If you received a 7% yield in a currency that lost 7% versus your home currency, your effective purchasing power has grown by zero. Therefore, in this electronic age, money is zapped between instruments of varying maturities and varying issuers (both governmental and private), as well as varying currencies.

Euro-Bund, Euro-Schatz, and Euro-Bobl

The Euro-Bund is about 10 years to maturity and consistently ranks at number 2 in terms of volume. At times, this is the top contract in terms of volume. (It alternates with the Eurodollar.) Futures on the Euro-Bund are the most active contract at the totally electronic Eurex Exchange based in Frankfurt, with approximately half of all

Bunds held by foreigners. The contract size is 100,000 Euros (1 point= 10 Euros). The Schatz is a two-year product, and the Bobl is a medium-term government bond (four to five years in length) based on a hypothetical 5.5% bond with a EUR100,000 size. The Schatz and the Bobl futures are two of the world's most heavily traded contracts in the 2- and 5-year segments and also rank in the top 10.

Euribor, Euroyen, Euroswiss, Three-Month Sterling

These are the Eurodollar contracts of Europe, Japan, Switzerland, and the United Kingdom. A typical commercial user would be a company exposed to short-term interest rate risk in a particular currency, as well as banks, speculators, market-makers, issuers, and foreign exchange traders. These contracts are very active, very liquid, and are based on short-term rates for these major currencies. The Three-Month Sterling is also commonly referred to as **Short Sterling**. The contract size is £500,000 and it's traded on the London-based, totally electronic Euronext exchange. One point is also .01 of 1%, but the value of a point is £12.50. The **Long Gilt** is the major longer-term Sterling-based contract with a £50,000 value. The minimum fluctuation is 1/32, like the T-Bond contract, but because the contract size is half (and in Pounds Sterling), a minimum tick is worth £15.625. They are based on the standard negotiable bonds issued by the British Government, which is now the fourth largest cash government bond market in the world.

You just learned about the major interest rate contracts of the world, but also of note are the following:

- *Swiss government bond:* The most important of the Swiss interest rate futures, the contract has a value of 100,000 CHF (Swiss Francs). It is traded on The Swiss Options and Financial Futures Exchange (SOFFEX). This Zurich-based Exchange trades respectable volume, but the open interest levels are comparatively low, indicating commercial participation is less broad than some.

- *Swedish interest rate contracts:* The OM Stockholm AB is the Exchange where the major Swedish contracts, both short term and medium term, are traded.

- *Australian interest rate contracts:* The Sydney Futures Exchange is where the major Australian contracts are traded. There are liquid, 3- and 10-year bond contracts with a contract size of $100,000 (in Australian dollars), as well as an actively traded 90-day Bill contract.

- *Canadian interest rate contracts:* The Montreal Exchange has an active 10-year Canadian bond contract with a size of 100,000 Canadian dollars and a Bankers Acceptance short-term contract with a face value of one million Canadian dollars.

- *Brazilian interest rate contracts:* These are traded on the BM&F.

Major fundamentals that affect interest rates

Because of thousands of variables, it is somewhat difficult to analyze the fundamentals of any major economy. Basically, the trader has to sort through and prioritize the myriad information available. Each country has its own fundamentals based on internal politics, infrastructure, and economic vitality. All of the major industrialized countries release regular government reports, forming the basis of what fundamental analysts and traders use in an attempt to forecast how government policy and economic activity will move the markets. The majors are listed as follows, along with the other fundamental factors I feel are the most important when trading: Bonds, Eurodollars, and the other interest rate futures:

- *Unemployment:* This is one of the most important reports affecting economic activity; therefore, it reflects credit demand and interest rate expectations. Usually released at the beginning of each month, it shows changes in unemployment for the preceding month.

- *Inflation:* Inflation rates are important in forecasting interest rates, because inflationary expectations get built into the price of borrowing money. If you loan money out at 10% for 10 years, and the average inflation rate over this period is 10%, your real return is nothing. If the inflation rate is 5%, you have a real return of 5%. If the inflation rate is now 4%, and the market thinks it will remain that way for years to come, then 10-year notes might be priced at 5% by the marketplace, which would yield a real return of 1%. However, if inflation heats up to, for example, 7%, and the market thinks this will continue, the yield on 10-year notes might rise to 10%, thereby depressing T-Note prices and T-Note futures. Two major U.S. reports and similar reports in Europe and Asia reflect inflation rates. The first is the **Producer Price Index**, commonly referred to as the PPI. This index measures the cost of materials at the wholesale or producer level. In other words, it measures the cost of raw materials purchased by manufacturers. Because higher costs are generally passed on to the consumer, this can be a good leading indicator of inflation at the retail level. The second report is the **Consumer Price Index**, the CPI, which measures inflation at the personal, or consumer level. The basic rule of thumb is that increasing rates of inflation lead to higher interest rates as the cost of money increases and the government looks to curb inflation and inflationary expectations.

- *Crude oil and gold:* Many bond traders closely watch the prices of these two important commodities as indicators of inflation, which in turn affect interest rate movements.

- *Housing starts:* The entire economy is greatly affected on a trickle-down basis by the rate of home construction. This is a good indicator of the demand for long-term mortgage money and affects Treasury Bonds to a greater degree than Euros or shorter- term contracts.

■ *Industrial production:* This is the level of factory output. It can indicate how economic activity, and subsequently the need for credit, is expanding or contracting.

■ *Business inventories:* This is a good indicator of the degree of future demand for short-term credit by business. Demand for credit to finance inventories could be a reason for higher interest rates. If inventories are low and the economic activity is picking up, this also could be a leading indicator of rising rates. This number affects the shorter-term contracts to a greater degree than the longer.

■ *Gross Domestic Product (GDP):* Gross Domestic Product in the United States, and in each of the major industrial countries, measures economic growth rates across the entire spectrum. Changes in GDP affect trader expectations. At times, these changes have a profound effect on price, whereas at other times, the report is virtually ignored.

■ *Balance of Trade:* Released monthly, these reports have a profound effect on the currencies and, at times, interest rates. A general rule of thumb is that a strong dollar is supportive to bond prices. It draws in foreign buying of domestic securities.

■ *Disposable income:* This is an indicator of the consumer's buying power, another indicator of general economic activity affecting credit demand.

■ *Retail sales and car sales:* For obvious reasons, both of these reports give clues as to consumer confidence and liquidity.

■ *Index of leading indicators:* This government-constructed indicator is supposed to provide advance warning of the future health of the economy. It is composed of data such as the average work week, layoff rate, new orders for goods, business formations, building permits issued, stock prices, and so on. Typically, a falling indicator points toward a weakening economy, which leads to lower rates and vice versa. The reports listed up to this point are all concurrent, or lagging indicators, whereas this one is supposed to be leading, or predictive. Its accuracy is questionable in my mind, but the release of an unexpected number in this index can affect prices *now*, regardless of whether it proves true in the future.

■ *Debt offerings:* As the supply of new securities offerings increases, by either the government's need for money or private financing, the price of all of these securities is hurt to a degree. This is generally a short-term factor. The future supply of new issues is published in the *Wall Street Journal* and *The Financial Times*.

■ *Federal Reserve:* The Federal Reserve (also called the Fed) is the Central Bank of the United States and is the most influential in the world. The central banks of the other major industrialized nations (such as the European Central Bank or ECB) act in much the same way; they all have a profound affect on interest rate policy and can move markets. It seems, at times, the Chairman of the Fed can sneeze, and the bond market falls 16 ticks. The Fed can purchase or sell government securities. When it sells securities, it reduces bank reserves, and therefore, the supply of money available for lending. In a roundabout way, this reduces the available funds for credit, and interest rates should rise as a result. The purchase of securities has the opposite affect. Traders can read the minutes of the FOMC, which is the Federal Reserve's Open Market Committee. The Committee meets monthly to discuss economic conditions and to establish U.S. interest rate policy. One drawback is that these reports are not issued until a month *after* the meeting; however, federal policy does not usually change on a whim. Fed action gradually affects interest rate movements over an extended period of time. The Fed (and other major central banks, which operate in much the same way) can affect interest rate movements in a variety of ways; one of the most important is setting the **discount rate**. The discount rate is the interest rate the Fed charges to banks that borrow from it. A commercial bank that is short on reserves because of high loan demand might need to borrow from the Fed. The Fed can set the discount rate wherever it wants, and by raising this rate, it makes it less attractive for commercial banks to borrow. The commercial banks, in turn, raise the rates they charge their customers (consumers and businesses), and as the price of credit goes up, generally the demand for credit goes down. Many times, the market anticipates a change in the discount rate because the writing is on the wall. I've seen many examples of this in the marketplace. The price of bond futures might be falling for weeks on anticipation of a rise in the discount rate, and the day the news is announced, the bonds spike down but then close higher on the day. This often confuses novice traders. How can bonds close higher on a day the discount rate is raised? Basically, the answer is that it is already "discounted" in price. The Fed (and all central banks) changes the discount rate only rarely, but it is engaged in daily activities that also affect rates. If you trade interest rate futures, you need to know the phrase "The Fed is doing Repos." **Repos** are repurchase agreements, which are transactions involving the sale of a securities with an agreement to repurchase at a stated price in the future. In effect, a Repo is a short-term loan. When the Fed is doing Repos, it is lending money and increasing reserves. This is generally a sign of easier monetary policy, or lower rates. **Reverse Repos** are the opposite, in which the Fed is decreasing reserves—a sign of tighter money and higher interest rates.

- *Fed funds rate:* This is an interest rate charged among banks for reserves they lend to each other. If the Fed believes this rate is running too high or too low, the banks might enter the market to buy or sell government securities. This action affects reserves and the Fed funds rate. The Fed funds rate can change daily, and even numerous times during a day. Many traders feel this is one of the most influential determinants of Fed policy and resulting interest-rate movements.

■ *Money supply:* These figures are released weekly. At times, they are closely watched, and they are an important determinant of futures prices. Other times, they seem to be on the back burner in trader's minds. It all depends on the "flavor of the week," or what traders seem to be focusing on at the time. M1 measures checking accounts and cash–basically money available for ready spending. M2 and M3 measure other deposits and are less readily available.

Which is the most important fundamental to watch? They are all important, and none of them is important. The problem is, no single economic indicator always dominates the market; they change. At any one time, the market seems to focus on certain indicators as the primary movers, but this changes over time. In the early 1980s, I remember the weekly money supply figures were watched closely and anticipated with glee or dread, because they were certain to move the market in the coming session. Today, only the most die-hard fundamentalists look at them. In the future, perhaps they will rise to prominence again.

Stock indices

In the 1920s, there was an old Wall Street maxim that went something like this: "Well, you can't buy the averages." This just isn't true anymore—now you can. As a speculator, if you have an opinion on the market in general, as opposed to any individual stock, you can buy or short the entire market or market groups, by buying or selling the futures contracts, or options, on specific indices. As a private investor, you are able to temporarily protect against market declines, or lock in portfolio profits without having to sell good, dividend-paying stocks that are part of your longer-term investment goals. Too many of the "herd-stock buyers," that vast group that started investing in stocks in the early 1980s at the beginning of the most recent historic rise, are oblivious to one simple fact. The history of markets has demonstrated that every bull market comes to an end at some point. When the bull falters, the bear takes over and reigns supreme until the bull rises again.

For hedgers, stock index futures and options can be likened to "bear market insurance," and this is a classic hedge. I've counted more than 70 listed stock index futures contracts on 20 different Exchanges. Today, the volume of equity indices represents the largest percentage category of futures contracts traded. The following sections describe the major stock indices traded today on the futures Exchanges. All of these have active and liquid options.

S&P 500 Index

This is the daddy of all the U.S. stock indices in terms of volume, capitalization, and liquidity. Traded on the Chicago Mercantile Exchange (CME), the S&P 500 represents the 500 biggest U.S. stocks, accounting for about 80% of total U.S. shares traded. It is a weighted index composed roughly of 400 industrial companies, 40 utilities, 20 transportation companies, and 40 financial companies. It is "weighted" because a bigger company carries proportionately greater weight in the index. The value of the big contract is 250 times the index. In other words, if the index is trading at 1000, the value of the contract is $250,000 (1,000 times 250, or 250,000). For every full point, such as a move from 1100 to 1101, the contract gains or loses $250 (as does the buyer or seller of each contract). Actually, the E-Mini S&P is the most actively traded contract in terms of dollar volume and is one of the day trader's favorites, because it is *extremely* volatile with major price swings almost every day. Because of high volatility, the margin requirements are fairly high to hold an overnight position. Day trading margins are generally much smaller, but a trader is always obligated for the difference between entry and exit. In other words, if you lose, you must pay the piper by the end of the day.

Euro Stoxx

This index, traded at the Eurex, is consistently the number two stock index contract traded in terms of value. Actually, the number one contract in terms of *volume* is the **Kospi200** traded at the Korean Kofex. In fact, the South Korean Exchange just opened in 1999, and many days, it is the volume leader. However, in terms of value (because this is a lower-value contract), the volume figures are deceiving. The number three contract in terms of value is the **E-Mini Nasdaq 100**. This is based on the NASDAQ top 100 U.S. stocks, mostly hi-tech, bio-tech, and similar offerings. Unlike the other indices, the value of this contract is 20 times the index, and a full point is worth plus or minus $20. (There is also a less actively traded "big" contract five times the size with a full point worth plus or minus $100.) Then there is the **DOW**, based on 31 major U.S. industrial stocks (in both a large and mini variety). Other actively traded stock index contracts include the Japanese **Nikkei 225**, German **DAX**, French **CAC40**, Swedish **OMX**, Dutch **EOE**, and Australian **SPI 200**. These are the major exchange-listed contracts, but for those interested, there are additional Exchanges (listing both stock index and interest rate contracts) in Austria, Belgium, Chile, Denmark, Finland, Hungary, Israel, Italy, Mexico, New Zealand, Norway, the Philippines, and South Africa. There are also single stock futures listed in both Europe and the United States; however, the liquidity is in some question as we go to press.

One additional point: Unlike many of the physical commodities, the stock index and currency futures are routinely cash-settled. This means that, at delivery time, there is a cash transaction only. The buyers and sellers trade cash credits and debits in their accounts based on the difference between the "spot" (index) price and the settlement (closing) price of the futures contract. There is no need to make or take delivery or a basket of stocks.

Major Stock Market Fundamentals

An owner of a single stock participates in the profitability and the risks of that particular company. An index trader is not concerned with the vagaries of any particular company but the actions of the market as a whole. Mega-market-moving fundamentals are as follows:

- General economic activity

- Interest rates

- Inflationary expectations

■ Political considerations

■ Investor attitudes

Let's face it, any one thing (war, a leader's death, an interest-rate hike, a major company's earnings) or any of one thousand things could affect the stock market on any particular day. Any and all the factors mentioned as fundamental considerations for the interest rate markets also affect the equity markets. The stock markets of the world can move together; however, any one market can certainly move opposite the pack based on internal considerations. One thing seems clear: Attitudes and economic trends tend to last for a while; therefore, the major trends of the stock market tend to last for a while. It's those minor trends that can kill you or make you rich.

Currencies

The very first financial futures contracts were based on foreign currencies. It should be noted that the spot (or forward market) is much bigger than the futures. The forward market, also known as the Interbank market, is dominated by currency dealers at major global banks. Traded electronically and by telephone, the spot market's volume towers over the listed Exchange volume. However, this vehicle is not available to the average investor. The average unit is $1 million, and although currencies also can be traded at retail FOREX-type outlets, the only major leveraged Exchange listed contracts are traded in Chicago. This book is geared toward the average futures trader; it is the active futures contracts that will be discussed.

Euro	Contract size €125,000
Yen	Contract size ¥12,500,000
Swiss Franc	Contract size SF125,000
British Pound	Contract size £62,500
Dollar Index	Contract size $1,000xindex (traded at the NYBOT)
Canadian Dollar	Contract size C$100,000
Mexican Peso	Contract size MP500,000
Australian Dollar	Contract size A$100,000

Other actively traded currencies include the New Zealand dollar, the South African rand, the Russian ruble, and certain Asian currencies. When the Chinese allow the Yuan to trade freely, no doubt it will become an actively traded currency, too.

Major currency fundamentals

The price of a currency is determined in the same way as the price of any other commodity. Currency users have risks. If a currency depreciates in value and a manufacturer is to receive this currency in payment for a product that he will deliver six months hence, he loses money. If not hedged, his entire profit margin could be wiped out. If the people in the United States demand more Japanese-made goods, the demand for the Yen goes up in relation to the dollar, and Americans will have to pay higher prices to induce holders of Yen to sell. If interest rates go up in Germany in relation to the United Kingdom, the Euro will look relatively more attractive as an investment than the British Pound.

- **Trade balances:** This refers to imports and exports, and is probably the most important determinant of a currency's value. When imports are greater than exports, you have a **trade deficit**. When exports are greater than imports, you have a **surplus**. A shift in the trade balance between two countries tends to weaken the currency of the country with the greater deficit.

- **Wealth:** Wealth is a country's reserves, in the form of gold, cash, natural resources, and so on. Basically any factor that affects a country's ability to repay loans, finance imports, and affect investments affects the market's perception of its currency and the currency's value.

- **Internal budget deficit or surplus:** A country running a current accounts deficit has, on balance, a weaker currency than one that runs a budget surplus. This is tricky, however, in that the direction of the surplus or deficit affects perceptions and currency valuations, too.

- **Interest rates:** Funds move around the world electronically in response to changes in short-term interest rates. If three-month interest rates in Germany are running 1% less than three-month rates in the United States, then all other things being equal, "hot money" flows out of the Euro into the dollar.

- **Inflation:** Inflation in each country, and inflationary expectations, affect currency values. What good is a 10% short-term rate in some country if inflation is running 15%?

- **Political factors:** Taxes, stability, whatever affects the international trade of a country, or the perception of "soundness" of the currency affect its valuation.

Central Bank intervention to support (or not support) a currency is definitely a market-moving factor. At times, a country can move alone to support its currency, and sometimes an orchestrated group effort is underway to attempt to support some currency. The Central Banks are huge, but not always larger than the speculative community. If the ultimate fundamentals are opposed to artificial support, a currency can still move contrary to the wishes of the Central Bank. This was demonstrated when Soros was able to break the back of the British Pound and successfully challenge the Bank of England in the late 1980s—he profited to the tune of $2 billion.

Obviously, some of these factors are subjective, whereas others are hard to predict in advance. Ultimately, capital flows are the major fundamental that determines what a currency is worth, and these are determined by the consensus of the world's traders. Technical analysis is discussed at length in Chapter 9, "The Most Valuable Technical Tool (TMVTT)." In my view, it is a more efficient means of evaluating a currency's worth than the fundamentals, which can be contradictory and confusing at times.

Energy

There are three major energy exchanges. The International Petroleum Exchange of London trades an active Brent Crude Oil and a Gasoil (heating oil) contract. The Tocom (Japanese) trades active gasoline and kerosene contracts. The predominant Exchange, however, is the New York Mercantile Exchange.

When I first entered the business, a part of my training program at Merrill Lynch was a tour of the Exchange floor. The New York Exchanges are housed in the same building, and after touring the wild and woolly COMEX (where the metals are traded—now a wholly owned division of the NYMEX), we passed a pit with four or five traders, not one of which was shouting out bids or offers. (In fact, a few of them were reading the paper.) We were told this was the NYMEX, the "poor man's Exchange," also called the "Potato Exchange," where platinum was the major contract (we really didn't know what that was at that time). Potatoes also were traded here, however inactively due to a delivery default. In addition, they had a "boneless beef" contract that, on a good day, traded 50 lots. You could have bought a seat for $2,000, but then the $100 per month dues made this appear to be a losing deal. A few years later, they had the foresight and good fortune to register their No. 2 Heating Oil contract with the CFTC and start trading it in 1978. Now, this is one of the world's major Exchanges, and you can't buy a seat for less than $1,500,000. (If only we had known in those "poor man" days and had picked up a few of those cheap seats!)

Crude oil

Crude oil is the world's largest cash commodity in terms of dollars and volume. (The annual value exceeds $500 billion.) In fact, 20% of the world's entire trade is in oil. (Only money and its derivatives are bigger.) The NYMEX has a light, sweet crude contract, which in many years becomes the highest volume nonfinancial futures contract traded. Light, sweet crude is preferred by refiners due to its low sulfur content. Most of the world's supply is sour (high-sulfur) crude, but because the sulfur content varies widely, the NYMEX contract based on West Texas Intermediate has become the pace setter for world oil prices in general. Brent Crude traded on the IPE is also liquid and active, a bit less than half the volume of the sweet crude. Both are 1,000-barrel contracts. Here's a bit of oil trivia (some of which might surprise you): If you think you have a pretty good idea who the top oil players, the top producers, and the top users are, you just might have to rethink some of your assumptions. Try not to peek at the following table—can you name the top five global oil producers? Can you name the top five exporters? Although most people are able to get three or four in each category, I have not found one person who could name all five in either category. The following table lists the International Energy Agency's rankings, current at press time.

▪ Key Countries in Oil

Million barrels per day

Producers	Consumers	Exporters	Importers
Saudi Arabia 8.5	USA 19.7	Saudi Arabia 7.1	USA 11.1
USA 8.1	Japan 5.3	Russia 5.1	Japan 5.6
Russia 7.7	China 5	Norway 3.1	Germany 2.6
Iran 3.6	Germany 2.7	Venezuela 2.5	South Korea 2.5
Mexico 3.6	Russia 2.5	Iran 2.4	France 1.9
Norway 3.4	Brazil 2.2	UAE 2.1	Italy 1.7
China 3.4	South Korea 2.2	Nigeria 1.8	China 1.6
Venezuela 3	India 2.1	Kuwait 1.7	Spain 1.5

First, a note about this table: These rankings are dynamic (constantly old and constantly changing). In fact, as this book goes to press, it looks as if China's consumption could exceed 6 mbd and surpass Japan as the number two consumer. This chart gives you a feel for the major players, but be aware that the figures will be dated the very day you read this. That said, here are the most common misconceptions.

Did you know the United States was the second largest crude-oil producer in the world? When asked, most people don't place the United States in the top 10. The U.S. problem is not a lack of production; the United States produces more oil than any other country globally except Saudi Arabia. The problem is that the United States gulps the stuff, every day burning through more than twice as much as it produces domestically. The United States consumes four times more than the second-largest global consumer, Japan. Were you surprised Kuwait is not a top seven producer? How about Nigeria? How about the most common exporter misconception: Iraq? Iraq is the second largest country in the world in terms of proven reserves (112 billion barrels), so why isn't Iraq listed in the top seven? During the Saddam era, Iraq produced far below its potential because its pipelines and pumping stations became dilapidated after decades of neglect. Before the 2003 war, Iraqi production was 1.7 mbd—it went down to zero during the war and will rise up to 2.5 mbd, assuming western oil companies make massive investments. Because of the enormous reserves, Iraq has huge potential for future production; however, because of higher domestic consumption than the UAE or Norway, Iraq will not be listed in the top 10 exporter category for years to come.

The new star in terms of production, because of western investment in improved technology, is Russia (plus some former Soviet states). Exports have increased there by 20% in the past three years. This makes OPEC far less important than 20 years ago (Russia is not an OPEC member), and as OPEC loses market share, it's lost its price control as well to free-market forces.

China's production (were you surprised to see China in the top seven?) has also been increasing; however, its consumption is increasing at a far faster rate. Japan has the biggest problem because it has no domestic production at all and is totally dependent on imports. Japan's economy (and consumption) has been stagnant for a decade. China has the same problem as Japan and the United States because it is dependent on imports to fill the gap, but its rate of consumption versus its production is accelerating at the fastest rate in the world. The ramifications of the increasing industrialization and economic growth of China will have the most profound of all dynamics on oil prices in the coming years. Realize China has five times as many people as the United States, yet today it uses just one-fourth of what America does. What happens as this gap closes? It's clear that while oil prices will continue to fluctuate, in the next few years, demand will increase at a faster rate than new supply. Unless alternative energy sources take hold (not likely anytime soon), the cheap prices of years past are going to remain a memory. Consider this: When Saudi Arabia promised to open the spigots in April 1986, prices fell to under $10 per barrel. Less than five years later, when Saddam Hussein invaded Kuwait, prices topped $40 per barrel.

Heating oil

For many years, the NYMEX heating oil contract was the second most liquid energy contract, although in recent years, it has been overshadowed by natural gas. It is also known as the number two fuel oil and accounts for about 25% of the yield of a barrel of crude. This contract also is used by hedgers of diesel fuel and jet fuel, both of which are chemically similar to heating oil. The contract size is 42,000 gallons, and a 1¢ move equals a profit or loss of $420. When the crude fell under $10 in 1986, the "heat" (as they call it on the floor) briefly broke the 30¢ per gallon mark. When Saddam was in Kuwait, the price broke above $1.00 per gallon.

Unleaded gasoline

Futures prices for this major transportation commodity might appear to be too cheap, but they are based on the wholesale price for delivery at the New York Harbor. The price you pay at the pump has all those costs added to get it to the station, including local and national taxes. Unleaded gasoline is by far the most important product, accounting for almost half of the yield from a barrel of crude. The contract size is also 42,000 gallons, with a 1¢ move (100 points) equal to a profit or loss of $420 per contract. When crude oil broke under $10, gasoline futures hit 30¢. Prices briefly hit $1.11 during the Gulf War, and it didn't take long into the twenty-first century to exceed that historic high.

Natural gas

For many years, U.S. natural gas prices were subject to government price controls; it has only been recently that the chains have been broken. The contract, which started trading in 1990, is now the second most actively traded energy contract. Of all natural gas that is produced, industry uses about one-third, homeowners use one-fourth, and utilities consume the balance. A fifty-year supply of natural gas is under ground, and it is virtually "free" to tap, except for the transportation and storage costs with middleman profits in between. The contract size is 10,000 MMBtu (Million British Thermal Units), with price quoted in dollars and cents per MMBtu.

Prices were about $1 in 1992 and above $10 during the winter of 2000 when it was freezing cold in both North America and Europe, then under $2 a year later, and again over $10 during the winter of 2003.

Major energy fundamentals

Thirty years ago, seven major oil companies owned 50% of the world's oil reserves and produced two-thirds of its crude and products. Today, these same seven own less than 10% and produce less than one-third of the products. OPEC is still a factor but no longer the major price-setter. The major price-setter is now the marketplace. The following factors are important and must be considered in any fundamental analysis of the energy markets:

- *Weather:* Watch the winter weather in particular. The winter of 1989 to 1990 is a classic example. In November of 1989, heating oil was trading at 57¢ per gallon. The day the January 1990 contract went off the board, it hit $1.10. This was the coldest December in more than a century. The winter of 1996 to 1997 was one of the coldest on record in the midwestern United States, where natural gas is the primary energy source for residential heating. Prices of natural gas soared from $2 to an all-time, then-record high of more than $4 in record time. Who would have thought the prices would exceed $10 just a few years later?

- *Seasonality:* It gets cold in the winter and warm in the summer, but one of the most reliable seasonal tendencies is not what you might expect. In my research, more than 80% of the time, heating oil makes a bottom in March, rising in price into May. The same scenario applies to gasoline (which logically makes more sense because of inventory building prior to the peak summer driving season).

- *API and DOE Reports:* The American Petroleum Institute and Department of Energy release weekly reports with supply-and-demand figures for crude, natural gas, and heating oil and gasoline. These reports are anticipated widely by the industry, and many times they move the electronic overnight markets prior to next day's open.

- *Politics:* Oil is a strategic commodity and an economic necessity. The Arab Oil Embargo, the Iranian Hostage Crisis, the Iran-Iraq War, and the two Gulf Wars are just five examples of how politics can dramatically affect the price of oil.

- *OPEC:* Although OPEC is not as important as it once was, it still can be important at times. The members of OPEC include Saudi Arabia, Iran, Kuwait, the UAE, Venezuela, Indonesia, Nigeria, Algeria, Libya, Gabon, and Qatar. If these countries collectively make a decision to increase production to meet world demand or decrease it because they perceive prices are too low, the price of crude oil will react. In October of 1985, King Fahd of Saudi Arabia said he would increase production, and he did. Prices were then at $31 per barrel. Less than five months later, they broke below $10.

Agricultures

Futures were invented in sixteenth century Japan in the rice trade, and the agricultural markets continued to dominate futures trading throughout the first 70 years of the previous century. Today, agriculture accounts for less than a quarter of global futures trade. Agriculture is, however, still important with the two Chicago exchanges (the CBOT and the CME) dominating this sector.

Grains and soybeans

All living things require fat, protein, and carbohydrates for survival. While meat is generally thought of as the predominate protein source, much of the world's human population, and a majority of the world's livestock populations, obtain their protein from the soybean. Corn is the predominate carbohydrate source used for animal feed.

Soybeans

Our British friends call and spell them soyabeans. Soybeans were mentioned in ancient Chinese records prior to 2000 B.C. The United States was the world's largest producer until 2004, accounting for about 50% of the world's output. Prior to the 1980s, the United States accounted for 80% of the world's output, but Carter's grain embargo prompted the Japanese, who were looking for a more reliable supplier, to fund the Brazilian soybean industry. Today, more than 50% of the world's soybean crop is grown in South and Central America, primarily in Brazil and Argentina. China accounts for most of the rest of the world's production, but it remains a major importer most years. Called the miracle crop, soybeans are used in thousands of applications, primarily crushed for meal (used as an animal protein feed) and oil (for human consumption and as a cooking oil). This is one of the major commodities traded at the world's third largest Exchange, the Chicago Board of Trade. It is generally the most volatile of all the grains although, technically, it is not a grain but a legume, also known as an oilseed. The contract size is 5,000 bushels, with prices quoted in dollars and cents per bushel. A 1¢ move is worth $50 per contract. In a typical day, the limit the price can move up or down is 50¢. However, this is a variable limit, and if the market closes, the limit is raised.

Soybean meal

The richest protein source of all the oilseeds, soybean meal is a feedstuff suited for cattle, hogs, and poultry. One bushel of soybeans weighs about 60 pounds and yields about 48 pounds of meal. Sixty percent of U.S. production is used domestically, with the balance exported. A contract's size is 100 short tons (2,000 pounds per ton), with prices quoted in dollars and cents per ton. A $1 move equals plus or minus $100 per contract, and there is a limit up or down of $20 per day. The limit is variable, and if the market closes the limit one day, it is raised for three subsequent days.

Soybean oil

The other major "product" of the soybean, the soybean oil contract, is sized at 60,000 pounds. One bushel of beans produces about 11 pounds of oil. This is an edible vegetable oil and competes in the world market with other edible oils such as palm, peanut, canola, corn, olive, sunflower, and even fats such as lard. Prices are quoted in cents per pound, with a 100 point or 1¢ move equal to a profit or loss of $600 per contract. The limit is 2¢, but this is variable and can be raised.

Canola

The major oilseed grown in Canada, canola also is the most active of all the contracts traded on the tiny (ranked 40th of the top 40 futures exchanges) Winnipeg Commodity Exchange. (In 2004, the Winnipeg Exchange was the first in North American exchange to drop open outcry in favor of becoming totally electronic.) A contract is for 100 tons; however, the Exchange trades "job lots" of 20 tons, too. Canola, the oil of choice among the health conscious, generally moves in the same direction as soybeans, although at a different speed.

Palm oil

This product is the world's second most heavily produced vegetable oil, and it is traded in Malaysia. Production is dominated by Malaysia and Indonesia. Palm oil competes directly with soybean oil and canola oil, but it generally trades at a discount because of health concerns about saturated fat in tropical oils. Palm oil is attractive to countries with expanding, low-income populations.

Corn

Traditionally the most active of the grain contracts, corn is the major U.S.-grown crop. The contract specifications call for feed corn, not the variety used for human consumption. In recent years, in excess of 80 million acres have been planted annually in the United States, producing crops that can exceed 10 billion bushels in a good year, accounting for one-half of the world's production. The United States consumes 70% of its crop domestically (80% of this is used to feed animals, with 20%—and growing—used to produce ethanol), with the balance exported. The limit move is 20¢.

Oats

The oat market is generally a slower moving, thinner market than the other CBT grains. Oats is the only major crop that the U.S. imports, primarily from the Scandinavian countries, Argentina, and Canada. Milling quality (used in oatmeal and other forms of human consumption) and feed oats are the two major varieties of oats. The contract, which is for 5,000 bushels, tends to act more like a feed contract based on the delivery specifications that favor delivery of lower-quality oats. A 1¢ move per bushel equals plus or minus $50 per contract. The allowable limit, like corn, is also 20¢ per bushel. Some traders believe the oats futures are a *leading indicator* of corn and wheat prices; that is, oats tend to move up or down prior to a move in the other prices.

Wheat CBT

Wheat is the "staff of life'" and is grown in more than 80 countries. The United States, Russia, the Ukraine, Canada, China, Argentina, and India are the major producing countries. The Chicago Board of Trade contract is the highest volume contract in the world. The deliverable grade is Soft Red Wheat, used for cakes, pastries, and cereals. This crop is grown in the area around southern Illinois and Missouri. The Kansas City and Minneapolis varieties are deliverable on the Chicago contract; however, because they generally trade at a premium price and have freight considerations, this does not happen often. However, if Chicago prices ever trade at a greater than 20¢ premium to Minneapolis (the cost of freight from Minneapolis to Chicago), it has not been unheard of for a major grain company to load a unit train of wheat (100 rail cars) and send that train south. The contract size, as it is for all the CBT contracts, is 5,000 bushels, so a 1¢ price move equals plus or minus $50 per contract. The price limit is variable and starts at 30¢ per bushel.

Wheat KBT

The Kansas City Board of Trade is where Hard Red Winter Wheat is traded. This is the most important class of wheat grown in the United States, accounting for half of the production, but the volume here is lower than in Chicago. This wheat is grown primarily in Kansas, Oklahoma, and Texas. It is planted, like the CBT wheat, in the fall and harvested in early summer. It lies dormant over the winter, and that's where the name comes from. Hard Winter Wheat is the bread wheat. The contract size is 5,000 bushels. A 1¢ move equals $50, and the limit is 30¢.

Wheat MGE

The primary contract of the small Minneapolis Grain Exchange is the Northern Hard Spring Wheat. This wheat is a high-protein, milling-quality-type wheat grown primarily in Minnesota, North and South Dakota, Montana, and Canada. It is used in specialty bakery products such as croissants, French rolls, and bagels. It is planted in late spring (hence the name) and harvested in late summer. Because it is a higher protein wheat, it generally trades at a premium, from 20¢ to 40¢ per bushel, to the Chicago Exchange. I have seen it under Chicago (1996 was a very poor winter wheat crop and a bumper spring wheat crop) and as much as $1 over. (The 1988 drought devastated the spring crop after the winter crop was already harvested.) White wheat, the fourth major wheat variety, represents 10% of the U.S. crop and is grown in the Pacific Northwest. It is used in crackers and pita bread, and is also traded at the MGE, but in relatively thin conditions. The Spring Wheat contract is liquid, however, and like the others is for 5,000 bushels with a 30¢ limit.

Major grain and soybean fundamentals

For the grains and the soybean complex, fundamental analysts set up a table and debate where the ending stocks ultimately will be at the end of the crop year. If it looks like stocks are too low, higher prices are needed to "ration demand." If stocks appear too high, lower prices are the result, as farmer selling overwhelms demand. The supply-and-demand table for soybeans, for example, includes the following:

■ *Beginning stocks:* This is what the government says will carry over from the previous year.

■ *Production:* This is the crop estimate for the current year. During the growing season, the USDA releases a weekly Crop Progress Report, which shows the condition of the crop.

■ *Imports:* Because the United States is an exporter, this is generally a small number for the U.S. table.

■ *Total supply:* This is the beginning stocks plus production plus imports.

■ *Crush:* This is the domestic demand by the "crushers," who buy raw soybeans and crush them into the products, meal, and oil.

■ *Exports, seed, and residual:* These are the other sources of demand. Three to four percent of the crop is held back for next year's seed use. Export data is released twice weekly by the USDA. There is a Monday report, called "Export Inspections" (after the close), and a similar Thursday report, called "Export Sales," which hits the newswires prior to the open. Exports also can be affected by the strength or weakness of the dollar and other major currencies. If the dollar falls dramatically, it makes these commodities cheaper to foreign buyers and helps to stimulate export demand (and vice versa).

■ *Total demand:* This is the sum of the crush, exports, seed, and a "residual" number for other use.

■ *Ending carryover stocks:* Total supply minus total demand equals the carryover, or ending, stocks. This is the important number everyone talks about. A supply-and-demand table can be set up for a single country or the world.

eg **Let's look at a typical table for 1996 to 1997 soybeans. (The numbers are in 100 million bushels.)**

Beginning stocks	183
Production	2383
Imports	4
Total Supply	2570
Crushing	1410
Exports	905
Seed	73
Residual	42
Total Usage	2430
Ending Stocks	140

This table theoretically could be constructed before the crop is in the ground. If production falls by just 100 million bushels, the ending stocks would fall to 40 million—an unsustainable number. ("Pipeline supply" is considered just over 100 million.)

This would be perhaps one week's supply. If you knew there were 60 million acres planted that year, the result would be just a 1.6 bushel yield decrease. On the other hand, if yields increased by 2 bushels per acre, because of favorable growing conditions, the ending stocks would rise from 140 to 260 million bushels (which is a comfortable level). Basically, a fundamental analyst constantly adjusts these numbers based on weekly export and crush numbers and his determination of how the crop is maturing. Benchmarks for where prices have gone before are based on various carryover levels, but every year seems to be completely different.

■ *Deliverable stocks of grain:* The CBOT distributes this is a weekly report about the quantity and change in terms of bushels of corn, wheat, soybeans, and oats, which are in the elevators licensed to deliver on the Chicago Board of Trade. The report is useful in determining whether there is the potential for a "squeeze," where the shorts are not able to find the grain to deliver. If all the corn is primarily on the farm and very little is available for futures delivery, this is short-term bullish (even though the longer-term fundamentals could be bearish). If there is a large supply deliverable and the commercial players have no export business, the best place for them to sell might be a futures delivery (to speculators who really don't want the grain), and this is bearish. These numbers are most useful for analyzing the nearest futures month.

■ *Government policy:* Government farm programs can expand or restrict acreage in general or for a specific crop. Price support programs can pull supply off the market, and "export enhancement" programs can stimulate exports.

■ *Weather:* This is the big factor when analyzing supply. Nothing affects soybean, corn, and wheat prices to a greater degree. A "weather market" occurs when drought or flooding moves the market. These can be the most emotional of all markets. In the spring in the United States, and in fact in most of the Northern Hemisphere, the market watches the planting progress (for soybeans, corn, and spring wheat). In the summer, the market monitors the crop development, and in the autumn, it keeps track of the harvest progress. In the North American winter, the market watches the planting progress and crop development of the South American crops (during their summer). In the spring, it watches their harvest progress. A wet harvest can cause delays and hurt yields. In the winter, the market watches the weather affecting the dormant winter wheat. The wheat needs snow cover, or else it is susceptible to "winterkill," if the temperatures drop too low without the insulating effect of snow. Weather is so important that there are services for hire providing weather advice and predictions. I'm not sure any of them are any better than the USDA, which releases its "Weather Bulletin" every Wednesday after the close during the weather period. Still, some of the private forecasters do get hot from time to time.

■ *Seasonality:* All other factors remaining equal (a bold statement), the grains and oilseeds do exhibit certain seasonal tendencies. (Recall the Voice from the Tomb from Chapter 2.) Soybeans and corn tend to put in a high in the May to July period, at the height of the "weather scare" period, and bottom out at harvest time in the October to December timeframe. Cotton exhibits the same seasonal tendency. Winter wheat tends to bottom out in the June to July period (harvest time) and peaks in January to March when supplies are depleted to an extent, but before the new crop is available.

Meats

Live cattle

The United States is the largest producer and consumer of beef. Just as the chicken starts with the egg, the steak starts with the **cow/calf operation**. This is a breeding operation that uses grazing land, cows, and a small number of bulls to produce calves. Calves spend their first six months of life with their mothers, at which time they are weaned. Some are placed in feedlots immediately, but the majority pass through an intermediate stage called **backgrounding** (also termed a "stocker" operation). Backgrounders place weaned cattle on summer grass, winter wheat, or some type of roughage. This phase of the calf's life might last from 6 to 10 months or until the animal reaches a desirable feedlot weight of 600 to 800 pounds. After the animals are ready to be placed in the feedlot, they are termed **feeder cattle**. Usually, feeding continues until the animals weigh from 1,000 to 1,300 pounds, at which time they are slaughter-ready animals. This is what the CME Live Cattle contract consists of: 40,000 pounds of slaughter-ready animals. The customer for these animals is the meat packer who buys the livestock and sells the meat and other products, such as hides. Prices are quoted two ways, either cents per pound or dollars per hundredweight (hundred pounds), which really are the same thing. A limit the price can move daily and is equal to 300 points (that's 3¢ per pound or $3 per hundred pounds) above or below the previous day's close. Variable limits come into effect after a lock-limit move.

Feeder cattle

Almost all feedlot cattle are steers (castrated males) and heifers (females who have not calved). Because some heifers are retained on ranches to replace cows that get too old, there are always more steers than heifers. Feedlots can be as small as 100 head or as large as 100,000. Some feedlots are farmer-owned, and some are commercial operations. The commercial operations (cattle hotels) account for less than 5% of all lots but 80% of all cattle marketings. The feedlot operator might buy feeder cattle for his own account, or for a fee, he might "custom feed" for farmers or other cattle owners. These feedlot-ready animals make up the CME feeder contract, which has a size of 50,000 pounds. The specifications call for approximately a 750-pound steer; therefore, the contract represents about 60 animals. Prices are quoted in either cents per pound or dollars per hundredweight. Unlike the cattle contract, the feeder contract is cash-settled, just like many of the financial futures. It is based on an Index, which the contract will equal on the last day. The Index is compiled by the USDA based on a weighted average of feeder cattle cash market sales. The feeder contract also has a 300-point limit. Like oats, some traders believe feeder cattle prices are a *leading indicator* of live cattle prices. They move first—hence the phrase, "Feeders are the leaders."

Lean hogs

Like cattle, the pork industry can be divided into segments, but there are important differences. The preslaughter phase of hog production is usually combined into what's called the "farrow to finish operation." In the hog industry, the background-ing phase does not exist. In other words, the hog generally stays on the same farm from birth to finish. (Eighty percent of all hogs are produced this way, with 20% coming from a breeding-only operation to the farm.) Hogs are taken to market when they weigh 220 to 240 pounds, and this takes about six months. Most beef is sold as fresh meat; however, a large portion of pork is processed further and becomes stor-able as ham—smoked, canned, or frozen.

Pork bellies

Pork bellies are the raw material for bacon and can be fresh or frozen and stored (the CME contract is frozen) for up to a year. The hog contract represents 40,000 pounds of carcass and is cash-settled based on an index of prices collected by the USDA. A 1¢ move equals plus or minus $400 per contract. The belly contract is 50,000 pounds of frozen bellies; therefore, a 1¢ move equals plus or minus $500 per contract. The pork bellies are notorious for numerous limit moves and volatile, erratic behavior. The speculative open interest is much higher in this contract than most, often accounting for more than 85% of total open interest. Here's a trivia question for you: How many bellies does a hog have? The answer is *two*.

Major meat fundamentals

Accumulation or liquidation? During the **accumulation** phase of the cattle cycle, ranchers are building their herds by holding back cows. This method can temporar-ily create a short supply of market-ready animals, but it is bearish longer term. During **liquidation** (for example, in times of drought, which kills off the grazing pastures, or high feed prices), cows are sent to market. This is bearish from a supply and price standpoint in the short run but bullish longer term. This tactic works the same way for hogs as cattle. During the expansion phase, an increased number of gilts and sows (female breeders) are withheld from slaughter to become part of the breeding herd. During contraction, females are culled from the breeding herd, and the female portion of the total slaughter rises.

- *Seasonality:* Although this does not happen every year, feeder cattle sales tend to peak in the fall with the end of the grazing season. At the same time, calf/cow operators tend to sell off unproductive cows, which increases the total beef supply and depresses prices. Hog prices tend to be the highest in the summer months, because the December through February timeframe is tradi-tionally a low-birth period. Also, the demand for pork tends to peak during the summer months.

- *Corn and feed prices:* The general rule of thumb is that high-feed prices result in liquidation and low-feed prices result in accumulation. The other variable here is the market price of the finished product. If sale prices of cattle or hogs are high, then more money can be spent on feed. In 1996, when corn prices soared to all-time record highs more than $5 per bushel, many cattle feeders found it more profitable to sell their stored corn and take their cattle to market (including breeding animals). Others could not afford the high-feed costs, and this added to the liquidation. Prices of cattle spiked downward under the weight of the burdensome supply, but this turned out to be bullish for the longer term. This is pure economics. When it is profitable to raise or feed animals, this is what producers do; when it isn't, they don't.

- *Feeder costs:* In cattle feeding, the feeder's cost accounts for, in many cases, more than half of the total cost of production. Higher feeder costs lead to lower placements into feedlots.

- *Weather:* Tough winter weather can result in death loss and weight loss, which can reduce supply permanently or temporarily. At times, when the temperatures in the major feeding regions get extremely cold, cattle eat more and gain less. Animals that were to be ready for market at a certain date are "pushed back," creating a temporary shortage, with a glut later when they reach market weight. This fundamental is more important for cattle than hogs, because the majority of hogs are now fed indoors.

- *Consumer tastes:* This can be approached in a macro and a micro sense. The per-capita consumption of beef or pork and how it changes over time affects price—this is a macro fundamental. This has to do with dietary considerations and media news. On a more focused approach, hot summer days increase barbecue demand, and holidays increase the demand for hams.

- *Exports and income levels:* When a country achieves a higher level of income, the demand for red meat increases. Exports to Asia have become a much more important factor in recent years, and unexpected new export business can, at times, result in price spikes.

- *The substitution effect:* Beef, pork, chicken, turkey, and fish are substitutable commodities to a major extent. For example, if the price of chicken plummets, sales increase, which takes away demand from the other meats.

- *Cattle on Feed Report:* This is an important and much anticipated monthly report released by the USDA. Three major parts compose the Report: cattle on feed (the total numbers in the feedlots), placements (of cattle into feedlots the previous month), and marketings (out of the feedlots the previous month). Because a placement of a 700- to 900-pound animal into a lot will become a market-ready animal in 120 to 160 days, this report can give a good indication of future market-ready supplies. Marketings out of feedlots can vary based on economic considerations, because cattle feeders can move cattle ahead a bit or feed them a bit longer at times.

■ *Cattle Inventory Report:* This is a count of the total numbers of mature animals as well as the country's "calf crop." It is an important report but only released twice a year, in January and July.

■ *Hogs and Pigs Report:* This is the most important report for the hog and belly futures. The market often moves "limit," sometimes for days, after this report is released when it shows numbers higher or lower than expectations. It shows the total numbers (the pig crop), the breeding herd (numbers kept back for breeding), the farrowings and farrowing intentions (the numbers actually bred and anticipated breeding levels), and the market hogs (those intended for market). Weight classes also give clues as to total future supply. It should be noted that although the H&P Report moves the market, it is often wrong. However, this fact cannot be verified for up to six months in the future when the animals either show or don't.

■ *Cold Storage Report:* This report is released monthly and indicates the amount of meat in the freezers, from beef to chicken to bellies. It has a tendency to move the bellies, more than the others, after release.

■ *Out-of-Town Report:* This is a weekly report, released every Tuesday after the close, watched by belly traders who want to see whether bellies were put into the freezers (bearish) or removed (bullish).

■ *Daily Slaughter Levels:* This report gives an indication of how many animals are processed by the packers on a daily basis.

Sal, whom you met in this book's Introduction, tells a story of a successful hog trader, who had a brother-in-law who was struggling in the pit. The successful one wanted to help his sister, who was promised a new house by her husband (the brother-in-law), but he could never seem to come through. The day after a very bullish Hogs and Pigs Report, the struggling trader saw 200 long hog contracts in his account. Thinking it was some sort of error (and not inquiring why they were in his account), he proceeded to trade out of them right after the open.

After a $7 run up in hog prices, the successful one walked up to his brother-in-law and told him to go and buy that new house for his wife (the successful one's sister). The brother-in-law responded, "With what?" The successful one said, "What do you mean with what? Take the profits on those 200 longs I put in your account two weeks ago!"

Softs

The commodity subclass termed the softs has also been referred to as the breakfast commodities because it includes coffee, cocoa, sugar, and orange juice. I imagine cotton is also in this class because it's soft, but obviously its not consumable. And although lumber is hard (although it can be classified as a softwood or a hardwood) and has nothing to do with breakfast, we place it in this category because there is no other that fits.

Sugar #11

Sugar is grown in more than 100 countries around the world. Most sugar is consumed in the country in which it was grown and produced under government pricing arrangements. The sugar that is not subject to government restrictions is freely traded among nations, corporations, and traders. This free market is typically 15 to 25% of world production. A 5% change in production can mean a 25% change in free market supply. The two main types of sugar grown in the world are cane and beet. Both produce the same type of refined product. Sugar cane, a bamboo-like grass, accounts for about two-thirds of world production. Cuba, India, Thailand, and Brazil are the leading cane producers, whereas Russia and the EEC are the major beet producers. The largest sugar exporting nations are Cuba, the EEC, Australia, Thailand, and Brazil. The major importing nations are Russia, the EEC, the United States, China, and Japan. Sugar is traded in London, but the leading contract is in New York at the New York Board of Trade. There are two contracts, but the #14 is a domestic contract that reflects quotas supporting the internal sugar industry. The one to trade is the #11 contract, which represents the world free market. A contract is for 112,000 pounds, with prices quoted in cents per pound. A one-cent move equals a profit or loss of $1,120 per contract.

Coffee

This breakfast beverage is traded in London, but the most active contract is in the United States, which is also the major consuming nation. It is traded at the NYBOT. Coffee is classified into two types: Arabica and Robusta. The Arabica areas produce 60% of the world's output, with Brazil and Columbia accounting for one-third of the world's exportable supplies. The Central American countries of Costa Rica, Mexico, Guatemala, Honduras, and El Salvador are also important producers, as are Uganda, Indonesia, and Vietnam. This contract calls for delivery of Arabica coffee. Robusta, with flavors generally not as mild as the Arabica, is produced in the hot areas of Africa and Asia. The London contract is a Robusta contract. It takes approximately four years for a coffee bush to produce a useful crop. The fruit is green at first, and as it ripens, it changes to yellow and then red. It should be picked only when red, and the work is extremely labor intensive. Coffee beans do not ripen simultaneously, even when on the same branch, so the crop needs to be hand picked in most cases. In New York, the contract size is 37,500 pounds, or roughly 100 bags. A 1¢ move equals a profit or loss of $375 per contract. In the back months only, there is a 6¢ limit. The front two months can go wherever they want to. Note that most of the Central American varieties are deliverable on the contract at par, but if you deliver Colombian coffee, you receive a 2¢ bonus, because it is considered a premium product.

Cocoa

The cocoa tree is a tropical plant that grows only in hot, rainy climates. As a result, the major producing countries are (in order) Brazil, The Ivory Coast, Ghana, Malaysia, and Nigeria. The fruit of the cocoa tree appears as a pod on the tree's trunk, which when ripe is cut down and opened, and then the beans are removed.

Cocoa butter is extracted from the beans for use in cosmetics and pharmaceuticals, but its primary use is for the manufacture of chocolate. Cocoa is consumed primarily in countries of relatively high income. It was first brought to Europe as a luxury drink in the seventeenth century. The leading importing nations are (in order) the United States, Germany, France, the Netherlands, and the United Kingdom. These five countries account for about two-thirds of the world's consumption. Cocoa trades in London, but the NYBOT is also the leading Exchange for cocoa. The size of the contract is 10 metric tons of cocoa beans, with prices quoted in dollars per ton. A $1 move in price equals a profit or loss of $10 per contract, with a $100 move equal to $1,000.

Cotton

Since the Civil War, cotton has been the major cash crop of the American South, and the United States remains the world's largest producer to this day. However, U.S. production has not grown at the rate of the rest of the world. Other major producers include China, Russia, Pakistan, Mexico, India, and Egypt. The cotton fiber produces fabric, and the seed is used for cooking oil. The contract calls for 50,000 pounds of U.S-grown white cotton. A 1¢ move is equal to plus or minus $500 per contract, and there is a 2¢ per pound daily limit up or down.

Orange Juice

Oranges are second only to apples among fruit in production. (Apples, interestingly enough, are one of the few commodities not traded on a futures exchange.) The United States used to be self sufficient in production; however, a series of killer freezes in Florida created the growth of the Brazilian orange industry. Now up to 50% of U.S. consumption is imported from Brazil. The New York contract is based on a U.S. grade of Frozen Concentrated Orange Juice. In years of crop problems (primarily a freeze), prices can trade at more than $2 per pound. In years of high production, they trade below $1. This is a relatively thin contract, with a size of 15,000 pounds. A 1¢ move equals a profit or loss of $150 per contract.

Lumber

Woods are classified as hard or soft. Softwoods account for 85% of total lumber consumption. Most harvesting of lumber is done by the mill on land leased for timber rights by private parties or the government. The bark is removed, and logs move to the head saw. The contract calls for construction grade random length two-by-fours manufactured in the Pacific Northwest or Canada. The contract size is 80,000 board feet, with prices quoted in dollars and cents per board foot. A $1 move equals plus or minus $80 per contract. Like orange juice, this is a relatively low-volume, thin contract. The limit is $10.

Major Fundamentals for the "Softs":

■ **Stocks-to-usage ratios:** The level of sugar supplies in relation to demand, the stocks-to-consumption ratio, is the major statistic traders talk about when measuring the degree of "tightness" in the marketplace. For sugar, a ratio of 20 to 30% is considered low and consistent with higher prices. When prices spiked above 25¢ per pound in 1980, this ratio was in the mid-twenties. When the ratio rose above 40% in the mid-1980s, prices fell as low as 3¢. Because the free-floating supply of sugar is comparatively low, it does not take a big move in the stocks-to-consumption ratio to result in a major price move. Licht, a German-based trade house, is the primary reporting service for sugar statistical reporting. Candy sales are important, as is the price of corn. (High-fructose corn syrup is a competitor of sugar.)

■ *For cocoa, the "grind" is the term used to measure consumption:* Higher grinds indicate rising demand, and vice versa. From time to time, the International Cocoa Organization (ICO) forges an agreement intended to support prices. The ICO is a group of producing nations that purchases cocoa for its own account and stores it to push prices upward. When a shortage develops, it releases stocks onto the market. Coffee consumption is believed to be more inelastic, with a major price increase needed to curtail demand. However, the sharp rise in coffee prices in 1976 to 1997 was met by a commensurate reduction in consumption. Americans consume close to double what the Germans drink (they are number two), followed by the French, the Japanese, and then the other major EEC countries. Consumption trends need to be followed closely. In the late 1940s, the United States accounted for two-thirds of world imports, but because of changing preferences, this number is down to one-third. However, rising demand in Europe has completely offset the reduced American demand.

■ *Crop yields:* Weather, disease, insects, and political and economic conditions in the producing countries all affect production rates. For example, the great freeze in 1994 caused coffee prices to surge from less than $1 per pound to close to $3. For coffee, the ICO (International Coffee Organization) provides useful statistics, such as number of bags produced by country.

When I was a young broker at Merrill Lynch, I once heard a commodity broker tell a client that there could be a freeze in Brazil, which would hurt the coffee crop. It seemed reasonable to me because, at the time, we lived in Minnesota, and it was well below freezing. Only later did I realize that the North American winter is the South American summer, and there was no way they were going to freeze in the summer.

Metals

There are two major subsets to the metals category: precious and industrial. Although gold certainly is used in the jewelry industry and electronics and other industries, it is considered precious due to its traditional role as a medium of exchange (in other words, money). Silver is considered both precious and industrial. Metals such as copper (sometimes called the poor man's gold) are certainly considered to be in the industrial class.

Precious metals

Gold

Unique and precious, gold is its own asset class. Prices are quoted alongside securities in the major financial media. Gold is still a hedge against asset erosion in times of inflation and political unrest, and it is becoming increasing popular as an investment vehicle in China (as it has perhaps lost some of its luster in the West). In 1816, Great Britain, the world's major superpower, backed its currency exclusively with gold, which in turn forced other nations to follow its lead. The metal formally entered the world's monetary system in 1944 when the Bretton Woods agreement fixed all the world's paper currencies in relation to the dollar, which in turn was tied to gold. Then in 1971, Nixon canceled the dollar's convertibility to gold, which likely allowed the hyperinflation of a decade later. Today, many of the world's central banks, particularly in Europe, are divesting themselves of a portion of their gold reserves. Gold now trades freely in accordance to supply and demand. At times, it acts like an industrial metal (responding to jewelry demand), but it still is its own asset class with money flowing into the metal as a store of value when inflationary expectations heat up. South Africa is the world's largest gold producer, accounting for more than 25% of the world's production and 50% of the reserves. The next five major producers (in order) include Russia, the United States, Canada, Australia, and Brazil. The all-time futures price high as this book goes to press was $1,026 (reached in January 1980 on the October 1980 contract when the spot price hit $875). When the contract was listed in 1976, it came "on the board" less than $100. The COMEX is by far the world's largest precious metals market, with its 100 troy-ounce contract. Prices are quoted in dollars and cents per ounce, with a $1 move equaling a profit or loss of $100 per contract.

Platinum

Although an industrial metal (used in the automotive industry and in chemical, petroleum refining, and electronics), platinum is a precious metal, because only 80 tons of new production reaches the world annually. Ninety percent of the world's production takes place in South Africa and Russia; however, there was a major find in North America recently. South Africa still accounts for 85% of the world's reserves, with its two largest production companies, Impala and Rustenberg, setting the producer price. However, the NYMEX sets the price with its 100-ounce contract, which also is worth $10 or $1 ounce move. Platinum and palladium are traded on TOCOM (Tokyo Commodity Exchange). Platinum now generally trades at a premium to gold, and the platinum/gold spread is a popular speculation.

Silver

Silver is truly a hybrid industrial/precious metal. Because many of the world's dedicated silver mines cannot be operated profitably below $8 per ounce, until recently much of the production was the result of a by-product of copper, lead, and zinc mining. Mexico and the United States are the world's largest producers, followed by

Peru and Canada. Fourth and fifth in production are Australia and the former Soviet block countries. In recent years, silver consumption has outpaced new production, with the balance being met by above ground supplies. This probably cannot occur forever without either demand falling, production rising, or prices rising. The major Exchange for silver is again the COMEX, where a 5,000 troy-ounce contract is traded. Prices are quoted in dollars and cents per troy ounce, with a 1¢ move equaling a profit or loss of $50 per contract. When the Hunt brothers felt the world would run out of silver and attempted to corner the market from 1979 to 1980, they were able to run prices as high as $50 per ounce. They were 35¢ per ounce during the Great Depression in the 1930s.

Major metal fundamentals

■ *Gold:* Watch what the central banks are doing. At times they are aggressive sellers, and at times they are absent from the market. Keep an eye on the global political climate and how gold reacts to it. In times of instability, gold is considered a store of value. War, or a loss of confidence in traditional investments, can cause a shift of funds into gold. Watch China. As income growth increases there, gold demand increases, too. Most importantly, keep an eye on inflation and inflationary expectations. In the long run, the price of gold and all precious metals is most sensitive to inflation.

■ *Silver:* Watch the price of copper, zinc, and lead. Because much of the new production of silver comes as a by-product of these three metals, if the price of the three is depressed and production curtailed, silver output will suffer as well. The reverse is also true. Watch for alternatives to silver in photography. Because one-third of all silver use is still for photographic film, digital photo technology has curtailed silver use. Watch Indian imports. Silver is the precious metal of choice in India, and a strong economy there increases demand.

■ *Platinum:* Watch Japan. In Japan, platinum is the precious metal of choice, with more of it used for jewelry than gold. A strong economy in Japan is good for platinum prices. This is an industrial metal and a precious metal, and the demand for platinum is somewhat dependent on the health of the automotive, electrical, dental, medical, chemical, and petroleum industries (where it is used as a catalyst).

Industrial metals

Copper

The red metal is traded both in New York at the COMEX and in London at the London Metals Exchange (the tenth largest Exchange in the world). The LME contract trades about five times the volume of the U.S. contract; however, they are both very liquid and active. The LME contract has, at times, held the third spot in terms of volume for nonfinancial futures, after crude and corn. The LME contract is for 25 metric tons, or 55,000 pounds (prices are quoted in dollars and cents per ton with a

$1 move equal to a profit or loss of $25), and the COMEX is for 25,000 pounds or 12 1/2 "short tons." The price is quoted in dollars and cents per pound, with a 1¢ move equaling a profit or loss of $250 per contract. Copper is the third most widely used metal, after aluminum. The red metal is mined all over the world but primarily in the United States, Chile, Mexico, Australia, Indonesia, Zaire, and Zambia.

Aluminum

The British call this one (and spell it) aluminium (al-you-min-e-um). They include an extra "i" and extra syllable in the word. We Americans call it aluminum (al-ou-min-um). Aluminum is the world's second most widely used metal, after iron. The LME lists this very active, very liquid contract, which at times can be the fourth highest volume, nonfinancial future after crude, copper, and corn. During some years, the soybeans trade more, but it depends on the news and the weather. The contract size is 25 metric tons, or 55,000 pounds. Prices are quoted in dollars and cents per ton. In the United States, prices routinely are quoted in cents per pound. To convert from dollars per metric ton to cents per pound, you divide the price by 2204 (the number of pounds in a metric ton). The LME also trades a scrap aluminum contract; the aluminum alloy is a 20MT contract.

Zinc

Zinc is used as an alloy with copper to make brass. It also is used with iron or steel in a process called galvanizing, which is the largest use. The former USSR countries, Canada, the United States, and Australia are the major producers. The LME lists a 25 metric ton (55,000 pound) contract, which is also quoted in cents per pound. In 1988, zinc traded as high as 95¢ per pound. (It was 35¢ just two years earlier.)

Nickel

Most of the nickel production is used in stainless steel. It also is used as a coating for such varied applications as helicopter rotors and turbine blades. Nickel is also used in coins and rechargeable batteries. The major producers are Canada, Russia, and Australia. The contract also is traded on the LME, in six-ton lots, with prices quoted in dollars and cents per ton.

Lead

The major uses of lead include car batteries, ammunition, fuel tanks, and as a solder for pipes. The United States is the largest producer, followed by Canada, Mexico, Kazakhstan, and Australia. Because it is extremely toxic, there has been a concerted effort to "get the lead out" of many products in recent years. The United States, Japan, Germany, and the United Kingdom (the common link here is a major automotive industry) are big consumers. In the late 1970s, the price rose above 55¢, and to date has not been there since, averaging 30 to 40¢ in recent years. Lead also is listed on the LME in 25 metric ton contracts quoted in dollars and cents per ton.

Tin

Tin is manufactured into a coating for steel containers used to preserve foods and beverages and other forms of electroplating. China is the largest producer, followed by Brazil, Indonesia, Malaysia, Bolivia, and Thailand. However, more tin is smelted in Malaysia for export than any other country. It can be volatile at times, and in the late 1970s, prices soared above $850 per ton. That price was not exceeded again until 2004. Traded on the LME in six-ton contracts, prices also are quoted in dollars and cents per metric ton.

Palladium

Palladium is a member of the platinum group used in the automotive, electrical, and medical industries. Russia is the world's largest producer, with South Africa a close second. The two countries account for about 93% of the world's supply.

The all-time high price of $1,090 per ounce was reached in 2001, a period of shortage. From its peak, palladium lost more than $800 per ounce in only two years. But as new uses were discovered and demand increased, the price has started to rise once again. Palladium futures are traded in 100-ounce contracts on the NYMEX. Every $1 per ounce of price movement results in a $100 profit or loss per each contract purchased. It is a relatively thin market.

Major industrial metal fundamentals

- *Economic activity:* Watch the economies of the major industrialized nations that comprise the prime demand fundamentals of this group. Each of the metals, of course, has its own fundamentals (zinc and lead are generally mined together, for example), but industrialized demand is the key. If there is the threat of an economic slowdown, this will be reflected in lower prices.

- *LME stocks:* Every day, the LME releases its widely watched stocks report, which is a good measure of supply. It lists the stocks in the Exchange-approved warehouses for aluminum, copper, zinc, tin, and lead.

- *COMEX stocks:* These also are released every day for copper. At times, there is arbitrage between the LME warehouses and the COMEX, with stocks moving from one to the other.

- *Mining strikes, production problems, and war:* Copper, in particular, has been called the "war metal." Demand traditionally soars for the industrial metals in times of increased defense spending.

- *Inflation:* The industrial metals have, at times, been called "the poor man's gold," and they heat up in an inflationary environment.

True story

When I was a novice commodity broker at Merrill Lynch, my biggest client was a retired, former top executive of a major software company. When the company went public, his stock was worth more than $15 million. In retirement, his hobby was trading commodities. He traded a bit differently from most of us, in that he had the funds available to back his convictions until they eventually worked—and they usually did. I remember he once started to short wheat at $3 per bushel. The market went against him, and he added to the position at $3.50. He added to his short position at $4 and more at $4.50. When the crop finally came in, he covered the entire position at $3—a nice profit. This is not a recommended way to trade, mind you, but it worked for him. He was a strict fundamentalist and never looked at charts.

In 1979, when silver first crossed $8, he started to short the market with a modest position of five contracts. He was a former metallurgical engineer, and he had a theory that above $8, the technology was available to extract silver from the slag heaps alongside the mines, and the market would be flooded with supply. Remember, at this point we did not know that the Hunts and their Arab partners were accumulating silver bullion and silver futures in their attempt to corner the market. At 850, my client shorted another five and another five at 900. By the time the price crossed 1000, he was short 25 contracts with an unrealized loss of more than $125,000. He was determined to keep shorting; "whatever it takes," he told me, until he finally beat this one—this was his style. By the time the market reached 1200 (an all-time high), he was short approximately 50 contracts with an average price of 1000 and an unrealized loss of $500,000. I was getting very nervous and very concerned, but he was adamant. All we knew at that time was that there was a broker from the now-defunct Conti Commodity firm who would come into the pit, almost daily, purchase a huge position, and leave the pit for the day. Many times, his buying would put the market up the limit. (There was a 50¢ per ounce limit at the time.) When he left the pit, the market would drift a bit and usually close higher on the day, but not up the limit.

I started to have silver nightmares, afraid my big client would go down with the ship, but I didn't really know what to tell him. At the time, there wasn't a good fundamental explanation that could convince him he was wrong.

I then remembered that there was a Merrill Lynch executive who was also on the Board of Directors of the COMEX. The next morning I called him, explained I had this big client short silver with a big loss, and he just wouldn't get out. I still remember the call: His response went something like this, "Look, there's big money behind this market. If you're short, GET OUT. That's all I can tell you—don't call me again!" Then he hung up.

About 10 minutes prior to the open, with my heart pounding, I called John and told him about this conversation. I must have sounded daft as I told him, "The guy says, 'If you're short, GET OUT,'" because he calmly told me to "Reverse the position at the open." I said, "You mean, not just buy your 50 to cover, but buy 50 more?" He said, "Yes. If we're wrong to be short, then we should be long."

Now I was really nervous. What if I convinced him to cover and then he bought at the top? He could lose more than $1 million, and I could lose my best client. Still, it was too late to do anything but put the order into buy 100 contracts at the open. Guess what happened? The market opened limit up, at an all-time high price somewhere around 1250. Then it started to drift down. So he covered his 50 at a loss in excess of a cool half-million, and because of my phone call, he now owned 50 contracts at what was an all-time, record-high price—and the market was drifting down!

To make a long story short, the market drifted another 10¢ or so lower but then reversed up to close that day up the limit price (so at least he was not showing a loss on the new position at the close that day). As it turned out, the next $2 to $3 higher came fairly easily, and when he recouped his total loss, plus a modest profit, he got out of the 50, in the $15 to $16 range. Of course, if he held on to the 50 up to the highs, around $50, he could have made more than $9 million. Then again, he could still have been there on the descent back to $5. In any case, disaster was averted.

John never traded silver again, but he continued to trade actively until he passed away about three years later.

8

The advanced futures trading course (or how to analyze the markets technically)

If you work for the global commodity trading firm Cargill and have access to timely, accurate (and no doubt expensive) fundamental information, while this might not be all you need, the odds are it's better than what the rest of us are getting. It is Nestlé's business to know how the cocoa crop in the Ivory Coast is developing. Although you might read a brokerage house report that discusses the "witch's tail disease" and its potential to devastate the crop, Nestlé has its man in the Ivory Coast, with another in Brazil for that matter, walking the fields. Nestlé and Hershey both have a better feel for just how good or bad the crops are than you'll ever have (and they have no reason or obligation to share this information with the rest of us).

Let's say, for example, that the cocoa crop is deteriorating. A confidential communiqué is wired to Switzerland, and the people in charge of purchasing for Nestlé get busy. One aspect of their job is to hedge by buying cocoa futures in London or in New York. If the odds favor the supply dropping, there's a good chance of prices rising when the news hits the wires. Protecting against future price risk is what hedging is all about. The Nestlé traders will, as quietly as they can, accumulate new crop cocoa futures long before you know what they're up to, but there's a catch. Nobody is able to accumulate a large position, either on the long or short side, without leaving "footprints in the sand." Large, significant, "informed" volume must be reported according to Exchange rules and inevitably will move price. This is what technical analysis is all about—analyzing past and current price action to project future price action.

Does technical analysis really work?

I have more than 25 years of experience that proves technical analysis really does work. Solid technical analysis is perhaps the only tool that can give the individual trader a decent chance against the professionals. You might not have the research capabilities of the commercials or the execution advantages of the floor traders. However, with technical analysis on your side, what you do have is the luxury of moving faster than the big commercial operators, because your trading size will not affect price too significantly. You have one advantage over the "locals"—a better perspective. You're not subject to the false trend movements, what I call the "noise" that takes place on the floor every minute of every day, plus you're not stuck trading just one market (which might or might not be moving). You can sit back, relax, and look at your "maps" in the comfort of your home or office—you can analyze your charts.

Pure technicians believe that the only important factor necessary to the markets is price action. They do not look at crop size, export data, money supply, or employment numbers. They don't care if it's raining in Brazil or if the head of the European Central Bank just made a speech saying he's in favor of raising interest rates. Technicians only care about price action.

This is not to say that technicians don't believe that fundamentals move the market. They concede this fact. A technician might know that soybean prices are rising, because drought is devastating the Brazilian crop. He also will tell you that price will signal when the diminished supply has finally been rationed by diminished demand, and this could happen long before the drought has broken.

The technician believes that all the pertinent fundamental information, perhaps thousands of bits of data impossible for any mortal to assimilate, is reflected in price action. In essence, the price action reflects the consensus of the market players far better than the mainstream fundamental information available to the public trader.

Is technical analysis the best way to go?

Although I personally feel a mix of fundamental and technical analysis makes the most sense, certain technical approaches are more important, in my opinion, than the fundamentals. I know of many successful traders, people who consistently take money out of the markets, who are purely technical. This chapter discusses both methods, and I believe it is the most important chapter in the book!

Charts

The **price chart** is your road map, your primary trading tool. Charts come in different flavors, from point and figure to Japanese candlestick and the most popular, the bar chart.

Most of you are no doubt familiar with bar charts. Although they're fairly easy to construct, they are not always that easy to analyze for maximum profitability. The bar chart can be in any time frame the trader prefers. The day trader might use a five-minute time frame, whereas the long-term "position trader" might use a monthly time frame. All the charts are constructed basically the same way; the most popular is the **daily bar chart**. On a daily bar chart, each day is plotted as a vertical line (or bar), with the range of the day's trading represented by the length of the bar. In other words, the top point of the bar is the day's high, and the low point is the day's low. On a standard bar chart, the horizontal axis measures time, and the vertical axis measures price. A small horizontal "tick mark" (or "flag") is plotted on each daily bar "waving" to the right to indicate the closing price. Some bar charts also reflect the open via a small horizontal flag (or tic mark) plotted on each daily bar waving to the left.

_eg_ **For example, if on May 9, July sugar opened at 1104, proceeded to trade down to 1080, and then traded up to 1142 with a close, or "settlement price," near the highs at 1138, the daily bar for July sugar above May 9 on the horizontal axis of time would be the length of the range, in this case 1080 to 1142. This bar would be positioned to correspond with the vertical axis of price from 1080 to 1142. The flag representing the open would be a tick placed waving to the left "looking toward"' 1104 on the vertical price scale, with the closing flag waving to the right of the bar "looking away" from 1138 on the price bar. Because a picture is worth a thousand words, let's get on to the pictures.**

Many good charting services are available for purchase via mail or electronic means. Most of the professionals in the business subscribe to at least one real-time data service that updates its charts automatically. However, I know of more than one professional who still prefers the old-fashioned method. These folks have graph paper and a pencil. They chart each market they are interested in daily and _by hand_, saying this is the only way to get a real feel for the price action. I even know of a floor trader who charts ticks right in the trading pit, which is not an easy thing to do.

How to use price charts

Success in trading equals making money. Personally, I buy the technical approach, because I have been able to use it successfully in my own trading. If you're a skeptic, and it appears to you that charting is no more than crystal ball gazing, you still should become familiar with technical analysis because it will help you become a better fundamental trader. Most of the fundamental analysts I know still look at the charts. So many of today's market participants use the charts that they have now, in effect, become fundamental. At times, a particular chart movement or pattern becomes self-fulfilling. So many traders are looking at the same thing, that its very existence encourages them to simultaneously make a move that influences prices. In effect, this can make the anticipated move actually happen—a self-fulfilling prophecy. At other times, certain price actions on the charts create temporary "false" moves, which give the fundamentalist an excellent opportunity to enter or exit a trade. Bottom line, without a working knowledge of technical analysis, the fundamental trader is at a disadvantage to those who know what to look for.

In this chapter, I will touch briefly on some of the more popular and significant chart patterns. In Chapters 9, "The Most Valuable Technical Tool," and 10, "How I Use 'TMVTT,'" I will discuss in depth a specific technical approach I use in the markets. The following pages should give you a good basis for additional study, but I do not mean to imply that the price patterns discussed are the gospel—far from it. Every one of these price patterns will provide you with false signals at times. In a way, however, this can be beneficial, because even false signals are useful signals, *if* you know what to look for and how to react.

The trendline

The trendline is perhaps the most popular of all chart tools. I've mentioned numerous times in this book that if you can determine the trend of the market, you'll make money. This is what the trendline is designed to do: determine the trend of the market and keep you with the trend until it changes.

Trendlines come in two basic flavors: the up-trendline and the down-trendline. In an uptrend, the market tends to make higher lows and higher highs. A downtrend is characterized by lower highs and lower lows. You can prove to yourself that markets move in trends by simply picking up a diversified chart book and doing an "eyeball." Note how the moves of significance are characterized by a series of higher highs/higher lows, or lower highs/lower lows.

Certainly, hindsight is 20/20. It is not always easy to know just what the trend is in the thick of the battle or if you can accurately determine the trend, just how long it will last. This is where the trendlines come in.

A trendline is drawn on the chart you are analyzing along the tops or bottoms of the price bars in the direction of the significant trend. In a bull, or rising market, the trendline is drawn by connecting a straight line that connects higher lows. At least two points are necessary, but I recommend a minimum of three to add validity. In a bear, or falling market, the line connects two (but preferably three or more) highs.

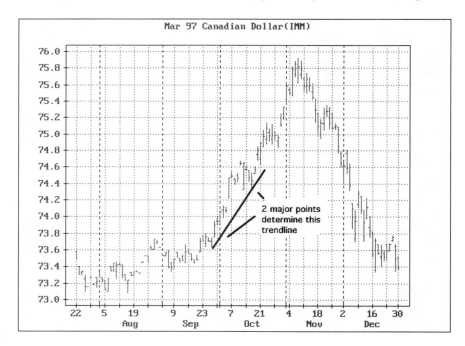

■ **Chart 8.1**   Two major points determine this trendline

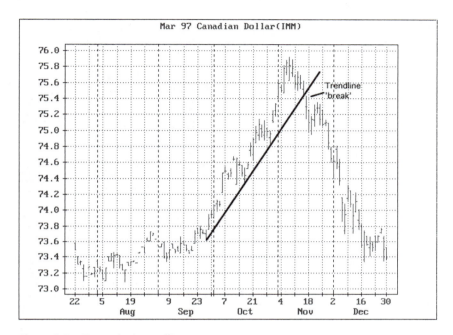

■ **Chart 8.2**   Extended trendline

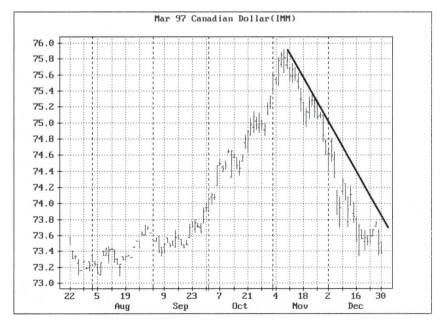

■ **Chart 8.3**   Down-trendline

The rule of thumb is that the more points you have connected, the more "valid" the trendline. But here's the rub: The more "valid" the trendline, by definition the more price data you have to use, therefore the older the trend and the closer it is to its inevitable conclusion. A broken trendline (price action moving below an up-trendline or above a down-trendline) is a danger signal that the trend has reversed. This is how technicians use trendlines. When an up-trendline is broken, longs should be liquidated and new shorts established. Shorts should do the opposite when a down-trendline is broken. Many traders place stops just under an up-trendline, or just above a down-trendline, to exit positions. If a trend is of significant duration, a *trailing stop* can be used, where the risk is reduced gradually daily as the stop loss is moved in the direction of the prevailing trend. In this way, the first risk is the greatest risk. The objective is first to achieve a break-even, and then if every-thing goes according to plan, a modest profit is locked in. Over time, additional prof-its are locked in until the trendline is finally broken. The best and most reliable trendlines are older and, therefore, by definition, longer.

The problem with using trendlines is that, in practice, markets are not always all that orderly. A straight line assumes some sort of symmetrical series of higher lows and highs, or the reverse. In the real world, markets can act this way for a time. Because of human nature, however, there will be sharp and meaningless reversals in trend, which in the long run generate false trendline reversal signals. False trendline reversal signals are more likely to occur when the trendline is too steep. Steeper trendlines are generally those of shorter length; therefore, they are shorter in dura-tion and, by definition, most likely to be violated.

When a trendline is broken, it certainly can be used as a danger signal. But what do you do if the market in short order resumes back in the direction of the major pre-ceding trend? You can construct a new trendline by using the new significant low or high.

When trendlines are broken repeatedly and new trendlines redrawn, the chart tends to look like a fan. A series of trendlines, all starting out at the same point, moves in parallel. This fan effect either indicates the major trend is still intact (albeit less steep) *or* the major trend is actually changing. Good interpretation and analyti-cal tools come into play at this point; some traders have a sixth sense when this occurs. Others need to rely on a completely mechanical approach. Bottom line, it is best not to become too reliant on any one technical tool. Trendlines are helpful, but I do not believe you can make money using them alone. Not all markets trend well, and no markets trend all the time, which is when trendlines will not work at all. Nevertheless, trendlines can indicate the basic tendency of a trending market and also can tell you when the trend has exhausted itself. However, by combining trend-lines with *other* chart patterns plus some of the more powerful tools covered in Chapters 9 and 10, you'll increase your odds for a winning combination.

Channels

Although channels come in various flavors, prices in a classic trend commonly tend to trade roughly within a channel. A channel is identified by constructing a line parallel to the major trendline. If a market is trending higher and a standard

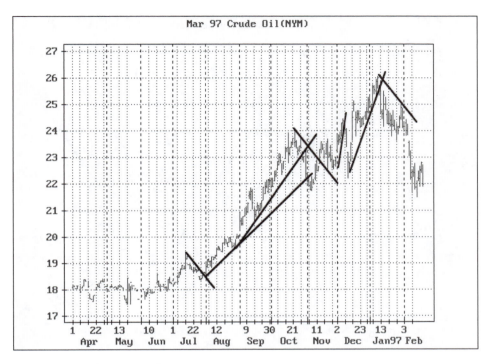

Chart 8.4   Redrawn trendlines

up-trendline has been constructed, the top line of the channel is drawn by connecting progressive highs. In a downtrend, a parallel to the down-trendline is drawn, connecting progressive lows. Presto, a channel is born. As long as the market remains within the channel for the most part, the market is behaving normally during a trending-type period. Nimble traders look to buy on the trendline and sell toward the upper channel line (assuming they're in an up-trend). Active traders might also look to reverse at the channel lines, but this generally is not recommended, because they would be fighting the trend.

At times, any market trades out of the bounds of the channel. This can be a significant clue to subsequent market action. The general rule of thumb is that when a market trades above the upper channel line (in an up-trend) or below the lower channel line (in a down-trend), the odds that the market is entering an accelerated phase have increased. In other words, a significant change in the normal supply and demand balance has taken place. With bona fide breakouts of channels, the market tends to move faster, with price action becoming more dramatic. Stops can be tightened, positions can be pyramided, and your "antenna should be up" for any signs of a subsequent trend reversal. The accelerated phase of any market can be the most profitable and most exciting time to play, but it also can be the shortest. Don't fight it; go with it, but remain alert. If acting right, after it has broken out, the market should *not* fall back into the channel, because this would be the place to exit and reevaluate.

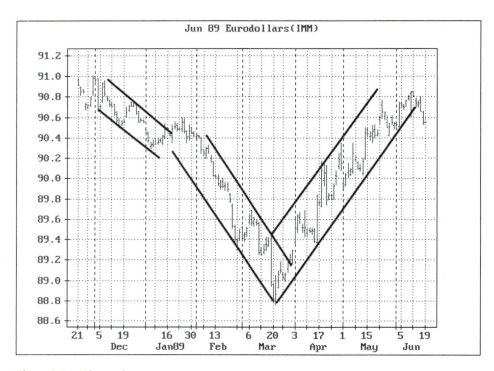

Chart 8.5 Channels

Support and resistance

Support and resistance levels are neon signs along the avenue that can clearly indicate at what prices the demand or the supply for a particular commodity rests. Think of them as floors and ceilings. Simply put, **support** is a significant area in which buying interest develops, has developed, or is expected to develop based on past history. Support becomes evident on a price chart, as the market "bounces off support" or "holds support."

eg **If copper trades up to 99¢ and then breaks down to 95, bounces back up to 97 and then breaks back down to 9490, and finally bounces up to 100, and then breaks back to 9510, where it again starts to move in an upward direction, traders would say, "Support is around 95."**

This is an area in which the buying interest, whether it be commercial copper users, fund buyers, or bargain hunters (it actually doesn't matter who) have either placed resting buy orders or step up to the plate to buy at the market. It also might be an area in which a big short, or perhaps multiple shorts, look to cover their positions to take profits or exit a losing position. It doesn't matter why the price holds at this level; this is a level where buying comes out of the woodwork, and as a result, it is termed a **support level**.

Support levels can be plainly seen by looking at price charts and appears basically where buying interest has shown before. Therefore, the expectation is that buying interest will be there again, should the market trade there again. If the market doesn't hold on a return run (as in the preceding example, copper breaks down to 94 the fourth time), this is termed **breaking support** and is a bearish sign. Those traders who previously had supported the market at around 95 are either gone (or all the significant shorts have covered), or if they were new longs, they are weaker this time than the new sellers.

The mirror image of support, the ceiling, is called **resistance**. This is a level at which a market has trouble getting above or has a hard time moving higher. If copper rallies to 100, then tails off to 97 and back up to 9995, and does this more than once, this is the level (at least temporarily) of resistance. In other words, resistance is an area in which the selling interest is greater than the demand.

Support and resistance levels can be drawn graphically by using a horizontal line on the bar chart connecting the *floor* points, in the case of support, and *ceiling* points in the case of resistance. These are important levels that indicate the areas you would expect a market to hold or to fail. Like trendline points, traders are cognizant of where support and resistance levels are. As a result, they can become a self-fulfilling

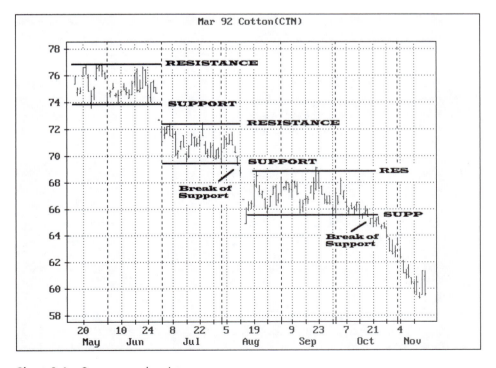

■ **Chart 8.6**   Support and resistance

prophecy, at least in the short run. If a market continues to fail at a certain resistance level, the sellers become bolder every time that price is reached, and the buyers assume this is the place to exit.

eg **For example, for years corn prices were unable to trade above $4, give or take a few cents either way. This was considered a ceiling price in years of big demand and in years of drought. In 1996 when China turned from a corn exporter into a major importer, corn prices broke the $4 "glass ceiling" (and didn't look back until it hit $5.50).**

It didn't take all that long either. After the resistance was taken out, the path of least resistance was easily north.

Extended periods of support and resistance both holding simultaneously can lead to one of the most powerful of all chart patterns, the "breakout from consolidation."

Breakouts from consolidation

A market bouncing off support is like a ball bouncing off the floor. If the floor is a deck four stories off the ground, the ball will bounce as long as it falls on the deck, but if it subsequently falls off the deck, it keeps falling. Alternatively, resistance is like a ceiling, but if a glass ceiling is smashed, the birds are free to fly away.

Support and resistance levels are extremely important to traders. When a market is in a relatively flat range (holding at support and failing at resistance), this is termed **consolidation**. Consolidation is nothing more than an inability by either the bulls or the bears to win the battle. When the market holds at some level, rallies, and then again retreats to that same level, it appears cheap. Those bulls who missed the first rally feel like they have a second chance at "cheap" levels and step up to the plate. The shorts, especially those who are scalping and sold at higher levels, see the market start to bounce and are induced to cover their shorts before their paper profits disappear. This additional buying, this short covering, adds fuel to the bull move.

The reverse occurs when the market rallies to the level of previous failure, which is called the resistance point. Some of the longs who purchased at support might feel the market is looking expensive and cash in. Bears, who missed selling the last rally, will consider this a "second chance" and start to get busy. The market starts its retreat, and other longs (who do not want to see their paper profits disappear) sell out, thus adding fuel to the bear fire. If a market fails at a resistance level on numerous occasions and over a significant period of time, and then one day trades above that level, this is a sign that the bears have lost the battle. The buying interest was finally strong enough to overwhelm the selling interest, and the defensive ceiling built by the bears has been shattered. (The opposite is happening if a support level is broken.) In simpler terms, there is a major shift taking place in the supply and demand fundamentals of the market in question. Look at the 1988 oats chart, the all-time monster oats rally that drove prices to levels never seen before or since. Look at how long and beautiful the consolidation was that preceded this bull move.

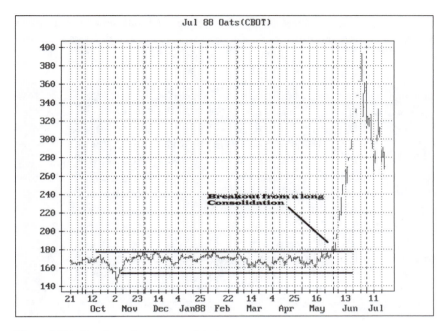

■ **Chart 8.7**   Breakout from consolidation

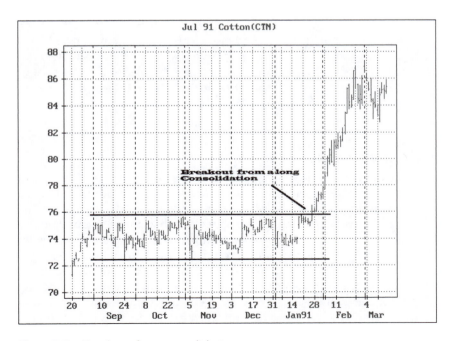

■ **Chart 8.8**   Breakout from consolidation

The preceding two charts are good examples of breakouts from long consolidations that marked the beginnings of major moves. I particularly remember the oats move of 1988. This is a true story.

I had a large client who was wealthy, stubborn, gutsy, and would not get out of his March oats because he felt they were too cheap. He had two million bushels (the limit an individual could own at that time), and I told him if he didn't get out, he would get delivery. No problem, he told me, even though when delivery takes place, a trader is required to put up the full value of the contract and is no longer on margin.

He took delivery of the 2 million bushels at about $1.60 per bushel in March. He wired the $3,200,000. From that day on, he told me my job was to be on the lookout for a good bid to sell the oats in the cash market, but none of the big boys (neither General Mills nor Quaker Oats) seemed interested. The market traded in the consolidation range for a few months, and then it got hot and dry.

The drought of 1988 is history now, but let me tell you how this all worked out. The oat crop in the Dakotas was devastated. The futures traded up to about $4 per bushel. On June 28, the all-time record high day for oats, I got a call from one of the large processors. When he asked if the oats were still for sale and when I told him yes, he offered $4 per bushel for the entire 2 million. I called my client, who told me to reject the $4 bid and offer the whole lot at $4.40—take it or leave it. When I called the processor back, he said, "Sold!" My client sold 2 million bushels of cash oats for 40¢ per bushel higher than the futures. As far as I can determine, this is the all-time record price at which oats have ever been sold. The client cleared a cool $5 million.

When I later asked the grain man why he was so quick to buy the oats at record high prices, he told me this: "I had the choice of closing down the mill and putting 200 people out of work because I didn't have any oats to make oatmeal, or paying too much and bumping the price of a box of cereal by 10¢. What would you have done?"

Support becomes resistance and vice versa

An interesting characteristic of support and resistance is that upon penetration, one tends to turn into the other. For example, if copper were in a consolidation between 95 and 100, and then blasted through 100 to trade up to 103, the assumption would be that the 100 level would offer new support. Human nature, again, comes into play here. The first blast through resistance most likely came with new money that created new demand. Those longs, having completed their initial purchases, are satiated, done for the time being. The market starts to drift back on profit, taking from those bulls who've not recognized the change in trend and now see a chance to cash in with profits at levels not seen for a while. New shorts are established by uninformed speculators who perceive these new high levels as expensive. Meanwhile, there are shorts who had successfully sold at the 100 level many times in the past, and this time they were caught behind the eight ball. If the market is able to drift back to their

Dec 89 Gold(CMX)

Chart 8.9   Support turns into resistance

break-even level, they are relieved, because they are able to liquidate (cover their shorts, which in effect is buying) without much pain. Meanwhile, new bulls who now clearly see the breakout view the 100 level as an excellent place to establish long positions. The "strong arms" who know what's going on also look at any break as a buying opportunity. Always remember that human beings make markets, and this is why support, when broken, becomes resistance and vice versa.

False breakouts

At this point, I would like to digress a bit. Although this information is good, and I believe it works more times than not, you didn't think it would be all that easy, did you?

When I first discovered technical analysis, I studied the profitable examples in the books and thought this trading thing would be a piece of cake. Unfortunately, like all of life, it doesn't work all the time. I must tell you, there have been and will continue to be false breakouts from consolidation. Many traders are well aware how powerful a tool these patterns can be, and as a result, they look for these breakouts. Many technicians place stops just under support to limit losses or establish new short positions. Floor traders know intuitively just where these stops are going to be. There is nothing sinister about this; they can make an educated guess where the stops are just by looking at a price chart, and they look at the same charts as everyone else.

eg **If a market has held numerous times at 95, and it approaches that level again, what's to stop a floor trader (or group of floor traders) from offering the market down to 9490? The objective is to uncover the sell stops. Remember, a sell stop is a resting order to sell at some predetermined level. If the stops are actually "resting" at 9490 (they could be held by numerous brokers representing hundreds of traders from various unrelated firms), the selling commences. At times, this action can feed on itself. The brokers with sell stops at 9490 immediately begin to offer to sell. The resting orders to buy at 9490 are filled, so the brokers offer lower (9480, 9470, 9460). However, everyone seems to be selling—all on stops. The floor brokers love this, especially in a quiet or thin market. They will come back in and bid at 9450 and 9440 and cover their shorts at a quick and tidy profit. Because there was really no fundamental substance behind this price action, the market quickly bounces back above 95 as the shorts are covered and commercial traders and bargain hunters step in.**

As a speculator, getting caught in a false breakout is frustrating. Seeing your stop hit and knock you out of a good position, only to watch the market quickly reverse in the direction you thought it was going in the first place, will cool your jets. All I can tell you is, if you trade long enough, this will happen to you, so keep your cool. Place your stops carefully, where you don't think everyone else's stops are. Breakouts from consolidation are such powerful indicators of potential trend changes that you should never become complacent when they occur just because false breakouts exist. My six rules for trading breakouts from consolidation should help.

Six rules for trading breakouts from consolidation
Rule 1

The longer it takes to form a consolidation, the more significant the breakout, and the bigger the expected move will follow. A breakout on a daily chart is more powerful than a 30 minute, and a breakout on a weekly chart is more powerful still. A breakout from consolidation on a yearly chart is the most powerful of all, signifying a major fundamental change in the supply and demand balance of that market.

Rule 2

After the breakout occurs, the market can retrace back to the breakout level, but it probably shouldn't trade back into the consolidation zone. If is does, the odds of a false breakout increase.

Rule 3

The breakout should remain above the breakout level for a significant amount of time. After it's above the resistance or below the support, you really won't be in much trouble if you went with the breakout. If profits are not forthcoming in a reasonable amount of time, be wary. A quick failure is a symptom of a false breakout.

Rule 4

Watch the volume on the breakout day, because a true breakout is generally associated with a sharp rise in the daily volume. At times, this high volume level might precede the breakout by a day or two; however, false breakouts are almost always associated with modest volume.

Rule 5

When trading a breakout using stops, never place your stops just under support or just above resistance. This is what all the amateurs are doing, and they become bait for running the stops. Generally, it is better to take a bit more risk and place your stop at a slightly greater distance.

Rule 6

Determine the count. A basic rule of thumb is that when a market breaks out from consolidation, it will move roughly the distance up or down equal to the horizontal distance of the consolidation phase. To determine the count, take a ruler and measure the horizontal distance of the consolidation, and then measure upward from the resistance breakout or downward from the support breakout, to give you an indication of the price objective for the coming move.

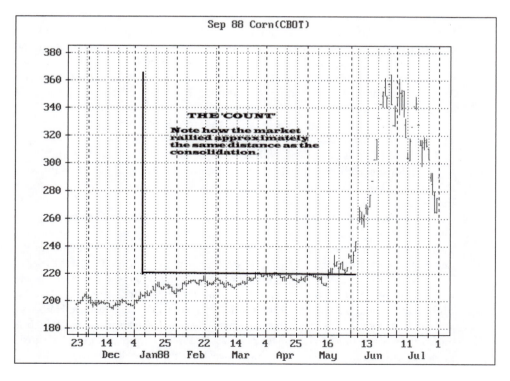

■ **Chart 8.10** The count

Classic chart patterns

Technical Analysis of Stock Trends, written by Edwards and McGee and first published in 1948, is often referred to as the "Bible of Technical Analysis." The basic premise is that prices of stocks and commodities move in repeating and identifiable patterns, the result of the ebb and flow of supply and demand. Although some of the concepts presented in the book at that time were new, many had been around since the turn of the century. Although markets might have changed dramatically since the 1940s, human nature has not; therefore, many of the patterns presented by these two groundbreakers remain valid today. Chart patterns fall into two basic groups:

- ▓ Those signaling a reversal in trend

- ▓ Those signaling a continuation in the prevailing trend

Reversal patterns include the head and shoulders, double tops and bottoms, rounding tops and bottoms, and reversal days. Continuation patterns include flags and pennants. Gaps and triangles are hybrids that can signal either or both. The following sections explain the classic patterns, which I have found remain valid today.

Head and shoulders [H&S]

This is perhaps the most famous of all the classic chart patterns, but I am going to spend some ink on this concept, because in my experience it is one of the most reliable. This is a reversal pattern—one that signals a major top or bottom is forming. When you can see a head and shoulders, it's time to get out and take your profits, cut your losses, or establish a new position in the new direction. An interesting characteristic of the head and shoulders is that it not only tells you a market is making a top or bottom but will tell you how far the ensuing move is going to travel. The H&S does not actually pick *the* top or *the* bottom but gives you the sign after the top or bottom is in place.

Because a picture is worth a thousand words, let's start with some images that illustrate the head and shoulders pattern.

The head (H) is a price peak with another peak lower than the head to the left (the left shoulder, or LS) and another peak lower than the head to the right (the right shoulder, or RS). The line connecting the lows of the declines from the shoulders and the head is termed the **neckline** (NL). In a classic head and shoulders, the neckline is horizontal (much like a support line); however, it does not have to be. It can also be upward-sloping, like an up-trendline or downward-sloping like a down-trendline. This is where your detective skills come into play. Many of the best head and shoulder patterns are mutants, which resemble the original in some modified way.

You can discern a head and shoulders developing when the left shoulder and the head are in place, and the market starts to rally from the neckline. If it fails at a lower high than the major high, the right shoulder is in formation. A classic H&S will have a right shoulder of the approximate same size and duration as the left, but once again, it does not need to be this way. It can be lower or higher, longer or shorter, but its peak will ultimately end up being lower than the head. *The pattern is not complete until the right shoulder is completed* and *the decline from the right shoulder's peak breaks under the neckline.* When that happens, the supposition as a top is in place. It is time

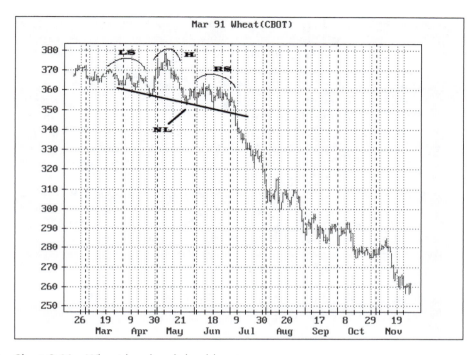

Chart 8.11 Wheat head and shoulders top

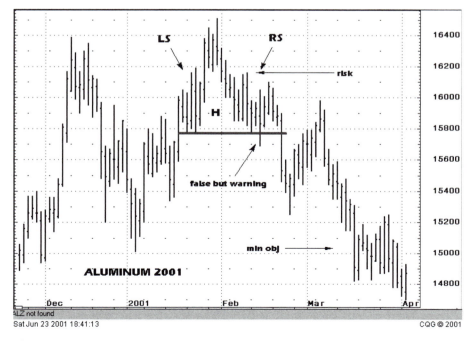

Chart 8.12 Aluminium head and shoulders top

to exit longs and go short. Many times, after the initial breakout below the neckline, the market rallies back up to approximately the neckline, giving the trader an excellent, low-risk shorting opportunity.

Head and shoulders patterns can also, at times, provide false signals. A false signal should be suspected if the market is able to again rally back above the peak of right shoulder. (This is the place to set your risk point initially.) This does not occur with the best H&S signals, because most do not rally beyond the neckline. Should the market again be able to trade above the peak of the right shoulder, you can safely assume all bets are off, and this one isn't "right." In the preceding aluminum chart, the corrective rally came back to slightly above the neckline but never exceeded the right shoulder.

There's a bonus that comes with the H&S. It gives us a target, which is generally reliable and more precise than most technical techniques. If you measure from the top of the head to the neckline and bring this measurement down starting from the neckline, you have a minimum target where prices will subsequently end up. The market can certainly move farther than this count, but it gives you a minimum objective that could prevent exiting prematurely.

H&S patterns occur in all time frames, and you can see them in the short term S&P chart frequently. Of course, with a smaller pattern, in most cases you need to shoot for a smaller objective.

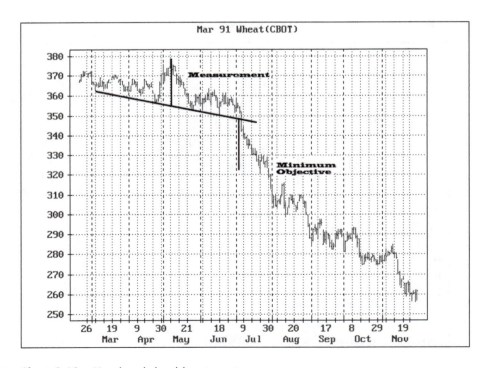

■ **Chart 8.13**   Head and shoulders target

■ **Chart 8.14** One minute S&P head and shoulders

■ **Chart 8.15** S&P head and shoulders

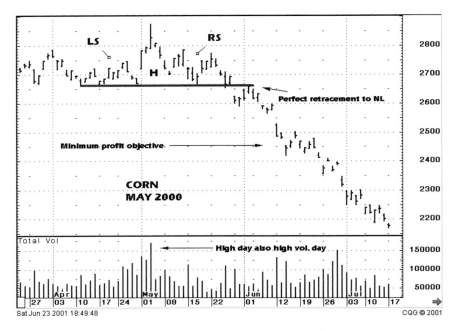

Chart 8.16   Corn head and shoulders with volume confirmation

Chart 8.17   Gold H&S bottom

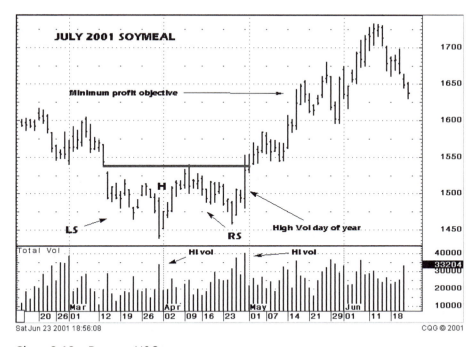

Chart 8.18   Reverse H&S

Watch volume to confirm the pattern. Many times, volume spikes at the head and is often higher than average at the break of the neckline.

Head and shoulders occur at major bottoms as well, and they look like the mirror image of those that form at the top. Some traders call these **inverted head and shoulders**, or **reverse head and shoulders**. In this variety, the head is at the lowest point, with two higher shoulders at either side. Other than the fact these are the mirror image of the tops, you trade them the same way.

Ten rules for successfully trading the head and shoulders

Rule 1   Never anticipate.

When I first discovered H&S patterns, I had a good trade, and it seemed I started finding them everywhere. I would start to sell after a right shoulder and a head developed, only to lose money. I would see complete H&S patterns develop and take action *prior* to penetration of the neckline, only to have my head handed to me. As Yogi Berra said, "It ain't over 'til it's over." Wait until the pattern is complete before you trade it.

Rule 2   The bigger the H&S pattern and the longer it takes to develop, the bigger the subsequent resulting move.

While an H&S pattern that develops on a five-minute daily chart may be useful for a day trade (and should be treated as such), one that develops over many weeks on the daily chart is much more significant to indicating the potential for a major move.

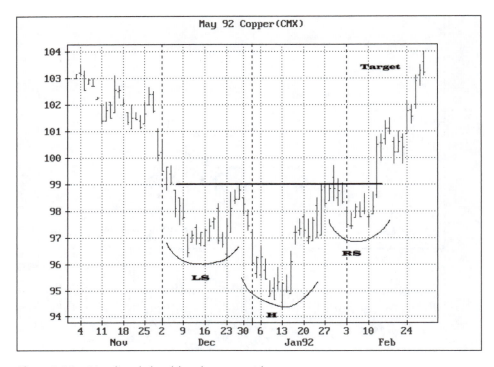

May 92 Copper(CMX)

■   **Chart 8.19**   Head and shoulders bottom with target

Rule 3   The count is a minimum measurement.

Odds favor the move carrying much further. However, a warning here: As with all chart patterns, you are not dealing with a certainty. If your count says the market will fall 400 points, and it falls 380 and starts to reverse, it would be a shame to let all your profits evaporate for a lousy 20 points.

Rule 4   After the market breaks the neckline, watch for the return move back to the neckline.

They occur in at least half of all valid cases and offer a place to enter with a close stop.

Rule 5   Watch the slope of the neckline.

Downward-sloping necklines for H&S tops increase the odds for a more powerful bear move to follow. Upward-sloping necklines for inverted H&S bottoms increase the odds for a more powerful bull move to follow.

Rule 6   Be volume cognizant.

The most valid of neckline breakouts are accompanied with higher than average volume. In retrospect, there have been times when I've seen the highest daily volume days of the year associated with head and shoulder patterns.

Rule 7   Watch for the head to form an "island."

This combines two powerful patterns and geometrically increases the validity of the signal.

Rule 8   When the pattern is complete, it should act the right way.

These patterns are fairly reliable and do not often deviate from their true purpose unless, of course, they are false. How can you tell if one is false? One good indication is that your margin account will start to show a loss. Don't freeze when it's not acting right—when in doubt get out. Be suspicious if the pattern occurs on low volume. Remember, the market can retrace to the neckline; this is normal and a good place to position. If the signal is any good, the retracement really shouldn't go much further.

Rule 9   If a false signal, look to reverse.

I've found that many times a classic H&S failure offers an excellent opportunity to get back in sync with the major trend. If the market again trades above the right shoulder's top (or below the right shoulder's bottom for a reverse H&S), odds favor, at the minimum, one last thrust to a new high or new low. I would buy the market at this point, with the objective of a new high, risking to under the neckline. For an inverted H&S failure, sell the market under the low of the right shoulder with a minimum objective of a new low, risking to above the neckline.

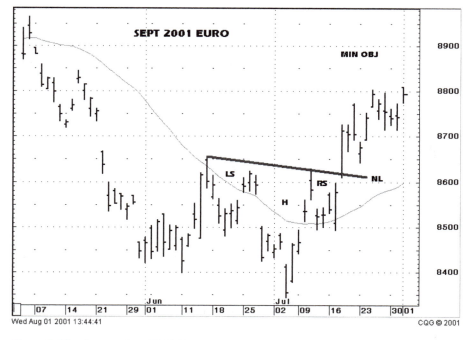

■ **Chart 8.20**   September 2001 Euro

■ **Chart 8.21**   July 2001 cotton

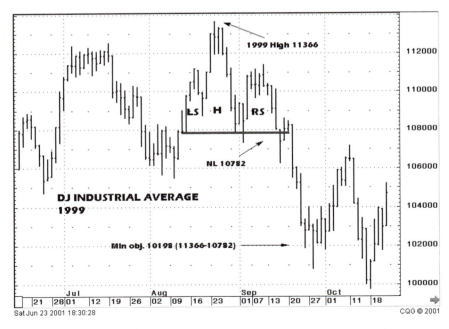

■ **Chart 8.22**   Dow H&S

Rule 10   After a false signal is confirmed, watch the market action closely as soon as new highs or lows are registered.

I've noticed that a head and shoulders failure, although not the final high or low, ultimately leads to a new contract high or low in short order. In other words, the H&S was telling you that you are close to the major top or bottom, but the bulls or bears were able to mount one last hurrah. If the market is unable to show much follow-through after this climatic top or bottom (following a H&S which didn't work), be ready to take action, because a major top or bottom will now be in place.

Double tops and bottoms

These are reversal patterns as well, many times associated with *major* tops and bottoms.

Double tops occur when prices rally from an area close to a previous high, but then the market fails with an inability to continue decisively into new high territory. I'm trying to be careful in my choice of words, because many novice traders (and one major newsletter that looks for these exclusively) believe a double top is valid only if a market fails under the previous top. I've found, in practice, many times double tops are formed when a market just nicks or at times moves slightly above the previous high, and then fails. Think of double tops as the letter M, with the right mast at times a bit lower or a bit higher than the left.

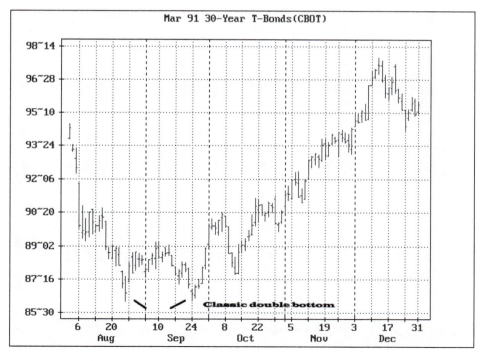

■   **Chart 8.23**   Double bottom

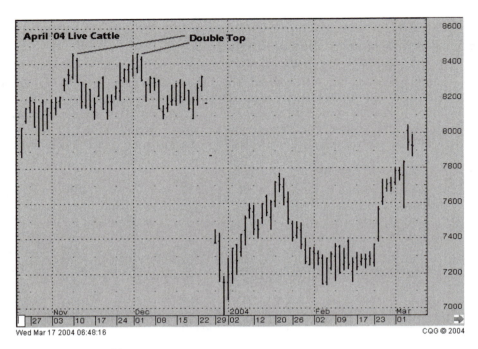

■ **Chart 8.24**   Double top

Double bottoms are the mirror image of the tops. Think of them as the letter W. The market makes a major bottom, rallies, fails, and holds slightly above or slightly below the previous bottom, and then reverses.

The one problem with double tops and bottoms is that they don't always occur at the top or the bottom. You have to be careful, because many times you'll see these in the middle of moves (which obviously doesn't help us in identifying a top or a bottom). As I've stated before, there is no Holy Grail. All you can hope to do is place the odds in your favor, using good money management to cut the losses on the trades that don't go according to plan. To avoid false signals, it is important to wait until the pattern is completed. This removes some of the profit potential but also improves your odds. Make sure you look for double bottoms and tops *only* after a *major* top or bottom is made, and then wait for the market to test the low/high and then rally/break significantly, which increases its validity. How much is "significant"? Unfortunately, I can't give you a number, but after you have been doing this awhile, and after studying hundreds of charts, you'll get a feel for this in various market situations.

Rounding tops and bottoms

Although you will come across these less often, they are eminently reliable reversal type patterns. Sometimes you might hear them referred to as **saucer bottoms**.

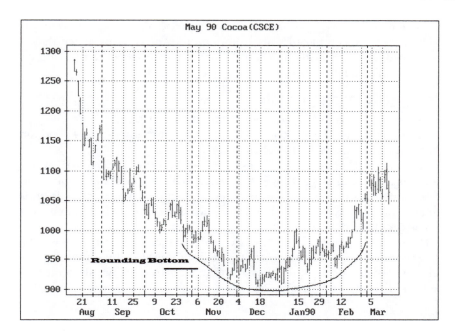

Chart 8.25   Rounding bottom

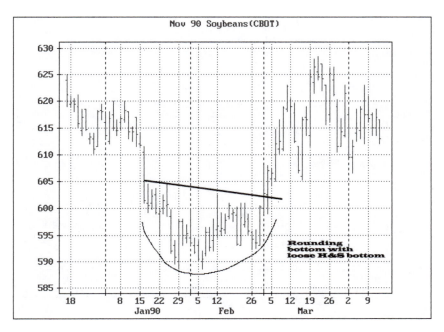

Chart 8.26   Rounding bottom with a "loose" H&S bottom

These usually are a long time in the making and again, it's important to wait for the pattern to be completed. False rounding tops or bottoms, when they do occur (evidenced by a higher high or lower low), often precede the final top or bottom (somewhat like a false H&S).

Flags, rectangles, and pennants

These are three relatively common continuation patterns. They generally occur in the first third, middle, or second third of major moves and can be good formations to pyramid from using fairly tight stops.

Rectangles, at times called "boxes," are formations where the market pauses and proceeds to trade in a tight range. A rectangle is like a consolidation but much smaller in length. Unlike a consolidation, a rectangle occurs after a move is underway—not at a top or bottom. It is generally a price movement that is contained between two horizontal lines as illustrated.

The upper line of the rectangle is your resistance line, and the lower line is the support line. The plan is not to anticipate but rather to go with the flow. In an up-trend, buy on the break of resistance, and in a down-trend, go short on the break of support. Rectangles basically represent pauses in the major trend; the market

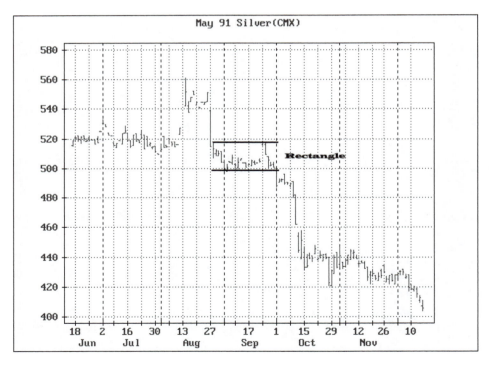

■ **Chart 8.27**   Rectangle

remains fundamentally bullish or bearish, but it has to undergo a "healthy" round of repositioning or profit taking before resumption of the move. Volume generally *dries up* during this box-like formation and increases on the breakout. Just like the neckline of the H&S, many times the market returns to the breakout level after it takes place. They provide an excellent time to pyramid a winning position. I look to add to profitable positions after the breakout, moving my stop on the *total* position to below the opposite boundary of the box.

One drawback of these is that they are continuation patterns, which at times can revert into reversal patterns. Once again, be warned: Keep an open mind, and be nimble.

A flag is a rectangle whose boundaries slant upward or downward. The boundaries are parallel, like a rectangle. The "flagpole" from which it flies is usually formed on large volume with the major trend. The "flag" is, again, a pause due to profit taking by the weak hands, a rest stop before the train once again rolls out of the station.

The general rule of thumb is that the slant of the flag will run *opposite* to the direction of the major price trend, but that's not always the case.

Actually, contrary to popular belief, I've found that many powerful moves out of flag congestions come from those slanting *in* the direction of the major trend.

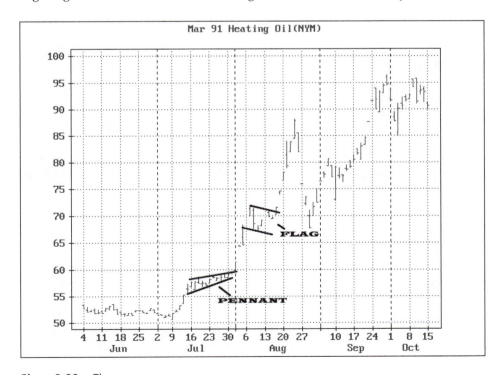

■ **Chart 8.28** Flag

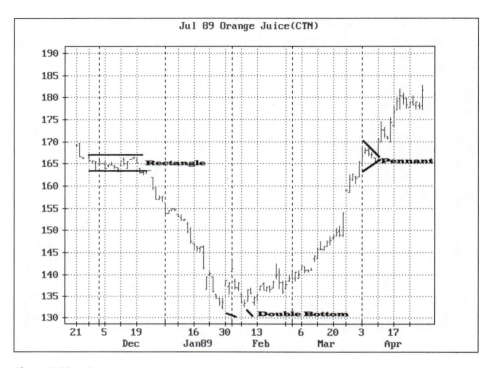

Chart 8.29   Pennant

Pennants work just like flags and rectangles. The basic difference is that the boundaries are not parallel.

All of these continuation patterns work best when they are tight, fast, neat, and formed on relatively light volume. Be wary of flags, pennants, or triangles that don't meet your expectations quickly.

Triangles

Triangles are congestion patterns that can signal either continuation or reversal. They come in three distinct varieties.

The *symmetrical triangle* has an upper line (looks like a down-trendline) that slopes downward and a lower line (looks like an up-trendline) that slopes upward. These lines converge at a point. Like all congestion patterns, there is a war going on between the bulls and the bears. Within the triangle, the sides are matched fairly evenly, neither side winning. However, at some point, as time goes forward, one side will win. The market will break out of the triangle, and this is the time to act, because the breakout signifies the direction of the next major move.

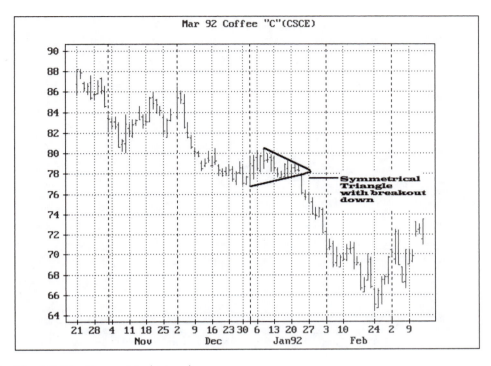

Chart 8.30 caption text (partial, inside chart):
Symmetrical Triangle with breakout down

Chart 8.30 Symmetrical triangle

The general rule of thumb is that the most valid signals will come when the market breaks out prior to reaching the end, termed the apex. The best breakouts generally come approximately two-thirds of the length of the triangle. Also, as with most of these patterns, volume should increase on the breakout. You know you're caught in a false move, a "trap," when the market trades back into the triangle after the breakout, and all bets are off when it moves over to the other side.

Ascending triangles and *descending triangles* are like their symmetrical brethren, except they work toward a breakout in the direction of their respective names. The ascending variety has a flat upper boundary with a rising lower boundary that can be defined by an up-trendline. The bulls are able to support the market at successively higher lows, while the bears are making a stand at the upper resistance level, with the result more likely to be a breakout to the upside. This is generally a continuation pattern, most likely to be seen during a major uptrend. The descending variety is the mirror image, with a lower horizontal support line and successively lower highs that can be connected by a down-trendline.

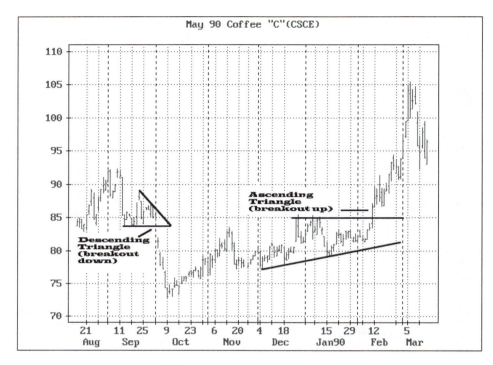

■ Chart 8.31   Ascending and descending triangles

Volume characteristics match the other patterns and it should jump on the break-out. The bigger the triangle, the odds are the bigger the move to follow. You'll also need to watch out for false breakouts.

Reversal days

Sometimes the market reverses direction in the same day. Prices rise to a new high for the move and end up closing lower on the day. Alternatively, prices fall to a new low for the move and rally at the end to close up for the day. They might signify a temporary halt in the prevailing trend, but my experience has been that many traders place far too much emphasis on common reversals. These reversals seldom are very valuable other than for a day or two at the most.

Of somewhat greater significance is the **key reversal**. A key reversal to the down-side occurs when a market makes a significant new high during the trading session, but it ends up closing lower than the previous day's low. A key reversal to the upside occurs when a market hits a new contract low, or significant low for a move, and ends up closing higher than the previous day's high. Key reversals possess greater validity if they are associated with high volume. The rule is to go in the direction of the reversal, with your stop above the high (or below the low) of the reversal day. A false signal occurs when the key reversal high or low can be violated within a few trading days.

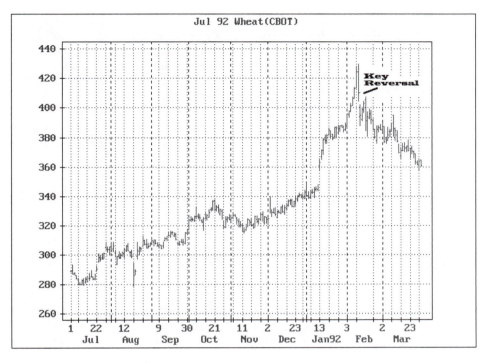

Jul 92 Wheat(CBOT)

Key Reversal

■ **Chart 8.32**   Key reversal

I have found reversals to be a reliable and important indicator in one circumstance.

George's reversal rule

The third reversal (after two previous reversal failures) works more often than not. I usually ignore the first and second reversals, relying on other indicators to identify a reversal in trend. However, I've found it helps to pay attention to that third consecutive reversal. The third doesn't have to occur over any particular time period; it can be short or long or even better, the third reversal might be a key reversal. (This was the case on Chart 8.25—can you find the first two reversals?) Look to enter a position against the major trend on the close of the reversal day, place your stop at the extreme of the day, and keep moving it as the market moves your way. The move will, on balance, be bigger when the market gaps in your favor on the opening of the following session. This point leads nicely into the discussion of gaps.

Gaps

A **gap** occurs when a commodity opens at a price higher than the high of the previous day or lower than the low of the previous day. By definition, the gap remains intact if it's not "filled" during the trading session. In other words, on a gap up day, the market never traded low enough to equal or exceed the high of the previous day on the downside. On a gap down day, the market was never able to trade high enough to equal or exceed the low of the previous day on the upside. The four major types of gaps are identified easily on the daily bar chart by a space.

Common gaps

The majority of gaps are more likely to be filled sooner rather than later. Most daily gaps are filled during the same trading session, and of those that aren't, more often than not, they are filled within a day or two. Because these are the most common variety, they are known as common gaps. They might occur, for example, as the result of a government report, but the news usually is not strong enough to change the major trend, and the gap is filled quickly. Common gaps are seen often in thin, or low-volume markets and are rarely significant. The trick is to be able to differentiate the common variety from the other three. The other three varieties are important technical tools that have powerful forecasting abilities.

Breakaway gaps

Breakaway gaps develop at a beginning of a new move. An **upside breakaway gap** occurs when prices jump up from a bottom, many times from some sort of congestion area. A **downside breakaway gap** occurs when prices jump down from a top, also many times from some sort of consolidation. A breakaway gap is significant because it signals a change in the supply and demand balance of the market in question. The pressure to push a market to the next level is so great that the market literally has to leapfrog to this new level, effectively trapping many market participants on the wrong side. It is those trapped on the wrong side who will eventually add fuel to this new fire as they liquidate. The shorts trapped under the upside breakaway gap are all holding positions at a loss and will eventually need to find a place to cover. Some of them will hope for a break to cover, but it won't come. Alternatively, numerous longs will be trapped above the downside breakaway gap, and at some point, they will be selling out. The inevitable result is more downside pressure.

How can you tell a breakaway from a common gap? Common gaps are filled fairly quickly. Breakaway gaps are not filled for a long time, sometimes never for the life of a contract. They signify the start of a new and major trend move. Many times they form out of a consolidation or during blow-off highs or lows. The breakaway day is accompanied by larger than normal volume, usually at least 50% greater than the average volume of the preceding two weeks. These are significant and powerful tools that you should be alert for constantly. Particularly, watch for them when a market appears. The market could be basing for a major bottom, or climaxing for a major top.

Measuring gaps

Measuring gaps are found at approximately the mid-point of a powerful trend move. They form one day, many times on news, but unlike a common gap, the market continues on its way without filling the gap. Once again, volume is usually large. Measuring gaps serve to trap many players who are on the wrong side even more deeply in the muck, and these traders provide some of the fuel for the next leg up or down. The interesting thing about these gaps is that they tend to occur when a move is just about half over. If the breakaway came at 100 and the measuring is at 140, you can project this move will run to about 180. The measurement rule is certainly not written in stone. At times, there will be more than one measuring-type gap in powerful moves, perhaps one at 33% of the move and another when the move is about 60 to 67%. However, the 50% rule is usually pretty close, so it can help you determine approximately where you are in the move. Exhaustion gaps can do this, too.

Exhaustion gaps

An exhaustion gap forms near the end of a move. In a major uptrend, the market gaps up to new highs, generally on bullish news. In a major downtrend, the market gaps down to new lows, perhaps on new bearish news, sometimes based on final panic liquidation. In both cases, many times these gaps follow wide-ranging or limit-type moves. In those markets that still have limits, the exhaustion day might even trade at the limit at some point in the direction of the major trend. Unlike the other gaps, however, this is the beginning of the end. The market has run out of steam, even though most of the participants do not realize it on that day. One way to explain this is that on the day of an upside exhaustion gap, the last of the weak shorts has thrown in the towel and are covering their positions. The last of the 'uniformed' longs is entering the party believing this market still has a long way to go. However, the news is always the most bullish at the top, and the market is satiated. High prices are starting to ration demand, and supply is beginning to come out of the woodwork. With a downside exhaustion gap, the last of the under-margined longs has given up. Many times panicky conditions prevail as the red ink flows. This, too, is the beginning of the end because low prices have begun to stimulate demand.

How can you determine whether a gap is of the exhaustion variety? Unlike the breakaway or measuring, the gap will be filled fairly quickly. More commonly, the market will churn for three to five days, but it will be filled fairly quickly—sometimes the next day. Many times, the high of the exhaustion top day will not be exceeded, or with a downside, there will be no lower lows. Volume will be high, but it was probably high in the days preceding the exhaustion day, too. Like the breakaway, these are powerful indicators. Keep your exhaustion gap antenna up when a market becomes wild-eyed after a long run up or panic-stricken after a long run down. Remember, it is always darkest before the dawn and brightest just before the sun starts to recede.

Islands

Islands can be formed in part by either exhaustion or breakaway gaps. An island bottom is formed by a gap down, price action at a basing level, and then a breakaway gap up. An island top is formed by a continuation or exhaustion gap up, some price action at new highs, and then a breakaway type gap down. Islands are easy to spot, because they look like islands in the sky (or the sea). They are rare, but powerful, and you'll know one when you see it!

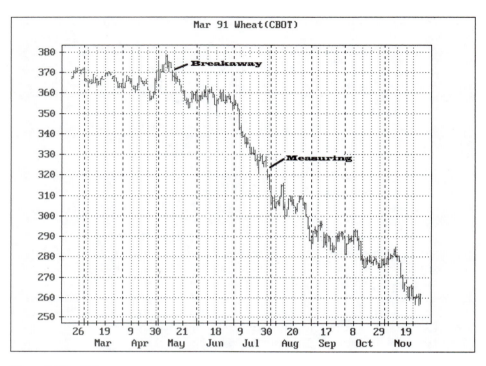

Chart 8.33   Wheat gaps

Chart 8.33 shows a well-defined breakaway gap, just days from the high right above the 370 level. A week after the gap occurred, it still was not filled. If you originally considered this a common gap, you needed to reevaluate by then. Also note that the high day was a reversal day, and this formation eventually turned into a head and shoulders top with a down-sloping neckline (additional evidence of a major top). After the market broke out of the rectangle below 350, there was little doubt (from a technical standpoint) that this market was done for. Note the measuring gap at approximately the 325 area. Measuring from the top at about 375, you could project a move down another 50¢ to minimum 275 (a level it did reach and eventually exceeded).

Chart 8.34 shows a breakaway gap on the top, forming an island top on a wide-ranging, high-volume day that closed on the lows. It looked technically weak on that day, but there should have been no doubt of the weakness after the market broke the downside of the rectangle below the psychologically important 500 mark. If you had identified 460 as a measuring gap, the objective would be another 80¢ lower, or 380. This silver market did reach this objective by the end of January, about a month past the chart as presented.

In thinner markets, like the bellies, you need to be careful to avoid labeling common gaps as significant. The upside breakaway in mid-September was not filled a

■ **Chart 8.34**   Silver gaps

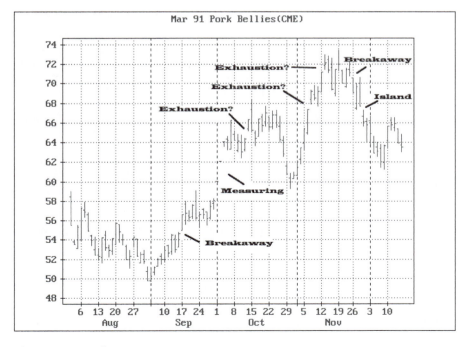

■ **Chart 8.35**   Belly gaps

week later; therefore, it marked a major bottom. The large early October gap was formed by a bullish Hogs and Pigs Report that pushed the market limit up for three consecutive days. Apparently, the "smart money" who originally had a hand in forming the breakaway knew something bullish was about to happen. If you take the approximate midpoint of the measuring at 61, an ultimate objective is projected at approximately 68 to 70. A gap a few weeks later could have been labeled falsely as exhaustion (because it was filled quickly after a reversal), but the measurement did not seem right. However, this did lead to a significant correction of more than $8. It would have been prudent to take profits and look for a sign of the resumption of the uptrend. Note, on the correction, that the measuring gap was unable to be filled, which is a bullish sign. I labeled two possible exhaustion gaps, and actually they both would have helped you identify a top formation even if you had labeled one falsely. After the final exhaustion gap filled quickly, the bulls were able to mount one last rally, briefly taking the market to new highs. This was the final gasp, however, and it quickly failed, leading to a downside breakaway gap that did form close to the top. Three days later, this gap was not filled and lead to another downside gap, which formed an island top. If you wanted to label this second gap (the one that formed the island) a downside measuring gap, it projected a move to about the 62 to 63 level, and this level was reached in less than two weeks!

Five rules for successful gap trading

Rule 1   Most gaps are common gaps and will be filled.

Do not look for significant gaps at non-significant times. If a market gaps on minor news, low volume, or what doesn't appear to be a major top or bottom, assume it will be filled. Scalpers can fade these common gaps and look to take profits when they're filled. If a gap is not filled fairly quickly (within two to seven trading days), begin to treat it as a significant gap (either a breakaway, measuring, or exhaustion—depending on where the market is in its cycle).

Rule 2   When a market is forming a long base, place a buy stop above the base to catch a breakaway type move.

Many times, the breakaway gaps occur when they're least expected; at times, they occur on no news. I've observed on breakaway-up days that the lows are generally registered right at the open. If you are stopped into a new long position in this way, place your sell stop at the low end (the fill) of the gap. If it is any good, it should not be filled, and you should be in close to the lows for maximum potential profitability.

Rule 3   Measuring gaps offer an excellent place to pyramid a position.

If you spot a measuring gap and are already in on a base position, it is time to double up and move your stop loss on the entire position to the fill of the measuring gap. Your average price is better than the market, and your risk on the new "add" is minor. When they work, you have a lot of profit potential remaining on the new, larger position.

Rule 4   Never anticipate exhaustion gaps—wait for them to be filled to take a new position.

Exhaustion gaps occur in the final stages of a major move. This phase is almost always volatile, and it is extremely difficult to pick a top or bottom. It is only after the exhaustion gap is filled that you can define what your risk is and that it truly was an exhaustion. I have seen occasions when the bullish sentiment is so frothy that it forms an exhaustion but still can work higher for days or weeks before it's filled.

Rule 5   When you see a significant gap (a breakaway, measuring, or exhaustion), don't wait!

This is not the time to hesitate; it is the time to act aggressively. If you wait, you'll be left holding the bag. Significant gaps generally offer good reward to risk, because you can define fairly closely what your risk should be.

Volume

I've mentioned volume repeatedly in this section, because when it is greater than average, it adds evidence to other technical signals. The one recurring theme you might have noticed is that significant days generally are associated with larger than average volume. Gap days, breakouts from consolidation, and neckline penetrations are all associated with larger than normal volume. To know what larger than normal is, you need to know what average volume is for the market you're trading. COMEX copper, for example, might trade about 8,000 to 13,000 contracts on an average day; more than 20,000 is a significant day. Yet, CME Live Cattle might trade 25,000 on an average day and 35,000 on a big day. Crude Oil might trade 80,000 to 100,000 on a normal day. They're all different, and you need to know what the average is. A rule of thumb is that a significant volume day is at least 50% higher than the 60-day average. You want to use total volume, and not volume by contract, which can fluctuate randomly for the thinner "back" months.

Here is a philosophical question to ponder at this point: Does price change trigger volume, or is it volume that moves the price? I think both. George Soros once said, "Price is the ultimate fundamental." How profound! Whenever you see volume pick up, ask yourself, "Who's in trouble?" The answer to this question will give you a strong clue for the move to come.

Three major volume rules

Rule 1   In a major up-trend, volume will tend to be relatively higher on rallies and lower on declines or trading-ranges (consolidations).

Rule 2   In a major down-trend, volume will tend to be relatively higher on declines and lower on rallies or trading ranges (consolidations).

Rule 3   Volume will tend to expand dramatically at major tops and bottoms. Major bottoms can be characterized by climax-type selling. Blow-off tops will be associated with climatic volume, too.

Open interest

Open interest (OI) analysis is one of the most powerful trading tools I have found. OI is a wonderful tool that stock traders do not have, but futures traders do. What follows is an open interest primer, followed by the advanced course.

The primer

Open interest is quite simply the number of contracts outstanding. It is the total number held by buyers or ("or" *not* "and") sold short by sellers on any given day. The open interest number gives you the total number of longs and the total number of shorts, because in futures, the short interest is always equal to the long interest. Each long is willing either to accept delivery of a particular commodity or to offset his contract(s) at some time prior to the expiration date. Each short is willing either to make delivery or to offset his contract(s) prior to the expiration date. With this in mind, you can plainly see that open interest is a measurement of the willingness of longs and shorts to maintain their *opposing* positions in the marketplace. It is a quantitative measurement of this difference of opinion.

Open interest numbers go up or down based on how many new traders are entering the market and how many old traders are leaving. Open interest goes up by one when one new buyer *and* one new seller enter the market. This act creates one new contract. Open interest goes down by one when a trader who is long closes out one contract with someone who is already short. Because this contract is now closed out, it disappears from the open interest statistics. If a new buyer buys from an old buyer (who is selling out), total open interest remains unchanged. If a new seller buys back or *covers* from a new seller entering the market, open interest also does not change. The old bear had to buy to cover with the other side of this transaction being a sell by the new bear.

eg **Here's a typical example. If one day heating oil has a total open interest of 50,000 contracts, and the next day it rises to 50,100, this means 100 new contracts were created by 100 new buyers and 100 new sellers. Or perhaps it means 10 new net buyers and sellers of 10 contracts each, or whatever it takes net to create the new 100. Of course, during that day many people closed out and many entered, but the net result was the creation of new open interest—50,100 contacts worth of shorts and 50,100 contracts worth of longs at the end of the day. Theoretically, one short who had 100 new contracts sold (probably the smart money) could have taken the opposing side of 100 others who each bought one (the majority, probably the "dumb money"), but the short and long interest are always the same on any particular day.**

Open interest figures are released daily by the Exchanges, but they are always for the previous day, so they are a day old. A trader can chart open interest on a price chart, and the direction it is changing can tell you some interesting things.

The advanced course

Open interest statistics are a valuable tool that you can use to predict price trends and reversals. The size of the open interest reflects the intensity of the willingness of

the participants to hold positions. Whenever prices move, someone wins and someone loses; this is the zero sum game. This fact is important to remember, because
when you think about the ramifications of changes in open interest, you must think
about it in the context of which way the market is moving at the time. An increase
in open interest shows a willingness on the part of the participants to enlarge their
commitments.

Let's say the market is moving lower, and open interest is increasing. You can
assume that some of the hurt longs have left the party, but they are being replaced
by new longs, and many existing longs are still there. If they were liquidating en-
masse, open interest would drop. If the short holders were on balance, taking profits, and leaving the party, open interest would drop then, too. However, because the
open interest is increasing and the price is dropping, you can assume the bulls are
losing money. Still, many bulls must be hanging in there, or they are recruiting bud-
dies at an increasing rate. What are the ramifications of an open interest decline? It
is a sign that the losers are in a liquidation phase (it doesn't matter which way the
market is moving), the winners are cashing it, and new players are not entering in
sufficient numbers to replace them.

Six profit rules for analyzing open interest

Rule 1   If prices are in an uptrend and open interest is rising, this is a bullish sign.

The bulls are in charge. They are adding to positions and making the money, thereby becoming more powerful. Undoubtedly, shorts are being stopped out, but new
sellers are taking their place. As the market continues to rise, the longs get stronger,
and the shorts get weaker.

Rule 2   If prices are in a downtrend and open interest is rising, this is a bearish sign.

The bears are in charge in this case. They are adding to their positions, and they are
the ones making the money. Weaker longs are being stopped out, but new buyers
are taking their place. As the market continues to fall, the shorts get stronger, and the
longs get weaker. Another way to look at Rules 1 and 2: As long as the open interest
is increasing in a major trend, it will have the necessary financing to draw upon and
prosper.

Rule 3   If prices are in an uptrend and open interest is falling, this is a bearish sign.

The old longs, the smart money (after all, they have been right to this point), are taking profits—they're liquidating. New buyers, who will not be as strong on balance,
replace them to some extent, but the declining open interest is an indication that the
weak shorts are bailing, too. They will be replaced to an extent by new shorts, who
are stronger than the old shorts were.

Rule 4   If prices are in a downtrend and open interest is falling, this is a bullish sign, the mirror image of Rule 3.

The smart money, the shorts, are covering or liquidating. They will be replaced to a degree by new shorts who are not as strong as they were, but the declining open interest indicates that the weakened longs are throwing in the towel to a major degree. They will be replaced by fresh longs, who were not as weakened by the lower prices as the old longs were. Another way to look at Rules 3 and 4: When the pool of losers is depleted, the party is over.

Rule 5   If prices are in a congestion range and open interest is rising, this is a bearish sign.

The public generally plays the long side. Rising open interest in a trading range affair assumes that the commercials and professionals are taking the short side, and the uniformed public most likely will lose out in the end.

Rule 6   If prices are in a congestion range and open interest is falling, this is a bullish sign.

The professionals, who are more likely to be short, are covering. The weak hands are throwing in the towel.

Chart 8.36 illustrates the drought market of 1988. Note how open interest and volume rose dramatically on the bull move from April until the end of June. Volume remained high, but open interest started to decline, as did the market. When the last weak short was out and the smart money was long gone, the new folks took it down in a hurry!

Look at Chart 8.37, the silver chart. June through July was a nicely trending market, trending down, and open interest was building the entire time. As long as open interest continued to climb in a bear market, the bears were in charge. The guide here to ride and profit on this downtrend was Rule 2. Now note how open interest topped out and started to decline during the consolidation (sideways action) throughout August. The guide to cover shorts and start to position yourself for the coming bull move was Rule 4. Now note how open interest dove dramatically on the three-day bull move, resulting from the trauma and uncertainty following September 11. Although the market players had no way of knowing the events that would occur, open interest still somehow gave ample warning of the bull move to come.

How could this be? I think it was a case of the market already being positioned for a bull move (this is what OI indicated); it just required a spark, whatever that might be. Although the bull move was dramatic, you can now use hindsight to know that it was short lived and not the start of a new major bull move. Once again open interest, Rule 3 indicates that this was a move that would not last and had to be sold due to the sharp collapse in OI. Although open interest was erratic following the shakeout in September, it basically had been rising during the severe bear move through November. Once again, you can look to Rule 2 as our guide; aggressive players could confidently short this market through October and into mid-November. (The OI line during this period resembled August.) The fact that OI

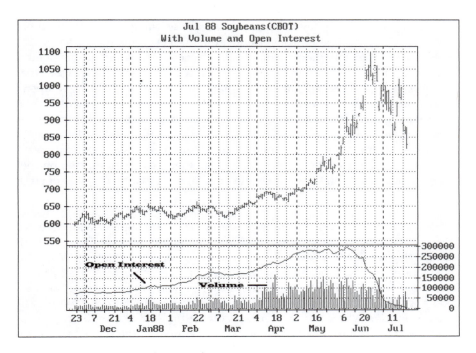

■ **Chart 8.36**   Soybean volume and open interest

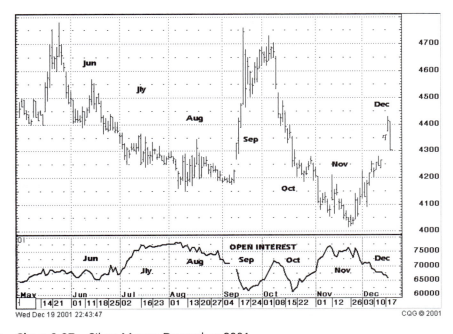

■ **Chart 8.37**   Silver May to December 2001

stopped its climb in November was an early warning signal of the bull market enjoyed this past month. Concurrently, the market formed a classic H&S bottom, which did ultimately meet its minimum objective. However, at this point a trader needs to be cautious with this bull run, because OI has been declining as the market has been rising (Rule 3). Monitoring volume in conjunction with these open interest rules can provide you with additional fuel for your profit engine. For example, if prices are going up, while volume and open interest are increasing, this is quite bullish. The capital is there to sustain and accelerate the move. Alternatively, when prices are going down, and volume is increasing with rising open interest, this is a bearish sign. Finally, it is important to note that chart patterns are, on the whole, more reliable with higher volume and open interest than with lower of either.

RSI

Oscillators are a group of technical indicators that are popular with traders as overbought or oversold indicators. The most commonly used oscillator is the Relative Strength Index, or RSI for short. RSI was developed originally by Welles Wilder in the late 1970s. You'll hear the words *oversold* and *overbought* touted by your broker, advisory firms, newsletters, and so on. Here's what they're talking about: Markets do not go straight up or straight down forever without corrective moves. There comes a point where the market is ready to turn, either temporarily or for good. Overbought basically means the market is too high in the respect that it's running out of buyers; in effect, it's about to fall of its own weight. Oversold is the antonym. The market is too low, running out of sellers (at least for the current time period), and ready for a bounce. Oversold is not a very scientific term and is bandied about somewhat arbitrarily. The RSI attempts to quantify the degree of oversoldness or overboughtness. (Spell check wants to discard these two words, but I'll leave them in because I think you get the idea.)

For you mathematicians, the formula is as follows:

 RSI = 100 − {100/(1 + RS)}, where RS = Average of net up closing changes for N# of days/Average of net down closing changes for N# of days

The trader selects the number of days; nine is the standard, or default, in most programs.

To calculate the nine-day RSI, you need to average the change of the previous nine up days and divide this number by the average of the change of the previous nine down days. The RSI ranges from just above 0 to just under 100, but it is extremely rare to see a number close to either of these extremes.

The RSI spends most of its time fluctuating between 25 and 75. At extremes, it moves under 25 or over 75. These are the standard oversold (less than 25) and overbought (greater than 75) areas. How do you use it? When this number gets too small or too large, it is time to put your antenna up. The market is getting close to a reversal point. Some traders attempt to buy when the RSI wanders into oversold range and sell in the overbought range.

My opinion is that if you attempt to do this, you better have deep pockets. At times (trading range type markets), this *can* be an excellent way to pick tops and bottoms. However, in the major moves and at extremes (the most profitable time for the trend follower), the RSI can remain in the extreme ranges for long periods of time and for quite a few points. (And hey, it's "only" points, right?) This is the major drawback of the RSI. It works in normal markets, but when the market is in the blow-off or panic stage, it can remain in overbought or oversold territory for an extended period and become quite costly.

Still, I do think this can be a useful tool, but only when used in conjunction with other indicators. You need to know what type of market you are in (trading-range or trending, young or mature). If you can determine this, the RSI can help you identify what point in the life cycle of the market you're at. RSIs tend to get high in the mature stages of a bull market and low in the mature stages of a bear, but there is no magic number that signals the bottom. In fact, I've found it is better practice to watch for the RSI to turn up *after* it falls under 25 to signal a bottom and vice versa for the bull. Yet, even this tactic tends to lead to numerous false and money-losing signals, because the RSI is a *coincident* indicator. It moves with price. A minor upswing has to turn the RSI up.

Divergences

The best way to use RSI is to look for **divergences**. These occur when the RSI doesn't make a new low or a new high coincidentally with the market.

 For example, suppose that coffee rallies from 128 to 158; the RSI registers a high for the move of 83 at 158 (so it is in overbought territory). The market then falls back to 152, a normal correction, and the RSI falls back to 71. Subsequently, the coffee market continues its bullish ways and reaches a new high of 161. Up until this point, the RSI has moved with price. Each day, coffee registered a new closing high for the move, and so did the RSI. However, on this occasion, the RSI moved up to only 79, a lower high. The market made a new high; the RSI made a lower high.

This is classic divergence, and I've found the best signals come from RSI divergence. The very best signals come from triple divergence, in which the market makes a third higher high or third lower low, while the RSI makes a third lower high or a third higher low. I've also seen quadruple divergence and even more divergences. This can be another dilemma when using RSI. Double divergence can be seen many times just before a turning point, but in the most powerful moves (the ones you really want to be on), there is nothing to say the market cannot keep going in the direction of the major trend. This is something to look at daily, because it can give you some useful information, but I would use RSI as a confirming indicator only, not as a stand-alone trading method.

Stochastics

Stochastics are another popular oscillator. While George Lane is generally credited as the developer of stochastics, there are those in the industry (Larry Williams for one) who contend Ralph Dystant was actually the creator of this widely followed indicator. The stochastics formula is a bit more complex than RSI and readily available for those who want to see the mathematics. I won't discuss it here (you can let the computer figure it out for you like most traders do), but I will talk about the

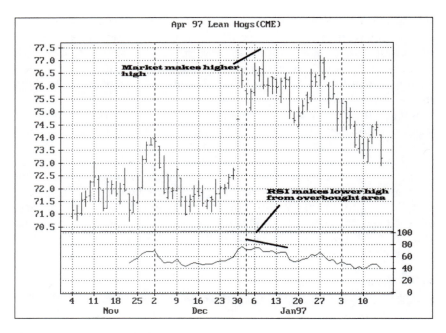

■ Chart 8.38   RSI bullish divergence

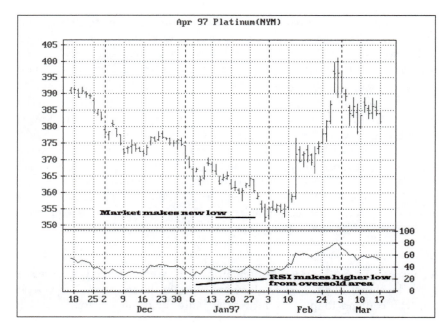

■ Chart 8.39   RSI bearish divergence

basics of how to interpret stochastics data. What the formula does is measure how the close impacts the trend. Here is the theory: In bull markets, the close is more likely near the day's high, and in bear markets, the close is more likely near the day's lows. The way the market *closes* determines how the stochastic trends. In essence, stochastics are a measurement of how the most current close relates to where prices have been during the period under study.

Stochastics consist of two lines: the %K, which is more sensitive, and the %D, which is slower moving. Like the RSI, the trader can choose the number of days for the formula. Shorter terms (five days is popular) are sensitive and act quickly, but lead to many more whipsaws. Longer terms (14 day is widely used) identify longer-term moves and eliminate some of the whipsaws of the shorter variety. If you plan to work with stochastics, the computer will plot the "fast" stochastic and the "slow" version. I've found the slow is a better way to go, because it is smoothed to eliminate many of the whipsaw and false signals of the former. The stochastic's values range between 0 and 100, just like the RSI. Overbought is generally considered to be a value in excess of 80, and oversold is less than 20. They can be used like the RSI this way, but they tend to give better signals when they diverge from price (just like the RSI). Divergence can precede the market. Bullish divergence is when prices hit new lows, but the stochastic makes a higher low than its previous low. Bearish divergence is when prices hit a new high, but the stochastic makes a lower high. Both of these occurrences can give strong indications of market tops and bottoms. Traders also look for the stochastic lines to cross to exit an existing position or enter a new one. The best signals come when divergence is present, and then the %K line crosses the %D line that confirms the divergence.

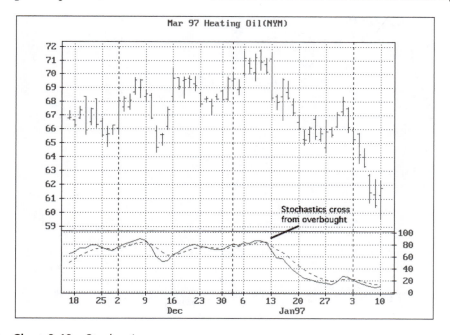

■ **Chart 8.40**   Stochastics

Elliot wave analysis

Ralph Elliot was an accountant who developed his theory on market cycles in 1939. Basically, Elliot believed there is a "natural order" to the markets and that they travel in predictable cycles. He believed the market rallies in five waves when in an up-trend and falls in three-wave corrective moves. When in a downtrend, the main trend is five waves down with three-wave corrective up moves. This five-wave pattern is made up of three odd-numbered waves: 1, 3, and 5, which are connected by two corrective waves, 2 and 4. Each major odd-numbered wave can be subdivided into five waves, and corrective waves can be broken into three parts (the abc correction).

At times, I have looked at longer-term charts of major trends and been able to see exactly what he was talking about. Other times it just doesn't happen. The main problem I personally have had with Elliot Wave is that I find it difficult, if not impossible, to determine what wave the market is in during the thick of the battle. If you

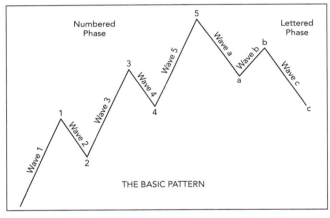

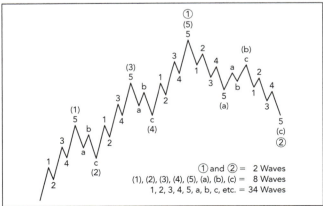

■ **Chart 8.41**   Elliot Wave

delve deeply into Elliot Wave Analysis, you'll find numerous rules that explain away every wiggle on the charts. There are subsets of subsets of waves, and when an Elliot Wave theorist misses the count, he revises his analysis to say wave 3 was actually not wave 3, but a subwave 4 of major wave 2, and this is the reason for an abc correction, which he didn't expect. I'm not trying to be critical here, because I do believe there is real validity to some of Elliot's work, but I have had trouble using it. Every trader must use what works for him. Two traders can have entirely different approaches, and both can still make money.

Point and figure charts

The point and figure (P&F) is another type of price charting; the difference is that P&F ignores time. Time is irrelevant; only price matters. Xs and Os indicate price signals. The point and figure chartist uses Xs to illustrate rising prices and Os for falling prices. As long as the price is rising, Xs are added. Os come into play when they are dropping. The decision to start a new column of Xs or Os is based on the market making a price change of a certain amount designated by the technician. This would be a **box**. The technician also must designate (in addition to the size of each box) what determines a reversal.

For example, a popular reversal size is three boxes. So, if you use a scale of 10 points for cattle, a reversal size would be 30 points. The values for the box and reversal are arbitrary, depending on how sensitive the trader wants his point and figure chart to be.

The larger the box size and reversal values, the less sensitive the chart is and vice versa. A 1¢ box for wheat is obviously more sensitive than a 10¢ box. If the chart is too sensitive and the boxes too small, you increase the chances of being whipsawed by insignificant fluctuations. If the boxes are too large, you miss out on significant portions of some moves and take too much risk.

Although I do not use P&F charts, I know some successful floor traders who do. This is why I want to at least mention them in this book, so the serious student who wants to pursue the P&F can do some of his own research. Because I don't use them, I can't help you in determining the correct values to use as price increments; however, like many technical tools, there is no magic answer here. It is mainly a function of trial and error, and it depends on the market and price volatility. The P&F traders I know tell me they generally like to use price reversals of a three- to five-box move. The box varies by the time frame of the trader.

Japanese candlestick charts

Candlesticks are the third major charting method, used by the Japanese before charting ever became popular in the West. Rice futures were active in Japan as early as the 1700s, and the traders of the day developed this earliest form of technical analysis. Bar charts use bars, point and figure charts use Xs and Os, and candlestick charts use rows of candles with wicks on either end. The body of each candle is the distance between the opening and closing prices. If the closing price is higher than the open,

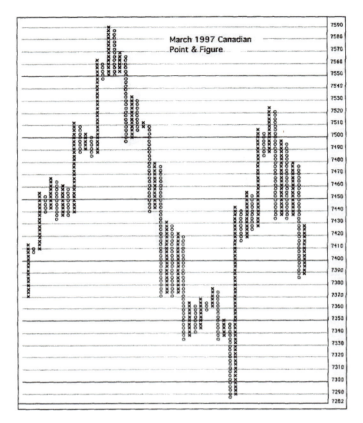

March 1997 Canadian
Point & Figure

■   **Chart 8.42**   Point and figure

the body is left empty or white (or it could be one color like blue). If the closing price is lower than the open, the body is filled in with black (or another color like red). The upper wick represents the high, and the lower wick represents the low. The wicks are not as important as the body. In other words, candlestick chartists are not as interested in the day's high or low as they are in the relationship between the open and the close.

I've studied candlesticks and have decided they do not fit my personal style. However, a number of interesting patterns appear to have some validity. They have colorful names, too. Candlestick chartists refer to "hanging men," "tweezers tops," and "dark cloud covers." In my studies, I didn't find most of these to be preferable to the more traditional bar charting patterns, with the possible exception of the engulfing patterns. They seem to be able to identify tops and bottoms better than standard reversal patterns. The engulfing line can be seen at major tops and bottoms, and there also can be continuation patterns seen in the midst of a major trend. In many cases, they do signal the end of a correction within a major trend.

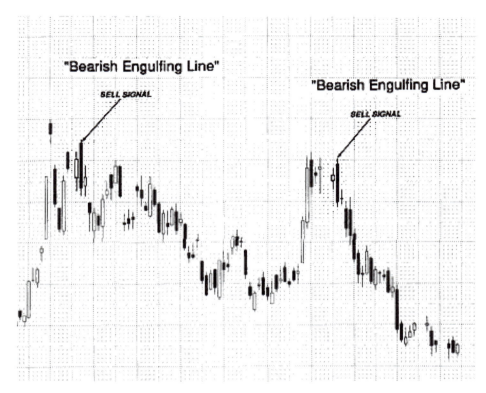

■ **Chart 8.43** Candlestick engulfing lines

The bullish engulfing line consists of a white (empty) body that totally engulfs, or covers, the previous day's body. In other words, the high of the body is higher than the high of the previous body, and the low is below the previous low. The white body is formed by a low opening met by strong buying, which pushes price to close above the previous candle. This is a bullish indicator that is seen often at major bottoms. Bearish engulfing lines are the mirror image seen at tops—a long black candle that totally engulfs, or covers, the previous day's candle. This is often seen at a blowoff top. It is a powerful signal for candlestick people.

Spread trading—a valuable forecasting tool

I've found that by analyzing the spread action in many of the actively traded physical commodities, a trader can get valuable clues as to how bullish or bearish a market is. Spreads also can be used to predict the market path of least resistance. Typically, commodity futures markets are "carrying charge" or "normal." (In London, they would say the market is in *contango*, and we are not talking about dance.) This is when the distant months sell at a higher price (or premium) to the closer months. Here's a typical example of what a "normal" copper market might look like:

March copper	99.05
May copper	100.15
July copper	101.95
September copper	103.25
December copper	105.10

Because it costs money to store copper from one month to the next (storage costs, insurance, and interest), this is reflected in the configuration of futures prices.

However, at times, markets take on the opposite configuration, in which the near month is trading at a premium to the distants, as illustrated:

March copper	103.50
May copper	101.25
July copper	100.05
September copper	98.15
December copper	95.95

This configuration is called an **inverted market**. In London, it's called **backwardation**. What can cause a market to invert? In most cases, an inverted market is the product of a perceived or real near-term shortage of the commodity in question. This can be caused by weather. For example, cold weather tends to push the nearby natural gas over the back or could even push the nearby cattle months above the distants, because cattle do not gain weight efficiently in cold weather and could conceivably be "pushed back." In other words, the cattle are not ready for market in a timely manner. Inversion could be caused by a mining strike, a government program, an excellent near-term export demand, or a classic short squeeze—actually, any number of things. The important point here is that the spreads can give you important clues as to the strength or weakness within a market.

Here's my general rule of thumb: When the bull spreads are working (the near months are gaining on the back months), this is a bullish sign, and you should play the market from the long side. When the bear spreads are working (the near months are losing to the back months), this is a bearish sign, and you should play the market from the short side.

As with every rule, there are exceptions. For example, November beans might be gaining on July beans in June, because the new crop, which will be harvested in the fall, is burning up due to drought; however, there are adequate near-term supplies. As a rule, this works. I'm usually skeptical if I am short a market and the bull spreads are working—something is definitely wrong.

Here's another powerful trading tip: Watch for spreads to cross "even money." I've noticed when spreads "cross zero." More times than not, this indicates a significant indicator of a change in the supply and demand balance of the commodity being studied. My advice is to go with the flow. If the spread in question crosses zero to the upside, play the bull spreads (long nearby, short the deferred), or play the market from the long side. If the market crosses zero to the downside, play the bear spreads (short the nearby, long the deferreds), or play the market from the short side. Here's a typical example, the spread between May 2003 sugar and March 2004 sugar. Note, this action took place during mid-2002 into early-2003 (the 2004 contract is listed two years prior to its expiration).

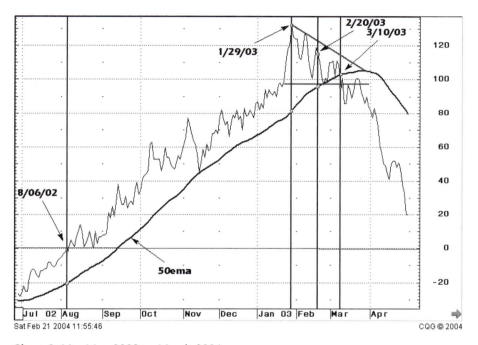

■ **Chart 8.44**   May 2003 to March 2004 sugar

This spread crossed the zero line in August of 2002, which turned out to be just a few weeks before a major bull run began in the sugar market. The price at that time was $574. The market on that day really did not "show its hand"; what I mean by this is there were no real indications of the major move that was to follow. Still, the spread (by the mere act of inverting) turned out to be an excellent leading indicator of a major bull run.

This particular bull spread continued to work nicely, peaking on January 29 at 132 points May over the March. On that date, May sugar closed at 822, so the market had moved 248 points to $2,777 per contract traded. The spread itself had rallied 132 points above the zero mark for a spread profit of $1,478 per spread traded. Considering the spread margins are generally much lower—in the case of sugar, only one-third that of an outright contract—trading three spreads for every one contract would have yielded an additional 50% profit. Of course, on that date there was no way to know this was the highest this spread would run; however, when the spread started to turn southward, our antenna should have been raised. My experience has

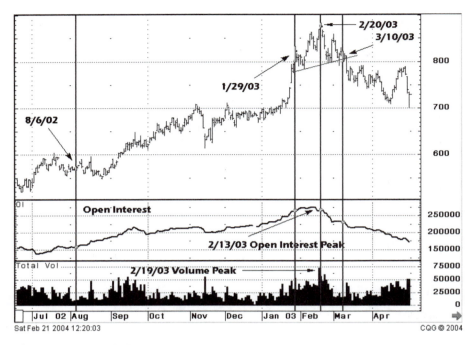

Chart 8.45 May 2003 sugar

been that more times than not, the spreads lead price action—spreads can be a powerful indicator. Note that after the spread peaked on January 29, the sugar market continued to rise and the contract high was registered February 20 at 884. On that date, despite the May contract making a new high, the spread was already fading, trading at 115, or equal to 17 points below its peak. On March 10, the day the spread broke below its 50-day exponential moving average, May sugar was trading at 801. This occurred simultaneously with the market completing a bearish H&S top pattern. This topping pattern confirmed on the breakout below the neckline just a few days later.

Certainly, there were other clues that the bull had run its course. For example, open interest was rising nicely during the bull-run, but it peaked on February 13, a full week before the price peaked. The combination of price rising with open interest fading with the bull spreads declining were two powerful signals that together could have been used to predict the end of this bull run. The icing on the cake was the volume spike on February 19, one day before the top. On that day, volume hit close to 74,000 contracts. High-volume days in sugar tend to come at turning points, and historically sugar volume tends to expand just prior to and coincidentally with the beginning of a bull move. A high-volume day in sugar is approximately above 50,000 contracts. Volume also expands when the move is one-third to one-half over and then again at or near the end of the move. This day turned out to be the third highest volume day in sugar's history to the date. The previous highest were January 5, 1999 and February 24, 1998. Both of these registered over 80,000, and both came at major tops with the market trading above 9¢ per pound. With greater speculative participation today, I've noted volume records continue to be broken. (Recently, a 100,000+ contract day was registered in sugar for the first time in history.)

Why technical analysis makes sense

Some pure fundamentalists dismiss technicians as merely "chartists," insinuating that technical analysis is black magic. I should point out that charts are an integral part of most sciences, from engineering to medicine. The reasons that technical analysis makes sense are fourfold:

1. "Footprints in the sand"—the smart money (who are generally the big players, because they are the ones making the money) cannot hide. They might be better informed, but their buying or selling has to show up in price, volume, and open interest.

2. The market discounts all fundamentals in price.

3. History does repeat, and if you don't learn from it, you are bound to fail.

4. Markets do move in trends, and these trends are more likely to continue than not. In the next two chapters, I will delve into a technical method I use for determining and then profiting from trends.

9

The most valuable technical tool (TMVTT)

"The market can remain irrational longer than you can remain solvent."
—Lord Keynes

Sorry to be the one to break this to you, but when trading futures or options, there just aren't any "sure things." You've all seen the infomercials, and I've tested many of the systems, but no matter what the ads say, you can never believe in any system that claims to win 90% of the time (or even close). If there's a Holy Trading Grail, I've not found it, and I have to ask myself, "Why would they share it with me anyway?"

One of the most important lessons I can teach you is this: There is no single pattern, system, method, or indicator that works in all market conditions. The best you can hope for is to find a tool (or tools) that places the odds in your favor. If your winning percentage is favorable, and if your wins on average are bigger than your losses, you'll make money. The good news is, excellent technical tools are available, and, when used properly, they can place the odds in your favor.

An old-timer once told me that when trading, if you can correctly determine the trend, you *will* make money. This makes sense because if you are correct on the trend, the market will move your way. Even if your timing is initially off, many times the trend will bail you out. There is one specific set of technical tools that have validity for trend determination, and these are the tools I've personally found the most useful and the most valuable: **moving averages**. In fact, let's call the moving average "The Most Valuable Technical Tool," or TMVTT for short. I've used moving averages successfully in my own trading, and in this and the subsequent chapter, I show you exactly what I do. This chapter covers the basics—what moving averages are, how they work, and how to use them properly in your own trading. In the next chapter, I'll present a specific trading approach by using certain averages that I believe can greatly enhance your bottom-line profitability.

Bottom pickers versus trend followers

Some traders say they are able to pick tops and bottoms with some accuracy, and there are certain indicators (the RSI, for example) and various patterns (the key reversal, or engulfing lines in candlestick charting) that are designed to do just that. No doubt that the trader who can pick tops and bottoms with any degree of success will make the most money; however, I've found in practice that this is a very (repeat *very*) difficult thing to do over time. Anyone who trades long enough might be lucky and catch a major top or bottom. I can remember two cases in my career (in more than thousands of trades) in which I've been lucky enough to catch one: one in soybeans and one in copper. I'm not talking about a daily high or low, or even a weekly high or low, but a *major* (yearly or quarterly) top or bottom. I'm talking about the *contract* high or low published in the papers and in historical charts. Catching one of these is an almost impossible thing to do, because in hundreds of trading days every year, there is only one major top and only one major bottom. For that matter, even minor tops and bottoms (that is, daily or weekly highs and lows) are hard to get, because they are the exception and not the rule. For example, during any two-week period, every market has its top and its bottom price, but how many thousands of other trades take place even in this fairly short period of time? There's an old trading adage that goes something like this: Bottom pickers get their hands slapped. As W.D. Gann has taught us, no matter how cheap or how expensive a market might appear, it's never too cheap to sell or too high to buy.

As a result, I've found it much easier and, therefore, ultimately more profitable to take a chunk out of the middle of a move, which is what moving averages are designed to do. Moving averages are *trend-following* tools. This means they do not anticipate the market; they *lag* it. Moving averages are designed to help determine two things:

■ What the current trend is

■ When the trend has turned

However, moving averages can tell us these things only after a trend is in place, and by definition, this is after the move is already underway. Therefore, it's impossible to pick tops and bottoms using moving averages. However, my advice is never to worry about missing the top, the bottom, or a portion of any move. Too many traders feel that if they haven't picked the top or bottom, it's too late to take a trade, and this is one of the primary reasons the majority never make any money. Gold might have fallen $100 per ounce over a year's period and already made its low, but after it's rallied $20 off the bottom, it doesn't look that cheap to most people anymore. This is because most people have short-term memories, and recent history is the history remembered first. The previous $80 down was a tremendous short sale. Anyone looking at a chart could have determined that. Looking back, so what if you missed the first $20 of *that* move? Or, what if you were trying to hang on to a long position for the previous $100 down? In that case, I bet you wished you had left that top $20 on the table (to save the grief and financial devastation the remaining $80 brought).

Remember, a trader's primary job is to identify the major trend, and if you can do this with any degree of accuracy, you *will* make money. So a primary portion of my advice is never to worry about missing the first part of any move. The second part can be highly profitable, and history has shown, in most cases, that it's that last part that's the most profitable. You also should remember that scores of legendary traders—Richard Dennis and his "turtles" come to mind—use trend-following techniques and have taken hundreds of millions of dollars out of the futures and other markets.

Moving average methodologies have been around for more than a century. The modern "father of moving averages" is recognized to be Richard Donchian. Donchian was with (the now-defunct) Shearson in the late 1970s, when I started in the business. He developed specific moving average trading techniques, and for more than 20 years, he successfully managed money using them. These techniques were useful then, and they are just as useful now. This is because the markets still tend to move in trends, and at the risk of sounding like a broken record, if you can accurately identify the trend of the market, you will make money.

A moving picture

Any one price is like a snapshot in time that can never tell us what the trend is. It does tell us something, but hardly the whole story. When you take 10 photographs in rapid succession, you can get a better picture of the whole story. If the story is the market, you get a better picture of the true trend by looking at the last 10 prices, as opposed to looking at just one. When you put together a series of, say, 20 blocks of 10 photos each, you then have a movie that is infinitely more informative than a photo or two. This movie is analogous to a **moving average line**, one that can be overlaid on a price chart. By observing the direction this line is moving and the strength (or velocity) of the move, the line can give you a sense of which faction is stronger at the time, the bulls or the bears. If the bulls are stronger than the bears, the moving average line appears to move up, and the current price trades above the MA (and vice versa). The tough question when using TMVTT is how many prices it takes to provide the best feel for the trend. If you use too many, the old data can tend to put the true trend out of focus; use too few prices, and you cannot really tell what it is you're looking at.

It's important to remember that when you utilize any trend-following method, you're not trying to forecast when a market move will start or end. Instead, you are using a completely technical approach that relies on a specific type of indicator to tell you what the trend is. By taking a market position in sync with this trend, you are attempting to place the odds in your favor. It would also be nice to have this indicator alert you, with some degree of reliability, when the trend has changed *before* you give back too big a chunk of your paper profits, or *before* any unrealized losses become too serious.

Moving averages can tell you when the trend changes. More importantly, they keep you on the major portion of a major trend, and this is where the big money is made. Still, nothing worthwhile is ever easy. In trend-less markets, moving average techniques generate false signals, and sometimes those periods have strings of smaller losses. And sometimes strings of smaller losses add up to bigger losses. In the next chapter, I will share with you some techniques designed to save you some grief; but be forewarned, there will be drawdown periods, and you must be capitalized adequately to ride these out. Finally, when using moving averages, it is extremely important for you never to lose your winning qualities of patience and discipline, particularly when the bad strings occur. This is the key to success.

A moving average primer

Moving averages come in various flavors and sizes. They range from simple, to weighted, to smoothed and exponential. Traders use them alone, or in combinations as crossovers, even triple crossovers. They use them in oscillators as moving average convergence/divergence, and in bands. The basic underlying assumption here is that, more often than not, markets move in a trending fashion. I should mention that not everyone believes this statement is true. A contingent of academics

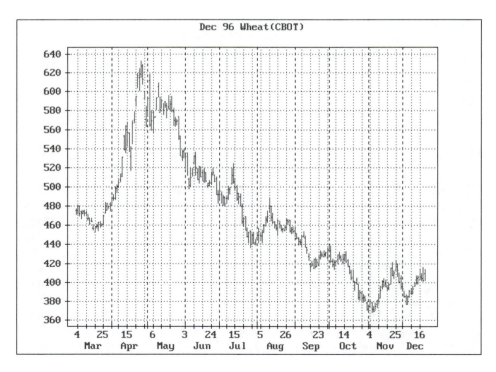

■ **Chart 9.1**   Early uptrend turns into major downtrend

feels market movements are random in nature (the "random walk theorists"), but I believe you can prove fairly easily to yourself that random walk is bunk. Although markets can be random in a short period of time, just look at any chart of any commodity of at least four to six months in length. You'll see the trends unfold before your eyes. When demand for a particular commodity, or a financial asset, is stronger than supply, prices (and therefore, the market) move in an up-trend. When supply is overwhelming demand at any particular point in time, the market trends downward.

Of course, it is easy to determine trends after the fact by looking at a chart. Isn't it easy to determine the various trends in the following historical charts?

However, it's not all that easy to determine the trend in the thick of the battle, and the news (the fundamentals) does not help you because it is always most bullish at the top and bearish at the bottom. Plus, whereas markets trend up or down, they certainly at times can move sideways. An erratic up-down type of affair, a trend-less market, temporarily wreaks havoc with any trend-following system. These are the periods you'll need to use discipline and patience to persevere. The good news is, I've found that markets are engaged in up or down trends more often and for longer periods of time than they are in sideways trends. This is why moving average methodologies can put the odds in your favor.

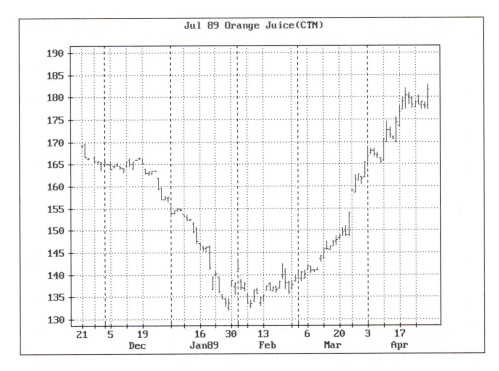

■ **Chart 9.2**   Early downtrend turned sideways turns into major uptrend

The simple moving average

The simplest moving average is simple to construct, and it's called (surprise) the **simple moving average** (SMA). It can come in any number of days or periods selected by the trader. Here's the formula:

$$SMA = \frac{P1 + P2 + P3 + \cdots + PN}{N}$$

P is the price of the commodity being averaged.

N is the number of days (or periods) in the moving average.

The value of an SMA is determined by the values that are being averaged and the time period. For example, a 10-day SMA shows the average price for the past 10 days, a 20-day SMA shows the average price for the past 20 days, and so on. The time period depends on the trader's time horizon, which can be years, months, weeks, days, minutes, or even ticks. Moving averages can be calculated based on opens, closes, highs or lows, and even the average of the day's ranges. I recommend using only the close (the settlement) price for each day. My theory is that this is the most important single price of the day, because this price is used to calculate margin calls. If the market closes on the high, or in the high range, most of the short players (unless they shorted right at the high or highs) will have funds transferred *out* of their accounts, with this money placed in the long's accounts. This action makes the shorts a bit weaker and the longs a bit stronger (at least for the next day).

eg **Let's construct a five-day SMA of crude oil based on the closing prices. Assume the closes for the past five days were 2105, 2110, 2115, 2120, and 2125. The five-day SMA is 2115. If on the sixth day the market closes at 2155, the five-day SMA rises to 2125, the average of the past five days divided by 5.**

$$5SMAday1 = \frac{2105 + 2110 + 2115 + 2120 + 2125}{5} = 2115$$

$$5SMAday2 = \frac{2110 + 2115 + 2120 + 2125 + 2155}{5} = 2125$$

In the formula, you always drop the oldest closing price and add the most recent closing price. In this example, when using the five-day, you would always drop the sixth-oldest day. With a 10-day, you drop the eleventh-oldest day, and so on. The direction of the trend is determined by the direction the SMA is moving and by comparing today's settlement price with the moving average. In this simple example, the trend is up, because the close on the most recent day—we'll call this Day 2 [2155]—is higher than the SMA [2125]. On Day 1 (the previous day), the close was 2125, and the SMA was 2115, so the trend is up. Even with this limited data, the odds suggest you should be playing from the long side. On

Day 2, the close was 2155, and the SMA was 2125, so the trend is up, and you stay long. When the closing price turns down and under the average, a sell signal is generated.

You can connect each day's SMA value on a chart, and this produces a line. You can chart this line and overlay it onto a price chart to generate trading signals. As long as the line on any particular day is *under* the closing price, the trader stays long, because the SMA has determined the trend is up. When the line *crosses over* the closing price, the trader goes short, because the trend has turned down. If long, and the line crosses over the closing price, the trader reverses the position by selling double the amount of contracts owned. The problem is, if you do this every time the line crosses price (and especially when using shorter term averages), you can get whipsawed easily (bounced back and forth with small losses, plus commissions, eating you up). Many times a market trades in a wild range, moving up wildly and down in the same session, but as I've mentioned before, I believe the closing price is the most significant.

As a simple rule when trading using SMAs, I suggest ignoring intra-day movements (many times these merely create "noise") and waiting for the *close* to penetrate the SMA to generate a signal. Even better, wait for a **two-day close** (two consecutive days of penetration of the moving average at the close) to signal a change in trend and, therefore, a change in position. Of course, by waiting for the close, you take on additional risk, because in a volatile market or a wide-ranging day, the price at the close could be far above or below the moving average. If, for example, you waited for the close on Black Monday 1987 (the day the Dow closed 500 points lower than Black Friday), you were in deep water. This is why good money-management sense says to additionally use an ultimate down-and-out point for any position (in other words, a physical stop loss). You should do this when using any technical system (or fundamental for that matter). When using a moving-average technique, place your stop at some point away from the moving average to create an approximate maximum percentage loss for those abnormal moves. Abnormal moves, although quite rare, do occur and Rule 1 is to *always* avoid the catastrophic loss (that's the loss so big it renders you unable to continue trading). Incidentally, option strategies can also help here. You can use puts to protect long positions and calls to protect short positions. However, most markets are normal, and in normal markets, there is a general rule of thumb for the first simple, yet effective, trading system:

- On the close, if the market price has fallen *below* the moving average line, a sell signal is generated.

- On the close, if the market price has risen above the moving average line, a buy signal is generated.

The signal can be taken at either the close of the signal day or the open of the following day. The preferred method is the close the day of the signal, because it has been proven that when a market closes at an extreme of a day's price range (which many times creates the signal), it follows through in the direction of the close on the following day. Sometimes the violation of the moving average can be a close call. On days like these, I would opt to wait one more day, rather than risk taking a false sig-nal. Still, you need to know on a daily basis exactly where the average you are fol-lowing will be coming into the close, and use a "stop close only" order to enter a new position or to exit an existing one. Alternatively, you can place a "market order" just prior to the close. Make sure your broker accepts this order type and has good floor communications.

How many days should you use in your moving average?

The length of the moving average has a great impact on trading activity and, there-fore, profitability. Some traders use 5-day moving averages, whereas some use 10-day or 20-day, and many funds use 50, and so on. For longer-term traders, par-ticularly stock market investors, the 100- and 200-day moving averages are popular. The length is an arbitrary decision that depends on the type of trader, but the sensi-tivity of any moving average is determined directly by its length. The length deter-mines how much time a moving average has to respond to a change in price. It is a matter of "lag time." This is a simple, but important concept—shorter moving aver-ages are more sensitive than longer moving averages. A 5-day is more sensitive than a 10-day, and both of these are more sensitive than a 20-day. The more sensitive the moving average, the smaller the loss will be on a reversal signal; however, there also will be a higher likelihood of a whipsaw, where a false reversal signal causes a trad-er to reverse a trade too soon.

A false signal occurs when a minor movement, which ultimately does not change the major trend, is enough to push the moving averages in the opposite direction of the settlement price, therefore resulting in a false position change. It is false simply because the trader will subsequently need to reverse once again when the major trend reasserts itself. In other words, it's important to use a moving average that is long enough so it is not overly sensitive. On the other hand, if the moving average is too long, the trader tends to take too big a loss (or give up too big a portion of unrealized paper profits) before he is even aware of a trend change. A longer mov-ing average keeps you in a trade longer, thereby maximizing paper profits, but it can eat into realized profits because it moves too slowly. So just like the story of the three bears, the moving average cannot be too hot or too cold; it needs to be "just right." I receive more questions about what is the "right" moving average to use than any other. I discuss the right moving average to use (in my opinion) in greater length in Chapter 10, "How I use 'TMVTT,'" but the bottom line of "just right" is not always that easy to determine and changes with market conditions. Voluminous studies have been done to determine which length is right for which specific market, but I believe these are useless simply because market conditions change for any and all markets. The silver market of the Hunt era is not the same silver market of today. Soybeans in a drought market act far differently from a normal weather market. In the next chapter, I will share just which moving averages I use and how I use them, but first it's important to discuss varieties other than the SMA.

Disadvantages of the SMA

The majority of traders who use moving averages use SMAs because they are simple. SMAs are easy to calculate (all you need is a calculator, or pencil and paper). Although

I use them, I don't always recommend them. This is because the oldest price has the same influence as the newest. Generally, the newest price reflects current market conditions better than the oldest, but with the SMA, they are weighted equally.

For example, suppose wheat is trading between 490 and 510 and the simple nine-day SMA is about 500. However, there was one day of data when the price was 475. When this low number becomes 10 days old and is dropped, the SMA jumps. This could generate a buy signal by indicating a new major uptrend, but the market tone might not have changed at all.

In other words, when one old piece of oddball data gets dropped, it has a tendency to jump the SMA. Many times, this jump results in an overstatement.

Alternatives to the SMA

Remember, any one price can be thought of like a snapshot in time. It tells you something about price, but it hardly tells the whole story. Ten photos in rapid succession provide you with a better picture of the story, and 20 blocks of 10 photos each paint an even better picture. If you are looking at a movie composed of 200 snapshots, the last 20 will most likely tell you more about what's likely to come next than the first 20. This is where exponential and weighted moving averages come in. They place more weight on the newest prices, and this can be more valid when determining the true trend than the older prices.

Exponential and weighted moving averages (EMAs and WMAs)

The exponential and weighted moving averages assign a greater weight to more recent events. WMAs increase the importance of the most recent price by a factor equal to the period used.

For example, with a five-day weighted, the fifth day is given a factor five times greater than the first. To calculate a five-day weighted average, multiply Day 5 by 5, Day 4 by 4, Day 3 by 3, Day 2 by 2, and the first, or oldest day by 1, and then divide by 15.

The EMA also weights recent events more than the distant, but it smoothes out the average for a more consistent result. The smoothing factor (SF) is determined by dividing 2 into the moving average plus one of the SMA you want to weigh and smooth.

For example, if you want to smooth a five-day SMA, you divide 2 by 6. The result, .33, is the smoothing factor. For a 10-day, the SF is 2/11 or .18; for a 20-day, the SF is 2/21 or .096.

The SF is a fixed weight applied to the current price, with the balance applied to the most recent moving average value. This will become clearer when we look at a specific example.

Let's calculate a five-day SMA and a five-day EMA for wheat. Remember, you need at least five days of data to produce the starting point for the SMA. ▶

Suppose the closing (settlement) prices for 11 consecutive days of wheat prices are as follows:

DAY	PRICE
1	440
2	446
3	461
4	446
5	463
6	458
7	472
8	470
9	464
10	476
11	481

You can easily see *in hindsight* that the trend was up during this 11-day period. (The market gained 41¢.)

However, hindsight is always 20/20, and it's not that easy to know just what the trend actually is when we're in the thick of the battle. This is where moving averages can help.

 The SMA is calculated as follows:

DAY	PRICE	CALCULATION	SMA
1	440		
2	446		
3	461		
4	446		
5	463	(440 + 446 + 461 + 446 + 463)/5	451.2
6	458	(446 + 461 + 446 + 463 + 458)/5	454.8
7	472	(461 + 446 + 463 + 458 + 472)/5	460
8	470	(446 + 463 + 458 + 472 + 470)/5	461.8
9	464	(463 + 458 + 472 + 470 + 464)/5	465.4
10	476	(458 + 472 + 470 + 464 + 476)/5	468
11	481	(472 + 470 + 464 + 476 + 481)/5	472.6

If you used the five-day SMA to generate buy or sell signals, starting on Day 5, you would have been a buyer at the closing price of 463 (because the price was *above* the SMA). You would have remained long on days 6, 7, and 8, but on Day 9, the price fell under the SMA, and you would have sold and reversed (gone short) at the closing price of 464. The result would have produced a marginal trade. Now you're short at 464 and would have to reverse again on Day 10 at 476 for a 12¢ loss.

This is a classic whipsaw. You got jerked out of what was a good trade in a definite uptrend when one low-ball price (the oldest) was dropped out of the equation. Now let's look at how the five-day **EMA** performed over the same time period.

eg **To calculate the smoothing factor for the five-day, you divide 2 by 6 (you use 6 because it is 1 more than 5), which is .33. You multiply this smoothing factor of .33 by today's price and then add this to 1 minus the smoothing factor, which is .67, times the EMA.**

Day	Price	Calculation	EMA
1	440	start	440
2	446	$[(.33 \times 446) + (.67 \times 440)]$	441.98
3	461	$[(.33 \times 461) + (.67 \times 441.98)]$	448.26
4	449	$[(.33 \times 449) + (.67 \times 448.26)]$	448.5
5	463	$[(.33 \times 463) + (.67 \times 448.5)]$	453.29
6	458	$[(.33 \times 458) + (.67 \times 453.29)]$	454.84
7	472	$[(.33 \times 472) + (.67 \times 454.84)]$	460.5
8	470	$[(.33 \times 470) + (.67 \times 460.5)]$	463.64
9	464	$[(.33 \times 464) + (.67 \times 463.64)]$	463.76
10	476	$[(.33 \times 476) + (.67 \times 463.76)]$	467.8
11	481	$[(.33 \times 481) + (.67 \times 467.8)]$	472.15

The results show that the price remained above the EMA during the entire period, even Day 9; therefore, no whipsaw resulted. You would remain long from 446 and still be long on Day 11 at 481.

Yes, you can still get whipsawed by using the EMA in a choppy market, but in general, I've found WMAs and EMAs to be superior moving averages with fewer whipsaws!

I should mention that popular these days with many computerized traders are moving average systems with a percentage band (such as the Bollinger bands), which uses an exponentially smoothed moving average plus a band above this EMA and minus a band below the EMA by the same percentage. A signal occurs whenever the closing price breaks outside the band. Exit occurs when the price crosses again into the band. Some traders like to trade within the bands, which is more like top and bottom picking. They sell at the top band and buy at the bottom. The risk point is set at some percentage outside of the band. I believe there is some validity to this, but because I find it difficult to pick tops and bottoms (I'm a trend follower), I will leave this to those who are inclined to attempt top and bottom picking.

Also, although it's informative to understand how the moving average is derived, you needn't stress over the calculations. Just about all of the trading software programs on the market today calculate SMAs, WMAs, and EMAs automatically. If you have access to real-time quotes, the software calculates these averages in real time, based on the last tick or the last bar, average of a bar, or close of a bar.

Bottom line

Moving averages are not the Holy Grail and are not all created equal. However, when used systematically and consistently, they will keep a trader on the right side of the big moves. Moving averages are a totally technical approach (rely on price only), and it doesn't matter what market you use them on. They work well in bull and bear markets and in the stock and commodity markets; however, they whipsaw the trader in a sideways or trend-less market. Still, this isn't as big a disadvantage as it might appear on the surface. My experience has shown that markets spend more time in trending modes than in trend-less modes. However, sometimes I've been involved in choppy, whipsaw-type markets that have lasted for many weeks. At times, a seasoned trader can sense a market is trend-less (the time to step to the sidelines), but if not properly capitalized or disciplined, a trader can be wiped out, or at the very least become demoralized and abandon the program. Usually he quits just before the big move starts. Remember, you need to catch the big moves when using a moving average system, or you won't win.

The next chapter goes into greater detail of how to use TMVTT; I will present a methodology I've found useful in my own trading for utilizing moving averages of varying lengths.

How I use "TMVTT"

My preferred approach to analyzing the markets is technical. In the long run, fundamentals do determine price; however, as Lord Keynes once said, "In the long run, we're all dead." As any journalist can tell you, it's easy to report the fundamentals after the fact, but you and I are not privy to inside information. Furthermore, as Richard Dennis once noted, "A known fundamental is a useless fundamental."

My primary goal is to determine the trends of the markets I trade. I believe if you are able to determine accurately the trend of any market, then you will, over time, make money. Just as it's easier paddling downstream than up and it takes less effort walking with the wind than into it, it's generally more profitable trading with the trend than against it. The best tool I've found for determining the trend with a fair degree of accuracy is the moving average. Since my previous books were released, I haven't lost any enthusiasm for moving averages—they remain the most valuable technical tool (TMVTT). However, I have modified and hopefully improved my methodology and will present the improvements in this chapter. In years past, I utilized shorter-term weighted averages. More recently, I've found (at least for me) that longer-term exponentials (in combination with shorter terms under certain scenarios) work best. What works best for you in your own trading is contingent on the time frame you're most comfortable with. I am going to share my approach, and I recommend that if you find this discussion useful, you should consider modifying it to fit your own trading based on your personal preference for risk tolerance.

Look at the crude oil charts shown in Charts 10.1 and 10.2. These are daily charts (each bar represents one day of trading) that encompass the entire trading period for 2003, a particularly volatile year because of the Iraq war.

Just glancing at these charts, you could determine that the trend was up December through March (leading up to the war), sharply down for a few weeks mid-March, choppy through May, and then back up into the summer. From the summer until year end, the market's trend was down, and then up, down, and then

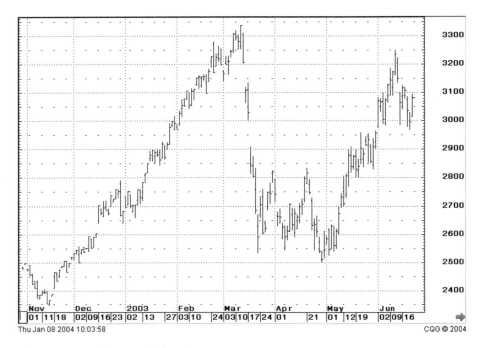

Chart 10.1   July 2003 daily oil

Chart 10.2   December 2003 daily oil

up again—you get the idea. Hindsight is always 20/20, of course, but in the thick of the battle, it's not all that easy to determine the major underlying trend. This period no doubt would have wrecked havoc with a fundamental trader, because the moves didn't appear to coincide with the news. Of course, one of the tenets of technical analysis suggests that if the markets appear irrational, you are missing something important, and the more irrational the trend, the more likely it's real. The primary question is this: How would you really have known what the trend was at any single point in time? A secondary question has to do with when the trend turned. TMVTT can help with the answers to these questions.

When constructing any moving average, I recommend basing the calculations on the closes and using either exponential or weighted averages. In my experience, although the SMA works just as well and generates similar signals, I've found either the WMA or the smoothed EMA to be slightly better. The real conundrum, and the one that directly affects the bottom line, is which length to use. Shorter-term averages are more sensitive. With a more sensitive average, the good news is that your average loss will be smaller, but the bad news is that the whipsaw factor increases geometrically. A long string of small losses is no better than a small string of large losses, and the latter is the problem that can surface when you're using too long an average. Losses are larger with longer-term averages, and so are the unrealized profits that are left on the table. However, the really big money is made in the big moves, and a longer-term average keeps you with the big trades during the big swings with a lower tendency to whipsaw.

So what's the "right" answer? If you knew for certain what type of market you were trading in (a long-term trending situation or a shorter term choppy consolidation), then you'd know exactly which average to use. The reality is that you are dealing with the unknown, and you can know for certain a market's true character in hindsight only. When looking ahead, the best you can hope to do is place the odds in your favor and then manage your position according to market action. The more I pondered this question, I came to realize there's a middle ground. There is a time for all seasons, and in certain market conditions, a shorter-term average minimizes draw-downs and improves on profitability. With this in mind, I developed my "best of both worlds" methodology, which I utilize in my own trading and present here.

Step 1
Calculate both the 23- and 30-day EMAs (this is for the daily chart)

In today's trading world, the big funds have become the most significant market-moving factor. Although there is no hard data on this, I am confident that a majority of fund managers utilize moving averages of various lengths and varieties. Those managers with a shorter-term perspective seem to prefer at or less than a 20 period, and those with a longer-term perspective tend to prefer at or above the 50. I'm not aware of many who use more of an intermediate term approach, higher than 20 but lower than 50. It's my experience that with an intermediate approach, you can attain somewhat of an advantage to stay out of the way of the thundering herd and, therefore, react in a more agile manner. As a result, I've found the 23 to 30 period to be a

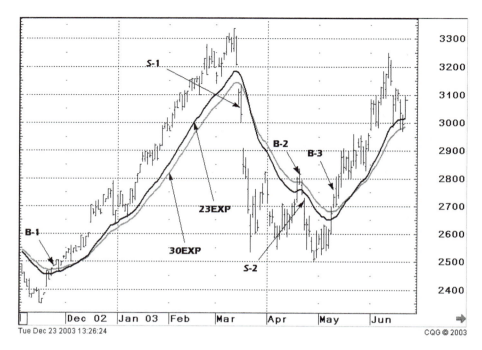

■ **Chart 10.3**   July 2003 oil EMA

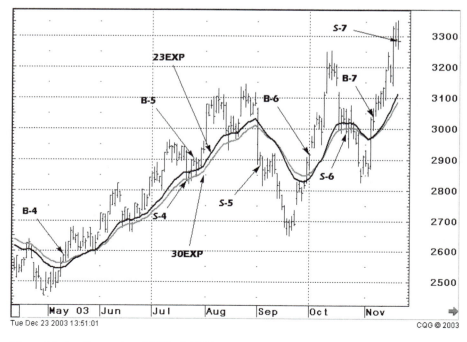

■ **Chart 10.4**   December 2003 oil EMA

perfect combination to use with the daily charts. Furthermore, I've found this time period to be dynamic. What I mean by this is that the methodology is useful over a diversified portfolio of non-correlated markets.

At our office, live quotes feed into our trading software. The computer calculates any moving average over any time period, and at the end of the trading day, we review the daily charts of the markets we trade with their respective 23 and 30 EMAs. The 23 and 30 tend to form a smooth channel or band that prices dance around. Charts 10.3 and 10.4 show what those 2003 crude oil charts look like with the moving average lines superimposed.

Step 2
Use the 23- to 30-day EMA band to determine the major trend of the market

The program rules are as follows:

■ To generate a buy signal:

1   On the daily chart, the market must first close above the band. (That's both the 23 and 30 moving averages.) This day forms what is called the **set-up bar.**

2   The market subsequently must exceed the high price of the set-up bar.
When both steps are met, a new buy signal is generated, indicating that the market is now in a confirmed up-trend.

■ To generate a sell signal:

1   On the daily chart, the market must close below the band (both the 23 and 30 moving averages). This is the *set-up bar* for a potential sell signal.

2   If the market then exceeds the low price of the set-up bar, a new sell signal is generated, indicating that the market is now in a confirmed downtrend.
Using these simple rules, 13 signals were generated for the 2003 crude oil contract year.

eg **If you hypothetically took every buy signal reverse every time a sell signal was generated, and then reverse again on a new buy, this is how you would have done (based on a one-contract position):**

Signal	Price	P/L (points)	Net $ P/L*
BUY-1	2483	July '03 contract	
SELL-1	3064	581	$5,710
BUY-2	2806	258	$2,480
SELL-2	2720	−86	($960) ▶

continues

Signal	Price	P/L (points)	Net $ P/L*
BUY-3	2746	−26	($360)
BUY-4	2591	Dec. '03 contract	
SELL-4	2829	238	$2,280
BUY-5	2899	−70	($800)
SELL-5	2884	−15	($250)
BUY-6	2911	−27	($370)
SELL-6	2986	75	$650
BUY-7	3039	−53	($630)
SELL-7	3286	247	$2,370
ANNUAL TOTAL			**$10,120**

*$100/trade deducted for commissions and "slippage"

Buy-1 through Buy-3 represents Jan.–May period (July chart)

Buy-4 through Sell-7 represents May–Dec. period (Dec. chart)

Sell-7 close out on last trading day for contract

The result (in this example, $100 per trade is deducted from the gross profit or added to the gross loss to cover commissions and slippage) is a net profit of $10,120. It's also interesting to note that out of 11 closed trades, a majority—6 actually—resulted in a loss.

This illustrates that it's not as important to have a high win-to-loss ratio as it is to have your average profit be higher than your average loss. In many ways, this chart also justifies the advantages of the technical approach over trading the news (fundamental analysis).

eg **The start of the war in Iraq was March 20, 2003, and on that day crude oil closed at 2687. The first sell signal was generated on March 17 at 3064, three days prior to the start of the war and almost $4 (representing close to $4,000 per contract traded) *above* the price on the day combat operations began. U.S. troops took control of Baghdad about three weeks later, on April 9. No one knew at that time how quickly the ground war would end successfully, but somehow the market knew it would be swift. After the ground war ended, the market did not collapse as many analysts predicted it would, with prices rising back to the annual highs by year's end. Saddam Hussein wasn't captured until December 14.**

Is it this easy? When it comes to trading, nothing is ever this easy, and I'm not trying to present this methodology as the Holy Grail. As you can see, even in good years, there are losing positions, and there are draw-down periods associated with this method during times of consolidating (quiet/sideways) markets. However, I've found this system to be, on balance, quite profitable, and it has identified the majority of the major trends for every exchange-traded market for the past 30 years.

Take a look at a more difficult market, the 2003 soybean bull-run, as shown in Charts 10.5 and 10.6.

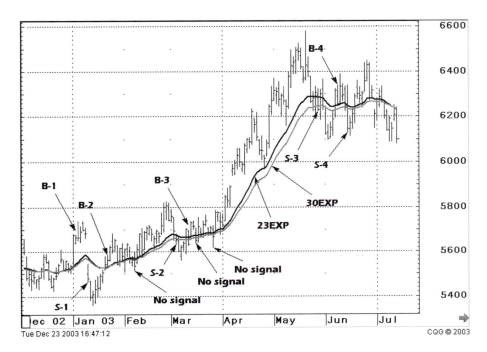

■ **Chart 10.5**   July 2003 soybeans

■ **Chart 10.6**   January 2004 soybeans

Signal	Price	P/L (points)	Net $ P/L*
BUY-1	569	July '03 chart	
SELL-1	546	−23	($1,250)
BUY-2	558	−12	($700)
SELL-2	563	5	$150
BUY-3	571	−8	($500)
SELL-3	622	51	$2,450
BUY-4	633	−11	($650)
SELL-4	613	−20	($1,100)
SELL-5	556	Jan. '04 chart	
BUY-5	552	4	$100
SELL-6	746	194	$9,600
BUY-6	763	−17	($750)
ANNUAL TOTAL			**$7,350**

*$100 per trade deducted for commissions and "slippage"

Buy-1 through Sell-4 represents Jan.–June period (July chart)

Sell-5 through Buy-6 represents June–Dec. period (Jan. chart)

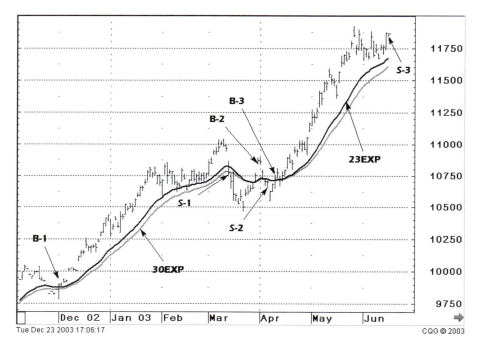

■ **Chart 10.7**   June 2003 Euros

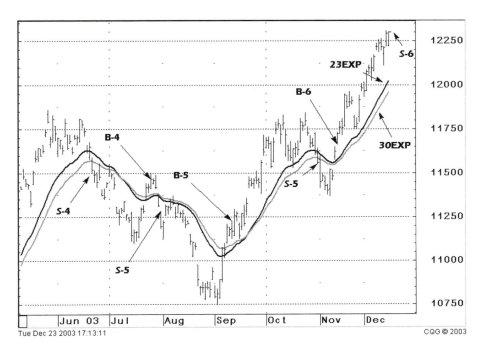

Tue Dec 23 2003 17:13:11   CQG © 2003

Chart 10.8   December 2003 Euros

The results of the program were good, with a net profit of $7,350 per contract trad-
ed, so why is this one considered difficult? Even though there was a total of 10 closed-
out trades, if you began trading the program at the beginning of the year, by mid-year,
you would have been down $1,600. It was absolutely crucial you took BUY-5, with-
out which there would have not have been a profit that year in the beans. The moral,
again, is to let the profits run and allow the market to take you out, because there's no
way to know in advance how long or how far any one move will last.

Remember, the objective is to determine the trend of a market and then profit from
this information. Thus far, I've demonstrated how this can work by using the oil market for 2003 (more than $10,000 net profit per contract traded) and what I termed a
"more difficult" market, the soybeans for the same time period (more than $7,000 net
profit per contract traded). Charts 10.7 and 10.8 illustrate an "easier" market, the Euro
currency for the same time period.

Signal	Price	P/L (points)	Net $ P/L*
BUY-1	9903	June '03 chart	
SELL-1	10757	854	$10,575
BUY-2	10844	−87	($1,188)
SELL-2	10675	−169	($2,213)
BUY-3	10759	−84	($1,150)

continues

Signal	Price	P/L (points)	Net $ P/L*
SELL-3	11847	1105	$13,712
SELL-4	11496	Dec. '03 chart	
BUY-4	11413	83	$937
SELL-5	11277	−136	($1,800)
BUY-5	11211	66	$725
SELL-5	11550	339	$4,137
BUY-6	11670	−120	($1,600)
SELL-6	12300	630	$7,775
ANNUAL TOTAL			**$29,910**

*$100 per trade deducted for commissions and "slippage"

Buy-1 through Sell-3 represents Jan.–June period (June chart)

Sell-3 close out last day of contract

Sell-4 through Sell-6 represents June–Dec. period (Dec. chart)

Sell-6 last trading day for contract

This was a fantastic market for our methodology, resulting in close to $30,000 net profit for just one contract traded. I termed this one "easier" because, for the most part, it was a beautifully trending situation. Remember, there is no Holy Grail, and this program unfortunately does not work this beautifully in all cases. But it can and does happen quite often, and the currencies in particular seem to trend better than most. Regarding my methodology, I'm not asking you to take my word for this; I urge you to prove it for yourself by using historic data on any market you want to test. Please send me an e-mail with your experience.

Additional rules for maximum success

The following sections describe additional and important rules to help you maximize your successes.

The accelerated trend

These methodology examples illustrate how moving averages assist you in determining the trend of a market and, as a result, can help you make money. However, because moving averages are a lagging indicator, they are not designed to pick tops or bottoms, and, by their nature, they leave money on the table. In fact, when a market is in what I term "the accelerated trend,"' at times my methodology can leave quite a bit on the table, so let's discuss one technique designed to minimize this problem. First of all, it's important to define what an **accelerated trend** actually is. In an up-trend, it looks like a parabola. The accelerated trend generally occurs at major tops and, at times, at blow-off bottoms. It's what W.D. Gann called "the third zone above normal." Here's how Gann (more than 50 years ago) described this type of market action:

"The third zone above normal is characterized by wild fluctuations and volume; great activity; a feverish public buys madly; the market advances for weeks with small reactions; the public is too full of hope to sell; people wait for reactions, get discouraged, and buy at the market; fortunes are made in paper profits, yet less than 10% will ever cash in. The first sign of the end comes with a sharp break on no news (possibly at the open). This is the warning. Then a second rally may come to approximately the high point and could hold awhile, but THE SATURATION POINT IS REACHED; THE END IS NEAR; EVERYONE IS LOADED AND WILL BE LOOKING FOR A BUYER WHO IS NOWHERE TO BE FOUND. Then follows the deluge back to normal and below! In Zone +3, HOPE & FEAR INCREASE TO THEIR HIGHEST LEVEL (and most people trade on hope & fear and not sound judgment). DO NOT WAIT UNTIL EVERYONE ELSE IS SELLING; GET OUT ON THE FIRST DANGER SIGNAL. When everyone wants to sell, profits run into losses fast. Profits from a whole year can be lost in 10 days! WILD ACTIVE MARKETS ARE BROUGHT ABOUT BY FEVERISH MANIPULATION; THEY INCREASE THE IMAGINATION AND EXAGGERATE HOPES; THEY TAKE AWAY ALL SENSE OF REASON & PROPORTION. In Zone +3, you must keep a cool head. Remember all things come to an end, and a train going 60mph will cause a greater smashup than one going 5— jump before she bumps."[1]

The daddy of all soybean bulls, the 1973 "Russian Grain Steal," illustrates a classic accelerated trend, as shown in Chart 10.9.

Our program would have worked nicely in this market. It signaled a buy in April at $5.62. The sell did not come until July at $9.50, an astounding 488¢ profitable trade, equal to more than $24,000 profit per contract traded. What is even more astounding is that the market peaked at $12.90. In other words, from the top to the sell signal, 340¢ was "left on the table," equal to $17,000 per contract traded. Yet, who could have picked a top in this market? After all, it was trading at uncharted territory the first time it moved above $6, and that was months earlier.

Nobody can pick a top, but I've found it useful to tighten the parameters when you can visually see (or even sense) a market is trading in Gann's third zone above normal, the accelerated trend. This involves using a shorter term, and therefore more sensitive moving average, the 10-day exponential. In this case, the market remained above the 10-day from the original buy signal on April 4 for 45 trading days until June 6, when it closed under at a price of $10.13. If you used a close below the 10-day as your "take profit signal," you would have sold out a month prior to the longer-term sell signal and reaped an additional $3,150 per contract traded. Here's the first additional rule for maximum success: Use the ten-day to liquidate and take profits only (that is, not to reverse trend) in an accelerated trend to leave a bit less on the table.

---

[1]Gann, William D. *The Truth of the Stock Tape: A Study of the Stock and Commodity Markets with Charts and Rules for Successful Trading and Investing*, 1923. Pomeroy, Washington: Lambert-Gann Publishing Co., Inc.

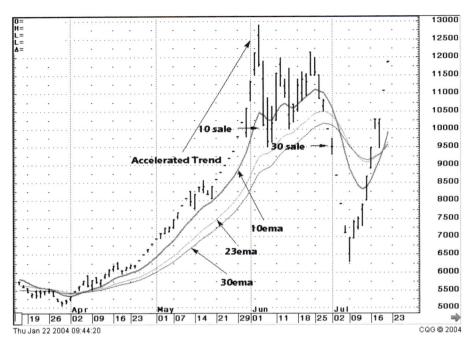

Chart 10.9   July 1973 soybeans

Diversify into a minimum of three unrelated markets

These markets should be broad and liquid to allow stop orders to be used with minimal slippage. Although this rule is not written in stone and you can make money using this methodology trading just one or two markets, this could take longer and generally requires greater patience if you happen to start at the wrong time. The premise here is that the greater the diversification, the greater the chance of catching a major move *somewhere*. At any point in time, one market might be in a major up-trend, one market might be in a major down-trend, and a third trend-less. The entire theory of this program is that the major moves are going to be profitable enough to offset the inevitable minor losses inherent in those choppy market situations. The odds of catching major moves increases with the number of markets traded. One caveat: They should be unrelated markets. Although the Swiss Franc and the Euro can move in opposite directions at times, they generally move in the same direction (although at different speeds) in relation to the dollar. Hogs and pork bellies can move in opposite directions, and they have, but because they are directly related products, they generally move in the same direction, although usually at different speeds.

In picking the optimal markets to trade, I personally prefer those that traditionally have the tendency for more dramatic moves. Unlike the slower movers, the more volatile markets have moves large enough to overcome the inevitable trend-less periods, plus the inherent costs of commissions and slippage. For example, I generally prefer soybeans to corn because of the increased volatility of soybeans. I like markets with good volume and major commercial participation. The commercial interests have deeper pockets and tend to support their positions longer.

In most market scenarios, I prefer to be in one currency, because the currencies tend to trend nicely. I usually trade the Euro, but any of the major currencies (the Swiss Franc, the British Pound, the Canadian Dollar, or the Japanese Yen) will do nicely. I also like to trade a grain, and I personally prefer the soybeans (technically not a grain but an oilseed), because they trend nicely and possess sufficient volatility.

Finally, I round out my portfolio with a meat, a metal, a stock index, or an interest rate product or an energy product. Crude oil and natural gas are liquid markets that tend to trend well.

Other deep and liquid markets, allowing for easy entry and egress, are the U.S. Treasuries, the S&P and Dow futures, and many other global financial futures products such as the Bund, Japanese 10-year bond, or DAX. Again, this program can theoretically work over time if used systematically on any single market; however, my experience has been that some markets don't trend as well or are thin, and the fills can be disappointing. (Lumber and pork bellies come to mind.)

Watch for breakouts from consolidation

If a market you're planning to trade has entered into a period of consolidation (range-bound, choppy, back-and-forth action, also known as a **trend-less** or **sideways** market), be patient—this is the one time when you should remain on the sidelines. Use patience, and wait until the market breaks out of the consolidation to take the next trading signal. Only after the breakout does it make the most sense to trade the methodology for maximum profitability. The reason for this is that the best trends are formed and *come out of* consolidation. Consolidation patterns are generally formed at major bottoms and (to a lesser extent) at major tops. If you can enter close to a major top or bottom, your odds for success increase.

Remember, consolidation is nothing more than an inability for either side (the bulls or the bears) to prevail. It is where the battle is being waged, but the war is not being won by either side. During periods like these, the methodology will not work well, so if you are able to identify these patterns, you will save yourself money and grief. Although it's not always easy to identify these patterns, it is possible, and your ability to do so will improve over time with experience. Also remember that the odds that you will accurately identify a consolidation period increase when you do *not* have an opinion or position.

My experience has shown that consolidation periods for most major commodities generally do not last more than three to four weeks. Periods of five to eight weeks can and do occur at times, however, and these are generally followed by the best moves and most profitable trading signals. Periods of sideways action lasting longer than eight weeks are rare. The general rule is that the longer the period of consolidation, the bigger the move to follow. After the breakout from a longer consolidation is complete, there will be fewer false signals.

Basically, when a market breaks out of a trading range, it means one group (either the bulls or the bears) has prevailed. The longer the period of sideways action, the

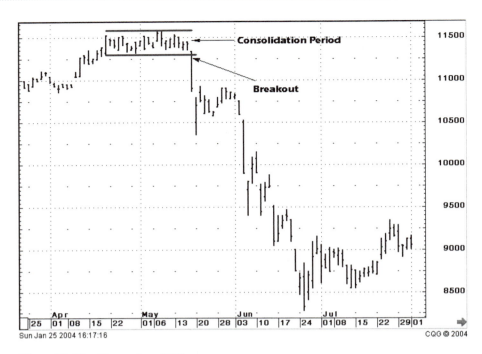

■   **Chart 10.10**   December 1996 copper

greater the number of participants on the wrong side of the market. The greater number on the wrong side, the more fuel available for a move in the direction of least resistance. In other words, the more shorts to panic in a bull move, and the more longs to panic in a bear. Certainly, false breakouts can occur; however, the longer the period of consolidation, the less likely a false result.

Footprints in the sand—look at the December 1996 copper chart.

This was to be a historic market, but few knew this when the year began. The fundamentals were bullish in the early part of the year, demand was outstripping new mine production, and scrap copper was in short supply. In the first quarter of 1996, the market was consolidating in a 106 to 110 range. It broke above the 110 upper barrier of consolidation decisively in April and trended higher, to a new 113 to 116 consolidating range, for the five-week period from mid April to mid May. At this time, no one had any idea one of the most infamous of all scandals was shortly to be announced: the Sumitomo affair. This turned out, at $2.6 billion, to be the largest financial loss to date. The news—a rogue copper trader from the international trading firm of Sumitomo had secretly racked up huge losses in copper over a 10-year period—would not hit the wires until early June. However, the market appeared to know something was going on weeks earlier, as it left its footprints in the sand.

Despite bullish news, the market broke out of the consolidation to the downside below the 11300 level. The news services attributed this to sell stops being hit exacerbated by fund selling. The fundamental news still appeared to be bullish (at least on the surface) according to the published news. However, the charts were saying that something was not right with this market when the breakout came below the consolidation. In addition, a 23/30 sell signal was generated just a few days after the downside breakout at approximately 10700. Of course, in the thick of the battle, this was not an easy market to short, because the sell signal did not come until 800 points under the recent highs. Still, the trend never turned up before a major break occurred, and this level was plenty high enough to ride the trend down. (In fact, there was another 2,700 points of downside profit to come before the methodology would flash the next buy signal.) In addition, the news was not officially announced in the *Wall Street Journal* for another two weeks, a time when the market was already trading well below $1 per pound.

Sumitomo, the company, didn't actually start to liquidate contracts en masse until the day before the announcement when the market, in one day, broke from 10500 down to under $1. This one trade could have made your year if you saw the footprints in the sand and took this short-sale signal. It did appear to be risky, measured from the break from the top, so it required guts and a belief in the methods. Incidentally, after the collapse, the market consolidated for a few months and eventually started back on a beautiful uptrend that recouped the entire loss of the run. In other words, the basic bullish fundamentals took hold again.

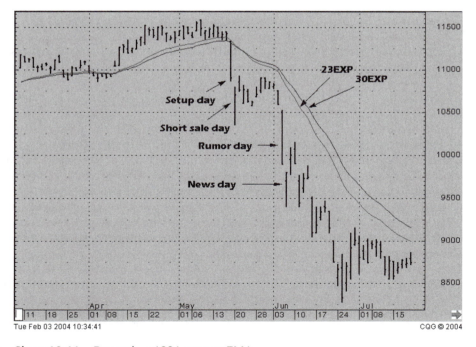

■ **Chart 10.11**   December 1996 copper EMA

You might think that I chose this example because it demonstrates how a trend-following program can work. Actually, I picked this example because I felt it could have been a hard trade to take. After all, you would have had to go short a bull market at a price that appeared cheap in relation to where it had been recently. I certainly could have picked examples from hundreds of profitable trends this same year across a wide variety of markets. You don't have to take my word for it. Prove this to yourself by picking up a chart book. Look at the charts, and then you can let me know if, generically, markets don't trend more often than not. Paper trade our averages as presented, and prove to yourself if this works or not. You might want to work with averages of your own to develop a trend-following system that performs better than mine. I'm sure they're out there, and I would very much like to hear about your successes.

Be consistent

The final rule for maximum success is to have the guts to take the signals. It is generally not a recipe for success to try to fudge the system or outguess the market. Gann once wrote, "The tape moves in mysterious ways the multitude to deceive." This statement is so profound. Just when a market looks the weakest, it might actually be the strongest. You must use your essential quality of patience to wait for a bona fide signal before entering a trade, and you must develop your essential quality of discipline, in this case to take all the signals. Discipline entails staying with the winning trades until you have a definitive signal to liquidate. Remember, it's fun to take a profit, but taking premature profits ultimately leads to failure.

I should emphasize that the impulse to take profits (and try to reposition better) will be quite strong. There will be numerous times you just *know* a market is overdone, and you just *know* you can re-enter better if you cash in *now*. When this impulse hits you, you'll probably, more times than not, be right. If you stick with your methodology, don't liquidate. When the market moves against you the next day, you could become frustrated, even demoralized. The temptation to fudge the system the next time becomes even greater. However, this is not a recipe for success—trust me. The reason has to do with the nature of the big moves. When using this system, the best trades will be those you'll have the good fortune to be on for the longest periods of time. There might be only a few trades each year you'll be able to stay with for months before liquidating, but these trades will make your year. Also, in an accelerating market, the best portion of the move comes at the end. This is when your biggest profits accumulate, and the temptation grows to book the profit. However, nobody I know can pick the actual top or bottom consistently, so remember that patience pays.

How do you acquire these essential qualities of discipline and patience? Write down your rules before you start to trade and then follow your game plan religiously. Know each day what needs to happen in the marketplace for you to take an action. If you don't get a signal, do nothing. The fewer number of trades you make, the greater the odds for maximum profitability increase!

This method is no Holy Grail; rather, it's a disciplined, businesslike approach to trading the markets. If you were actually able to pick tops and bottoms, you could do much better than this methodology, but in real life that's impossible. Remember, you're not anticipating the market here—you're following it. The best you can hope to do is get into long positions somewhere close to the bottom and out somewhere near the top—or vice versa. This methodology also has the advantage of being objective—actually most technical systems do. Historically, looking at people who have wiped themselves out, the majority of big losses are the result of having an opinion and not admitting or believing you can be wrong. This system tells you with certainty what the trend is and how to play it. Emotions and opinions are minimized. It is impossible to be on the wrong side of a major move when you are with the trend. If the market is trending, you *will* make money here. Just be cognizant of the fact that there are trend-less periods in all markets (even those that traditionally trend the best). The good news is that markets trend more often than not. Diversification helps here, and if you are astute enough to sense and avoid a market in a consolidation phase, or better yet catch a new move coming out of consolidation, you will maximize your profits!

11

A day trader's secrets

Why is day trading (defined as entering and exiting a position during the same trading day) so popular? In a word, it's seductive. Some people believe day trading is an easy way to make a killing, but these are the people who get killed! It appears to be liberating, but in reality day traders are slaves to their screens. The myth abounds that you can effectively day trade with a lot less money, because you need not worry about overnight margins. In reality, those who are inadequately capitalized ultimately drown in the financial sea. It might look exciting, but those who day trade primarily for excitement end up lost and dying of thirst in the financial desert.

After being involved in thousands of day trades, I can tell you this: Day trading is more demanding than position trading. It takes total focus and total concentration.

It is true that advances in technology and the Internet offer better opportunities for day traders. The democratic dissemination of information has leveled the playing field to a major extent, and today's traders no longer need to sit by the phone waiting for their broker to call them with fills. Yet, the odds are still stacked against the day trader, so the big question is why day trade?

Well, day trading has certain positives. The big one is that you do not have overnight exposure, with its associated overnight stress and risk. Day traders have a fresh start each and every trading day. They sleep like babies, not having to worry about Central Bank intervention or how tomorrow's USDA Crop Report or Unemployment Report might help or hurt them. The element of instant gratification that, trust me, can be emotionally rewarding is also a positive factor in day trading. No doubt, the shorter time frame does make for (all other factors being equal) lower risks, and without overnight margin requirements, the leverage can be magnified greatly. On the other hand, the greater the trade activity, the greater the costs, and I am not just speaking in terms of commissions. Because slippage (price fills other than what you anticipate you will receive or what you see on the screen when your order is submitted) is such an important cost of trading, it is imperative that you find a brokerage firm that has excellent trade execution capabilities for the markets you trade. Slippage, in my opinion, is of even greater importance to bottom-line profitability than fees, and it takes on an even greater significance when day trading.

In this chapter, I share with you my day trader's secrets, learned from more than 20 years of day trading. These secrets are absolutely essential to successful day trading. I will conclude by presenting a simple strategy that has worked for me.

Your nine essential day trader's rules
Rule 1
You will not be a scalper.

Pit traders can successfully scalp for a few ticks, because they have enormous scalper's advantages. They can buy the bid and sell the offer (you generally cannot), and they pay extremely low fees as Exchange members (fees that can make trading for just a tick at a time profitable). Floor traders can react instantly to big orders as they hit the pit, because they can hear the noise rising and know something is afoot—you can't. This logic applies to traders who work for Forex firms and those who create the bid/offer on so-called commission-free trades. These trades are not fee-free, because the retail trader is paying hidden fees embedded in the spread. On the other hand, off the floor can be a big plus, because you do not get caught up in the emotions of the pits, which often result in false messages.

Rule 2
You will be a day trader, not a daily trader.

A day trader, by definition, is in and out the same session, but nobody can do it successfully every day. The right kinds of market conditions are not present every day, and it is psychologically too intense to day trade day in and day out. One tremendous advantage you have is freedom of choice; you do not need to take every signal or trade every market. You do not need to be in a position before an important, but risky, employment report. You have the luxury to wait, watch, and witness the market's reaction before taking action. If a market is newsless and quiet, range bound, you can always relax and let your most important quality of patience work for you.

Rule 3
You will treat day trading as a business.

Day trading is not a part-time diversion. It is demanding. You need total focus and total concentration. To be totally focused, you must eliminate outside distractions. Lock your door if you have to. I know from personal experience, the more outside annoyances, the harder it is for me to trade effectively.

Rule 4
You will feel well.

If you do not feel well, you cannot day trade effectively. If you stayed out late last night drinking, are physically ill, or have emotional stress from outside influences, you should not trade. This is especially important when day trading. Day trading is much more demanding, and it is absolutely essential that you be sharper and quicker than your competition. When the optimal set-up presents itself, you must feel strong, because you do not have the luxury of hesitation.

Rule 5
You will be totally disciplined.

"Totally disciplined" means you follow written and well-defined rules systematically, which is the only way to avoid the emotionalism of the markets. In other words, you construct a game plan that you follow without bias. Let me repeat this: You have no biases. (I have always had my biggest losses when I have had a strong opinion about some market and overruled my technical signals.) If you do not follow your game plan, you will miss some of the best and most profitable trades. Sound familiar?

What should your game plan look like? It should have well-defined entry and exit rules from a program or system you have tested and have confidence you can win over time. Your well-tested system should have a positive outcome (not necessarily a high win-to-loss ratio, which is not easy to achieve for any system). If for every dollar you lose, your system, over time, makes $2 on winning trades (after fees and slippage), then a marginally positive win-to-loss ratio still results in excellent profitability. The best day traders are on autopilot, in "the zone," and just like a seasoned pilot, they operate without emotion using well-defined protocols. Your rules will be strict in terms of capital preservation, especially during drawdown periods.

Although your method might be better, let me present an effective set of money management rules. I do not tolerate a drawdown of greater than 5% in any single day. This is a moving target; in other words, if I have paper profits, this 5% drawdown number is off of a peak, so if I am up 1%, I move my stop up 1%. Five percent is a maximum risk; most days I risk much less. To determine where my stop is placed, I use a 4% number to calculate position size, with the extra 1% a cushion for slippage and fees.

Total discipline means you always use stops (just do it) and never cancel a stop just because the market is getting close to it. Finally, never add to a losing position.

Rule 6
You will never let a decent profit turn into a loss.

Here is what I do: If I have a reasonable profit on paper, I move my stop up, so that if half of these profits slip away, I am gone for that day. The reason is obvious: You escape with at least a portion of your profits.

Rule 7

You will become cautious after a "home run."

After you make a big hit, the temptation to overtrade grows geometrically. After a home run, look for singles (or better yet, take a vacation).

Rule 8

You will go only where the action is.

Being aware of the current trading environment is essential. Day trading requires volatility and liquidity. Not all markets are volatile enough to allow for ranges required for consistent profitability; you need a market that not only moves, but moves within a limited time frame. You shouldn't day trade markets such as oats or orange juice. Not all markets are liquid enough to minimize slippage. You shouldn't day trade markets such as lumber. Even large markets should be avoided when they are quiet or range bound. Look for markets in the news. Of course, sometimes you think a market is going to be a mover, but then it dulls up on you. Personally, if I am in a day trade that is going nowhere (after a reasonable time has passed), I use discretion and get out early. It seems the best day trades work either right away or relatively quickly, and many times with little or no grief.

Rule 9

You will day trade only markets suited to you.

Not every market is suited to everyone, and there is no rule that says you have to trade anything and everything. Although the S&P is today's day trader's favorite, it is generally not my personal favorite. At times it is too erratic, and in my experience, the slippage and risks are high. (The slippage is minimal, however, in the e-mini S&P.) Better suited to my personal temperament for day trading are the currencies, crude oil, bonds, and (when active) the soybeans and metals. Make a personal choice, because nobody is holding a gun to your head to trade the market du jour. You also need the right temperament to day trade. If you require numerous confirmations or can take action only after extensive research, you are probably not suited to day trading. In addition, I've found (maybe due to a simple mind) that simple is better. Keep it simple! Some of the most basic indicators can be incredibly profitable if you follow the rules I've outlined in the preceding sections.

The trend reversal day trading system

There are many wrong and fewer right ways to day trade profitably. The right ways come in different styles, and each trader has to discover his own style. Here, I present just one method that has worked for me. It combines two simple, yet effective and well-known, indicators: the RSI and the simple moving average.

For the record, I am a trend follower. In other words, I do not try to pick tops or bottoms, because I personally have found this just too hard to do. I would rather let the trend work for me and find it easier to target a piece of the middle. Remember what I said previously about not having a bias. This is particularly important when day trading. When using this method, you are interested only in exploiting the trend for that day; the major trend is irrelevant. A requirement is a volatile, high-volume market. You need to use discretion and best judgment to exploit the trending days and strive to remain on the sidelines during choppy, low-volume days.

How do you recognize the trending days? They tend to follow lower volume consolidation periods and develop on breaks or break-outs of significant chart points, generally with higher than normal volumes, and particularly on news days. You must be prepared and ready to act on days when news breaks, for example, when government reports are released. Always watch for gap opens. It is important to note that it is not the news, but rather the reaction to the news that is important. Your job is not to interpret news but to read the trend of the day correctly. You must act without hesitation when you get a signal. After you take the signal, you need to exercise patience. Even the best of trend days do not trend all day, because there are intra-day periods of consolidation that might only be rest periods, or what's termed "noise," and nothing more. You must always use stops, because no method works all the time. Finally, play it out to conclusion. At times, your biggest profits come in the final 15 minutes of the day.

Parameters

To set parameters, use a bar chart, with bars no shorter than 15 minutes and no longer than 45 minutes. A shorter time frame generates too much noise, and with a longer time frame, the risk is too high. For the following trade examples, I used 18-minute bars. Use 23- and 30-period simple moving averages and a nine-period RSI.

Rules

1   A signal is generated after a trend reversal. A trend reversal from down to up occurs when the market moves from trading under both averages to above both averages. A trend reversal from up to down occurs when the market moves from trading above both averages to below both averages.

2   A trend reversal can occur only after a set-up. For a long set-up to occur, the market must have one bar *close above* both averages (if previously below). For a short set-up, the market must have one bar *close below* both averages (if previously above).

3   When the high of a long set-up bar is exceeded, a buy signal is generated. When the low of a short set up bar is exceeded, a sell signal is generated. Use a buy stop to enter on the long side and a sell stop to enter on the short side.

4   Take a buy signal only when the RSI is less than 60. Take a sell signal only when the RSI is greater than 40. This rule filters buy signals in potentially overbought situations, and it filters sell signals in potentially oversold situations.

5   Your initial stop is a reversal signal, or a maximum 4% of your gross equity (5% including estimated fees and slippage). If by risking 4% of your gross

equity you cannot place your stop comfortably on the other side of the averages, do not take the trade, because the risk would be too high. (For most of the markets I trade, the risk is at least $400 gross per contract *not* including slippage and fees, which requires $10,000 in free equity per each single contract traded. When trading markets such as the large S&P, the risk is generally higher, requiring a larger account size.)

6   When the RSI moves below 25 on a short or more than 75 on a long, lower or raise your stop to the high or low of the previous bar. After you have reached this step, you are tightening your stop in the exuberance phase of fear or panic. In many cases, you will be stopped during the next bar period, but in most cases, you have locked in a profit (equal to at least your risk, and in many cases much more). This is a dynamic rule, in that you continue to move your stop to lock in additional profits as the market continues to move your way. If your new stop is not hit during the session, liquidate the position at the market on the close. It is important to hold the position all the way until the end of the day if you can. At times, this results in what I call a "mega profit" trade. You need only a few mega profits each year to really make your year.

eg   **Example 1: Long Bonds. This was a news day with no less than five major government reports, including the important quarterly GDP (all released 10 minutes after the open). The numbers were somewhat conflicting, and after the releases, the market continued to trend lower. But about one hour into the session, the market reversed and set up (Bar 8). The RSI on set-up was 52; so because it was under 60, this was a valid signal. We prepared to take the trade by placing our buy stop one tick above the high of Bar 8. A long position was initiated when the buy stop was elected (Bar 9) at 11320. A protective sell stop was initially placed at 11307. On this day, the RSI never traded above 75, so we were never able to tighten our stop. Because the initial stop was not touched, the position was liquidated at the close (Bar 23). It is interesting to note that the trend for this day had nothing do with the overall trend; in fact, the major trend was down, and the market did gap open lower on the following day (Bar 24). The fact that we were day trading made this overnight risk a moot point.**

Result: Long from 11320 and sold on close at 11330 for a day trade profit of 10 ticks per contract ($312.50 gross per contract).

eg   **Example 2: Short Euro. This was also a news day, one requiring action without hesitation. Prior to the market open, the European Central Bank raised interest rates. This was ostensibly bullish news, and the market gapped up at the open (but did so in a lukewarm sort of way). It traded modestly above the averages for the first six bars. The trend reversal came approximately two hours into the session (Bar 7 with the set-up and Bar 8 with the sell signal). On the set-up bar, the RSI was above 40 (at 45), so we took the signal and prepared to take the trade by placing a sell stop one tick under the low of Bar 7. The short was filled at 10500 when the sell stop was elected at 10502. The initial protective buy stop** ▶

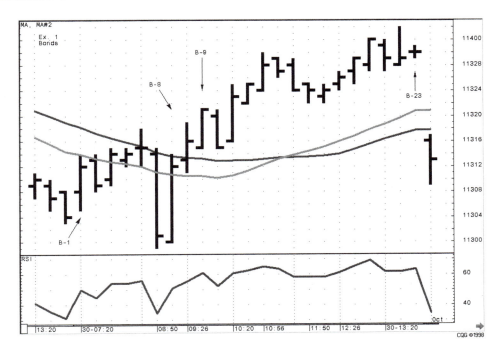

■   **Chart 11.1**   Long bonds

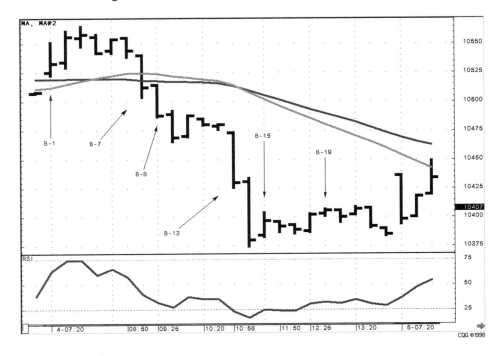

■   **Chart 11.2**   Short Euro

was placed at 10542. When the RSI moved below 25 (Bar 13), the stop was lowered to 10482 (just above the high of the previous bar). The stop was again lowered to 10474 or just above the high of Bar 13 at the start of the Bar 14 period, again to 10436, or just above the high of Bar 14 at the start of 15, and again to 10406 at the start of 16. If the market continued to trend lower into the close, we would have continued to lower our stop with each subsequent bar and cover at the close. In this case, however, we elected the stop and filled at 10406 during the Bar 19 period.

Result: Short from 10500 and covered at 10406 for a day trade profit of 94 points ($1,175 gross per contract).

12

Your state of mind (trader's psychology)

"Half this game is ninety percent mental."
—Danny Ozark, Philadelphia Phillies manager

"Please don't think . . . that I am showing off when I say that I know
the secret of how not to lose but win. I really do know the secret; it is
terribly silly and simple and consists of keeping one's head the whole
time, whatever the state of the game, and not getting excited. That is
all, and it makes losing simply impossible . . . But that is not the
point: The point is whether, having grasped the secret, a man knows
how to make use of it and is fit to do so. A man can be as wise as
Solomon and have an iron character and still be carried away."
—Fyodor Dostoyevsky, *The Gambler*

Dr. Leroy, the head psychiatrist at the local mental hospital, is examining patients to
see if they're cured and ready to re-enter society.

"So, Mr. Clark," the doctor says to one of his patients, "I see by your chart that
you've been recommended for dismissal. Do you have any idea what you might do
once you're released?"

The patient thinks for a moment and then replies, "Well, I went to school for
mechanical engineering. That's still a good field, good money there. But on the other
hand, I thought I might write a book about my experience here in the hospital, what
it's like to be a patient here. People might be interested in reading a book like that.
In addition, I thought I might go back to college and study art history, which I've
grown interested in lately."

Dr. Leroy nods and says, "Yes, those all sound like intriguing possibilities."

The patient replies, "And the best part is, in my spare time, I can go on being a teapot."

You've read this book and feel you're "ready to go," yet statistics on winners and losers indicate the great majority are missing an essential element for success. We all think we have the key to success before we begin trading. After all, our research is both fundamentally and technically sound, and the trading system we developed does appear to be a sure winner (on paper). Most traders embark on their journey confidently, so why then do so many traders encounter problems?

Trading is exciting, but it is also extremely difficult. In this chapter, I get you to focus on your inner self; you will cut to the quick regarding your personal qualities of work ethic, self-esteem, and the ability to focus and concentrate totally on the task at hand. This chapter is, in one respect, a treatise on discipline, one of the essential qualities for success. This, in turn, relates to the all-important subject of money management, a critical subset of discipline. I could have alternatively titled this chapter "The Psychology of Trading," or "Trading Consistently," but it all really boils down to one thing: your state of mind. For the successful trader, the mental game is actually more important than all of the other trading rules combined!

Motive

You want to trade futures, or you are currently trading—and you want to trade successfully. After all, that is why you purchased this book. Have you really sat down and analyzed your true motives? I know you want to make money—we all want to make money. But it should go well beyond that.

The hedgers in our markets are there for business reasons—to manage the risks inherent in the commodity and financial markets associated with their businesses. The other element, the speculators, should be in it for the same business reason—to enhance bottom-line profitability. Still, many are trading for another reason: the thrill, the excitement, and the adrenaline rush. These traders, and I think the numbers are significant, are looking for the same rush as the horse better or crap shooter. Although it is not impossible to make money as a Las Vegas gambler (some unique individuals do), most do not. My first question to you is this: What are your real motives? Only you can answer this question, but I will state clearly that if your real motive is action, and if you require instant gratification, you will fail. Your state of mind will prompt you to trade without regard to conditions. The conditions must favor your actions, or you will fail.

So what should your motives be? Not just to make money; this is not enough. You most likely are a competitive person, one who enjoys playing games and solving puzzles. You should strive to act in a disciplined, consistent, and unemotional manner. Prior to each trade, you need a well-thought-out plan for that trade. The plan expects a positive outcome, but it has a built-in contingency for the unexpected or, in other words, unprofitable outcome. You need to act in a confident and unhesitating manner. You need to overcome the six hurdles to successful trading.

Six hurdles to successful trading

1 Trading for the thrill of it

2 Trading for revenge

3 Lack of money management

4 No well-defined trading plan

5 Inability to pull the trigger

6 Inability to admit you're wrong

Condition yourself to be unemotional

If you are trading for the thrill of it, you trade when the conditions favor your methods, and you also trade when they don't. Because you are trading emotionally, you overtrade, which is an inevitable outcome of thrill trading. You also overstay your welcome on trades that are not going your way, and this invites disaster. It might work for a while, but there will come a time when thrill trading will wipe you out, plain and simple. The other side of this is those people who trade for the adrenaline rush but are subconsciously uncomfortable with risk. If you are one of these people, you tend to undertrade or place your stops too close, and this is not a recipe for success either. If you cannot condition yourself to assume the risk of a leveraged market, place your hard-earned money in Treasury Bills and go home. Undertrading is just as fatal a flaw as overtrading.

Revenge trading: another recipe for disaster

Has this ever happened to you? You have just been stopped out for a loss, a bigger loss than you had anticipated. Perhaps it was a gap open beyond your stop because of some unexpected news. It is early in the trading day, and you feel you must make it back. You cannot go home today with such a large loss. How would you explain it? The market owes you your money back, it will pay you back, and it will do so today! Have you ever had this feeling? I have, and let me tell you that when I am out for revenge, nine times out of ten it leads to disaster. Because the state of mind is unstable, trading angry inevitably leads to bad decisions. When you get this feeling, force yourself to take a step back and relax. The market will be there tomorrow, and there are always opportunities.

This is not the time to compound a problem; it is the time for your essential quality of patience to take over. Too many people let a loss affect their psychology on the next trade. I am not saying it is always easy to be unemotional; emotion is a human trait. But you must condition yourself to remain in control, and if you feel you might be losing it, force yourself to step aside for a time.

Preservation of capital is your primary mission

When you have no money management program in place, it is impossible to preserve your stake. Unless you tell yourself you will risk only a specific percentage of your account on any one trade, that one trade that looks so right will inevitably come along, and you will trade it too heavy. After all, the trade "looks so right," "everything is falling into place," and before you know it, you are dipping into the till once again.

Let me share a secret with you: They all look so right. I would not enter a trade unless it looked good, but there is no way to know in advance which trade is going to be the big winner. If you knew this, then these would be the only ones you would trade. I've found that only a few trades make my year each year, and it is usually not the trades I thought would be the big winners. If I had no money management plan in place, I would be long gone before ever capturing those major moves. You must preserve your capital, and this means taking small and consistent hits on the many inevitable losers. The goal is to still be in the game when those mega-trades finally materialize.

Your plan must be well-defined

Nobody enters a position expecting a loss; however, it will not come as news that even the top traders experience numerous losses over their career. If the best lose, why would you be any different? A well-defined plan defines success and failure both. Ask yourself, "Why are you buying gold?" If the answer is something like, "Because it just broke above the 30-day moving average," or "Because the CPI indicates inflation is heating up and in the long run gold is sensitive to inflation," you have not defined your plan. You have reasons why you entered but no clear exit strategy. You are trading on hope, and this is not a recipe for success.

You must define your loss point before you enter the trade, and if you are not prepared mentally to lose many times, you'll never win. It is essential to realize you'll lose countless battles in this trading war, or the war will never be won. You should have a profit objective. Stop loss points should be written in stone; however, profit points can be flexible, and you should have contingency plans when your profit objective is reached. The plan could be nothing more than something like this: "I am risking $500 per contract on this trade; my technical profit objective is $1200. If the market moves $500 my way, I will move my stop up to an approximate break even. If it moves $900 my way, I will move the stop up to approximately a $400 profit. If it reaches my technical objective, I will watch very closely for signs of failure. If the market shows these signs, I will sell at the market. However, if it moves through, I will tighten my stop to just under the previous low." This plan might or might not work, but at least it is a plan, and without a plan, you're ultimately doomed to failure.

You must act without hesitation (if a good reason to do so)

To paraphrase Steinbeck, "The best laid plans of mice and men . . . " When you paper trade, you always take the loss or the profit. In the heat of the battle, it is not as easy to pull the trigger. Remember, you must lose to win in this game. Too many times, even good traders do not take the loss when the planned risk point is reached. It is human nature not to be able to admit you are wrong, and it is seductive to wait just a bit longer or take just a bit more risk, hoping the market will turn back your way. In the great majority of cases, this just exacerbates the pain.

How do you overcome this shortcoming? Very simple—place a physical stop loss order with your broker the moment you enter the trade, and then just let the "market gods" determine your fate. Trust me when I tell you that you won't be stopped out of the best trades. Taking profits when the time presents itself, although not as critical, can be just as important. I always have a mental profit objective in mind whenever I try to work with a physical stop loss. It is not so bad to watch the market when it reaches the profit objective, because the best markets many times greatly exceed your minimum profit objective. However, if the market seems to hesitate at the goal line, cash in. Just do it, because many times the market will not give you that second chance. Whenever I am unsure, I just move the stop very tight and make sure I lock in a good chunk of the profit. The majority of times, I give up something, but sometimes I am able to squeeze out quite a bit more.

What about the "locals" running your stops? I have had stops in for a significant number of contracts and had the market come just one tick away, yet never has the stop hit. Conversely, I have had the market countless times stop me out and, thank God it did, as it never came back to that stop price again. Unless you place your stops in obvious places, which is never recommended, don't worry about it. Stops are valuable tools that give you an edge—use them!

Condition yourself to be humble

You cannot have an ego and be a successful trader. With apologies to Vince Lombardi, winning is not everything, and it certainly is not the only thing. I had a client with an S&P day trading system, one who made money four out of five trades. The problem was that fifth losing trade more than offset the other four winners. Yet, until he ran out of money, he kept trading it for small profits, because it felt good. Numerous clients try to pick tops and bottoms, but this is an almost impossible take, because every major move has just one top and just one bottom. Who cares whether any one trade makes money or whether you have more losers than winners? The name of this game is not how many winners you have but making money at the finish line. This is the ultimate triumph—consistently having winning months.

To have a winning month, my experience has been that you most likely have accepted losers all throughout that month. Most people have trouble admitting they are wrong, which is why they lose money in futures trading. In my own case, over the years, my biggest losses have come in those markets about which I have had a strong opinion. I would end up fighting the market, taking too much risk, and voiding my money management principals. At times, I would be forced out of a market just before the turn. In other words, I was right in my opinion, but my timing was off. The margin clerk, however, doesn't care if you are ultimately right. Other times, some new news I was unaware of would surface to demonstrate why I was wrong and the market was right. It is better to let the market tell you what it is saying, instead of you trying to dictate, because there is no doubt who is going to win.

Most people take profits too soon, because it is soothing psychologically to take profits. I always have profit objectives for my trades, but they are never written in stone. After all, there is only one top in every bull and only one bottom in every bear. I am not arrogant enough to assume I am the one who can pick those tops and bottoms.

Can you? A better plan is to see how the market acts when it does reach my profit point. Many times it goes much further, so if the market wants to do this, why not just let it? Forget about being right on any particular trade and focus on making money!

The traits that lead to success in trading are different from those you have learned during your lifetime, those that lead to success in everyday life. You have been taught that perseverance will ultimately lead to triumph, but in trading you need to lose repeatedly to win. This takes conditioning to train your mind to act in manner contrary to what works outside of trading. In life, it is generally a recipe for disaster to act impulsively; it is better to sit back and reflect upon your situation. In trading, however, you must condition yourself to act quickly without hesitation and unemotionally to cut a loss (or take a profit) when your predetermined point is reached. After you condition your state of mind, you have control over your trading emotions. You have greater confidence when taking losses and entering new positions, because you know your trading plan will prosper over time. Condition your mind to be disciplined, one of the essential qualities for trading success. The key is almost a reverse conditioning to your psyche. Unfortunately, you are going to have losing streaks. If your series of losing trades is a result of a lack of planning, and the margin clerk forces you out of the market, it is difficult to bounce back quickly. You lose confidence in your ability to recoup. On the other hand, if you know you followed your disciplined program of cutting losses according to a well-defined plan, you can't be devastated, because you followed your plan and know that over time it will work for you.

Money management

How can you trade in control, relaxed, unemotionally, and with confidence? The simple answer is to develop a consistent money management strategy with a positive outcome. Time and time again, I have heard from winning traders that a mediocre system with good money management triumphs over a superior system with poor money management. Money management is the vital element required for success, yet so few traders concentrate on it.

What's the best money management strategy? I think the beginning trader is looking for the Holy Grail here, but if there is such a thing, I've not found it. Going in, I strive to risk only 5% of available equity on any one trade (striving to be as close to this number as possible, including fees and slippage). However, I know that slippage and extraordinary events could potentially raise that number for any one particular losing trade. If I can keep my loss per trade to approximately 5%, it takes 20 losing trades in a row to wipe me out. Even at 10%, it would take ten losing trades in a row, and I have enough confidence in my system to believe the risk of total ruin under these parameters is small. Of course, I need to stick to these parameters, and this is where conditioning comes into play.

After I've defined my normal risk, I also need to define my normal reward. I personally am shooting for at least a three-to-one reward-to-risk ratio. Of course, many trades result in a smaller profit, or smaller loss, and because I try to never let a decent profit turn into a loss, I seem to have many **scratch trades** (small profit, small loss, break even).

Let's analyze the ramifications of this simple system. Suppose you had a small trading account of $10,000. (With the leverage inherent in the futures, you should probably start with more, but let's use this number to keep it simple and assume you're trading those less volatile markets.) You could have seven losing trades at $500 each and three winning trades at $1,500 each (three-to-one), and you would still be a nice winner.

$$7 * (\$500) + 3 * \$1,500 = +\$1,000$$

Think about this: You are wrong 70% of the time and still come out a winner. This is the beauty of a good money management program. You might ask, what about the time I placed my stop at a calculated loss of $500, a bad crop report came out before the market opened (bad for me), and that loss turned into $750? I understand this happens. However, my experience has been that these extraordinary events seem to even out over time. At some point down the road, there will be a favorable unemployment report, the market will gap open in your favor, and you will reap an additional $300 per contract profit over and above your original objective. Let's term this "even Steven." I don't know why the good and the bad even out; it is one of the mysteries of nature. But my experience has been that this is the way it works.

Finally, you must continually adjust your position size based on market volatility. A small account should concentrate on only those less volatile markets, so the risk can be adjusted to suit the account size. A quick and simple way to evaluate volatility is to obtain from your broker a list of margin requirements by market. The clearing firm has, to a major extent, determined the volatility levels for you, because margin requirements are adjusted based on volatility. Although there are always exceptions due to market inefficiencies, my general rule is that the initial margin for one position should not exceed 15% of your total excess equity available for trading. If you have a $50,000 cash account and the margin for soybeans is $1,250, a suggested maximum position size would be six contracts. If the perceived risk in this case is $500 per contract, you are risking $3,000 with six contracts, which is 6% of total equity. Therefore, you should pare down your position size by a contract if you want to stick with the 5% rule. Certainly some discretion is involved here, and if this trade is in your best estimation a 10 on a scale of 10, you might be willing to accept that extra point risk and go for the six. If the perceived risk as determined by your system is $750 per contract, then only three to four contracts should be traded for this position. If you always adjust your position size to volatility, then even in the bad times, you will have capital left to stay in the game. The name of the game is to avoid that catastrophic risk of ruin.

If you don't feel right, you won't trade right

Rodney Dangerfield once complained, "It's been a rough day. I got up this morning, put on a shirt, and a button fell off. I picked up my briefcase, and the handle came off. I'm afraid to go to the bathroom." If this is the way your day starts out, don't trade. Your state of mind is wrong.

In conclusion, you must control your state of mind and follow a well-thought-out money management plan, but the key is your state of mind. What if you are indecisive?

Consider this quote from Lee Iacocca when he was bringing Chrysler back from the dead:

"So what do we do? Anything. Something. So long as we just don't sit there. If we screw it up, start over. Try something else. If we wait until we've satisfied all the uncertainties, it may be too late."

Your advantage

Always remember, you are in competition, and the psychology on the other side is not as well-informed as you now are. Hundreds of thousands, perhaps millions, of traders who have a loser's state of mind are potentially on the other side of your trade. They might not realize it today, but their actions in the marketplace attest to this fact. The playing field has just titled your way if you change your behavior to act in a positive way. If you do this the right way, trading will be enjoyable and not filled with the anxiety so many face. Research your trading plan, develop good money management techniques, condition your mind for success, and you will succeed.

13

Twenty-five trading secrets of the pros

At the times I've done well in the markets, it usually was because I acted in a certain way. When I've done poorly, it usually was because I didn't. The "secrets" presented here are partially from experience (the "school of hard knocks"), but also originally gleaned from reading the masters. Two masters of yesteryear come to mind first—Jesse Livermore and W.D. Gann. Their heyday was during the 1920s; however, they both still live through their writings for me. Actually, a trader can learn more from their failures than their triumphs. The same mistakes made 50 and 100 years ago continue to be made by traders every day. Technology might change, but human nature never does. I thank these two men, because I know many of the "secrets" discussed in this chapter, although written in my words, originated from them. You personally might not use all of these "secrets," but if you can absorb only a portion of this wisdom, I believe you will be successful in your trading. Do I always heed these "secrets"? Mea Culpa—no. However, when I stray from the true path, I generally regret it. If you disregard what's presented here, you likely will become lost in the financial desert dying of thirst. (Perhaps that's a bit strong, but trust me, this is good stuff!)

Secret 1
The trend is your friend

Don't buck the trend. The way to make the really big money is to determine the major trend and then follow it. If the market will not go your way, you must go its way. When you are in a bear market and the major trend is down, the plan should be to wait for rallies and sell short, *not* try to pick the bottom. In a major bear market, you can miss the bottom several times on the way down and end up losing all your money. The same applies (in reverse) during a major bull market. Always go with the tide—never buck it. Let me repeat this, because it is important; it is easier walking with the wind than against it, it is easier swimming with the tide than against it, and the big money is made by going with the trend, not against it.

As Livermore told us, in a major bear market, it is safer to sell when the market is down 50 points from the top than when it is down just ten. The reason is, at down 50, all support is gone, and those who bought the breaks have lost all hope, are demoralized, and, in a leveraged market, are at the point where they all try to exit the same small door at the same time. The result, at times, can be an unexpected avalanche. I can give you many examples of markets that have trended long and far, made some people rich, and wiped out many others. You might have heard about the poor soul who lost his farm. I can almost guarantee that guy was bull-headed and fought the trend until he finally ran out of money.

For example, in the 1920s, the New Haven railroad was the premier blue chip stock of the day and sold as high as 279. Remember, in those days you could trade stocks on 5% margin, like we trade futures today. When New Haven sold 50 points from the top, it must have looked cheap at the time. How many would have had the guts to sell it short when it crossed below 179, 100 points from the top? Better yet, who would have had the guts or the vision to sell this investment grade security short at 79, or 200 points from the top? It must have looked extremely cheap at 79; remember that this was the General Electric of its day. Yet, the trend was down, and after the crash of 1929, it traded as low as 12. In the year 2000, a friend of mine bought a "new technology" stock at the offering price of $66. He added to his position at $150 a share, again at $200, and then again at $300. I suggested he use stops to lock in his profit, but he "knew" this company (his daughter worked there), and he told me it was going to $1,000. It kept going up, and he added at $450 and $500. It actually went as high as $600. As I write this book, it is trading at $1 (and he still owns it all). At least that one is still in business. Remember Enron? This was a blue chip energy company—the largest contributor to the 2000 Bush Presidential campaign. At that time, the stock was trading at $90 a share. Today, it is simply not around anymore. If you still own the stock, you can use the certificate as wallpaper.

How do you stick with the trend and not fight it? It isn't easy. That's why most people don't make money in futures. You need to have a strong will. When you can determine the trend of the market, don't change your mind until the tape shows the change. In any major move, there will, of course, be corrective moves against the trend. Some news will develop that will cause a sharp correction, but it will be followed by a move right back in the direction of the major trend. If you listen to this news, you will be tempted to liquidate prematurely. Avoid the temptation and listen to no one—listen only to the market. One way to do this is to *never* set a fixed price in your mind as a profit objective. The majority of people do this, and there's no good reason for it—it's a bad habit based on hope. Do not set a fixed time to liquidate either. This is the way the amateurs do it. They buy silver at $5, because their broker told them it's going to $6. Well, it gets to $5.97, turns and heads south again, and they're still holding looking for $6, watching and waiting as their unrealized profits melt. I've seen it, and this is just plain bull-headedness.

I've seen the opposite, too. The market closes at $5.95, looks strong, and is fundamentally and technically sound. The amateur has his good-until-canceled order sitting to sell at $6, because this is his price. The market gaps up on the open the next day at $6.05, and his broker is pleased to report he sold five cents better at this price. However, this is a form of top picking, and who is smarter than the market? The market probably gapped up above $6, because the buying interest was able to overwhelm the sellers. I've seen many cases like this one, in which the open was sharply higher but turned out to be the low of the day. In other words, it was the kind of market that never looked back until it hit $8. This is all a version of bucking the trend—something I do not recommend. Conditions do change, and you must learn to change your mind when they do. A wise man changes his mind; a fool never does. Just be sure that *if* you change your position, it is based on sound reasoning.

When you place a trade, your objective is obviously to profit. You cannot possibly know in advance how much profit to expect. Only the market determines your profit. Your mission is to determine the trend, hop on for the ride, and attempt to stay on until your indicators suggest the trend has changed, and *not before*.

Secret 2
When a market is cheap or a market is expensive, there probably is a good reason

This one goes hand in hand with "don't buck the trend." Livermore would tell us that he always made money selling short low-priced markets, which are the public's favorite and in which a large long interest had developed. Alternatively, he cashed in on expensive markets when everyone was bailing out, because the public thought the market was high enough for a healthy reaction. The public was selling soybeans short at $6 per bushel in 1973, because this was an all-time high and into resistance. Who could have guessed that soybeans weren't even halfway to what would be record highs—close to $13? Always remember that it is not the price that's important, it's the market action.

Secret 3
The best trades are the hardest to do

You need to have guts, and you need to be aggressive on entry. Quickly cut your losses when the market is not acting right. The news always sounds the most bullish at the top and appears to be the most hopeless at the bottom. This is why the technical tone of the market is so important. If the news is good but the market has stopped going up, ask yourself why, and then heed the call. Bottoms can be the most confusing. The accumulation phase, where the smart money is accumulating a position, can be marked by reactions, crosscurrents, shakeouts, and false reversals. After the bottom is in place, many traders look for the next break to be a buyer. After all, the market has been so weak so long that the odds favor at least one more break, right? But it never comes. The smart money won't let it. The smart money's objective after the bottom is in place is to move the market up to the next level. The best time to buy might actually feel very uncomfortable. However, the train has already left the station, and you need to have the courage to hop on for the ride.

Secret 4
Have a plan before you trade, and then work it

If you have a plan and follow it, you are able to avoid the emotionalism that can be the major enemy of any trader. You must try to stay calm during the heat of the session and remain focused. To do this, you have to be totally organized prior to the opening bell. Your daily mission, should you decide to accept it, is to make money each day or barring that, at least not to lose much. In normal markets, you should take normal profits. In those unusual markets (that occur rarely), you need to shoot for abnormal profits. This is one of the keys to success. The next is that you must always limit losses on trades that are not going according to plan! This takes willpower and is as essential a quality as having plenty of money. In fact, it's more important than having lots of money. Money is not to hold on with; that's for the sheep, and you don't want to be sheared. If big risks are required, don't take that trade. Wait for an opportunity where you can place a tighter stop. Livermore's method of trading was to look for opportunities where he could enter close to his risk point. In that way, his risk per trade was small in relation to the profit potential.

If you do not have the willpower to take the loss when your risk point is hit during the trading session, then you *must* use stop loss orders. Simply place your stop at the same time you place the trade. You probably have heard stories about the floor traders "running the stops," but I assure you that in the good trades, the majority of the time you will not be stopped out. This happens only with the bad ones.

Personally, I have a trading plan laid out the night before. I generally know what I will do if the market acts the way I anticipate it should and just as importantly what I'll do if it doesn't. It is a guide, of course, not written in stone and somewhat flexible. However, if a market is not acting "right" according to my plan, I know it is time to take action, either to take the profit if available, or cut the loss if not. Generally, I've found when I try to fudge the plan, I get my head handed to me. This doesn't always happen (and this is why it's hard to follow plans many times), but it happens enough to know the plan is smarter than I am in the heat of the battle.

When it's not going right, and when in doubt, get out. If you have a compass in the middle of the desert, and the oasis is north, don't get fooled into following the mirage to the west.

Nothing is better than getting out quickly when you're wrong!

Secret 5
Be aggressive

Be aggressive when taking profits or cutting losses if there is a good reason to do so. A good trader acts without hesitation. When something is not right, he liquidates early to save cash and worry. Never think too much. Just do it! And, don't limit your price—go at the market! Many times a market gives you one optimal opportunity to act and that's it—go with it. As Gann said, "The way to benefit through intuition is to act immediately"!

Secret 6
No regrets

When you liquidate a trade based on sound reasoning, never regret your decision. Just go on, and if it was a mistake to get out, all you can do is learn from it. We all make mistakes. Don't beat yourself up. You will lose your perspective and become too cautious in the future. How do you do this unemotionally? Try never to think about the price you entered, because this is irrelevant. If the market isn't acting right, don't try to get out at break-even after commissions. Always trying to break even can get expensive.

Secret 7
Money management is the key

Think about money management daily. You do not necessarily need to have a high win-to-loss ratio, but your average win must be higher than your average loss if you want to succeed. To do this, there must be (at least some) "big hits." You have to maximize some trades. You need these big wins to offset the inevitable numerous (and hopefully small) losses that are inevitable. I've found being able to cut losses early, by even a small incremental amount per trade, say $100, can make a major difference to the bottom line. This takes decisiveness, so be decisive if the trade is not acting right. Waiting for a few more ticks is generally not a recipe for success.

One more point here: It is bad practice to cancel or extend a stop loss order. You should never do this. My experience has been that 99 times out of 100, canceling a stop is the wrong thing to do. It's okay to cancel a profit-taking order at times, but the sooner a loss is stopped, the better. When you get out of a bad position quickly and with a minimum of trauma, not only is your capital base maintained, but your judgment also improves. Without a well-defined risk point, there's no judgment. (What it's called is hope, and you should never trade on hope.)

Secret 8
Success comes easier when you specialize

Every market seems to have its own nature and its own personality. Some markets tend to make tops and bottoms with a fast run up and reverse (called an inverted V top, or a V bottom). Some have rounding tops and bottoms, some double tops and bottoms, and some tops and bottoms with a long consolidation. You can read a market better when you become familiar with its idiosyncrasies. Familiarity comes from concentration and experience. If a market does not fit with your nature, find another one. Just leave the markets that don't seem to work for you, and stick with the ones that favor you. Plenty of markets are out there, one for each temperament.

Secret 9
Patience pays

As Gann once said, "People are in too big a hurry to get rich, and as a result, they go broke." Don't try to get rich in a few months. Don't try to catch all the fluctuations. Market movements of importance require weeks, even months to get ready. A few days (or longer) after a big move gets underway, there's generally plenty of time to buy or sell. At times, a man or woman with nerve, knowledge, and a bit of luck can turn a small amount of money into a fortune. However, this cannot be done continually. The very best trades come along only rarely. You need the patience to wait for the right trades. When they come, you need the patience not to be overanxious and get in too soon or overtrade. When you do get in and the market starts to move your way, you must have the patience to hold on tight until there's sufficient cause for closing out the trade. Remember that every act, either opening or closing a trade, must have a sound basis behind it. Never trade for the thrill of it. If you cannot see a definite trade, use your essential quality of patience and wait!

One last point on patience: After you are out of the market with a big profit, you don't need to be in too big a hurry to get back in. The best opportunities might be just around the corner, but they're not there every day. You need the patience to wait. Big account balances lead to the temptation to play for less than desirable trades. If you made a good profit, then look at it this way—you can now *afford* to wait a few weeks or months for the signs of the next big move.

Secret 10
Guts are as important as patience and more important than money

Some traders are too bold, and as a result, they overtrade. Others have trouble pulling the trigger, and this is a weakness that must be corrected. You must train yourself to trade in a way that there is no hope and no fear. When you enter or exit a position, do it decisively and without emotion. This is particularly important after a tough losing streak. I've witnessed traders who still have money left suffer a string of losses, and when the best opportunity of the year comes along (one they identified), they just didn't have the guts to act. In cases like this, guts are more valuable than money. You need the guts to press hard when you are right. You also need the fortitude to cash in when it is most pleasurable.

Secret 11
The "tape" (the quotes) will trick you

Gann once said that it's impossible for the man who day by day stands over "the ticker" to identify a big move before it starts. The tape will fool you every day while accumulation is taking place (and it takes time to accumulate or distribute a large position). Gann actually felt that the tape (today we call it the quote machine) is there to fool traders. "The tape moves in mysterious ways, the multitude to deceive" is the way he put it. Prices can look the weakest or strongest at the strongest or weakest times. Watching quotes all day causes you to change your mind constantly.

Trade too often, and this increases your percentage of being wrong. If you get in wrong, the quote machine tends to keep you in wrong longer than you should be, because every tick your way renews your hopes. If you get in right and you watch the screen too closely, there will come a minor move against you that will shake you out. This move, in the long run, means nothing, and as a result, you will lose a good position.

Secret 12
Be skeptical

Another way to put this is that it pays to be a contrarian. To be successful, you need to be a student of human nature and do the opposite of the general public. Sell on your first clues of weakness; don't wait until everyone is bailing out. If you're day trading the S&P, this rule could apply to moves of 15 minutes. If you're swing-trading, this rule could apply to a move lasting three days. It certainly applies to those moves lasting weeks or months. And be wary of tips. The tip-giver might be well intentioned, but tips invariably influence you in the wrong direction. Remember, the market doesn't beat you—you beat yourself. Following tips and not the market is just another sign of human weakness.

Secret 13
Be time cognizant!

In other words, know how much time the move has taken to get to the point it's at. The longer a market moves in one direction, the greater the velocity the buying or selling is in the final stage of the move. In many cases, the most significant portion of a major move takes place in the final 48 hours. You'll want to be there for that.

While we're on the subject of time, watch the volume after a market has made a long-term move. Volume tends to run higher than normal at the end of a move, because this is the "distribution zone" where the smart money is unloading their position to a public who is frenzied by the news.

Actually, it's important to know what "zone" the market is in. Market phases tend to act in a similar manner. Many times, at the bottom, a market can rally on small volume. This indicates there really isn't much for sale. The bottom can follow a period of panicky conditions, pessimism, and apathy. Even the prior bulls start to sound more cautious, and (hint) it could get worse before it gets better. It seems nobody is interested in buying. This is the time to watch your moving averages closely. If they flash a buy signal, then immediately cover shorts and start to buy. Tops are the opposite of bottoms. It seems nobody notices the market is saturated, yet the market might stop going up. After the first break from the top, many times there will be a low-volume "failure test of the high." When the market fails at a lower high, if you are not out already, this could be your last best chance to liquidate.

As a general rule, the big money is made in the last stage of a bull market when prices are feverishly active. The big profits on the short side are made in the last stage of a bear market, when everyone wants to sell, and it seems no one wants to be a buyer.

It is always darkest before the dawn and brightest at noon just before the sun starts to recede.

Secret 14
Watch the reaction to "the news"

This is important: It's not the news but how the market reacts to the news that's important. Certainly it's the news that sets the public perception, but you must be alert for divergences between the news and market action. It all has to do with expectation versus reality. Look for the divergence between what's happening and what people think is supposed to happen. When the big turn comes, the general public will always be looking the wrong way. Consider the following ways to analyze reactions to news (or even a lack of news):

- If bad news is announced and the market starts to sell off in large volume, it's a good bet the market's going lower.

- If the market doesn't react much to good news, it's probably been discounted.

- Moves of importance invariably tend to begin before there is news to justify the initial price move. When the move is underway, the emerging fundamentals slowly come to light. A big rally (decline) on NO NEWS is almost always bullish (bearish).

- It is generally not good practice to buy after a lot of bullish news or sell after an extremely bearish report, because both good and bad news is often already discounted in price. Of course, you should always consider whether the trend is down or up when the news is made known. A well-established trend generally continues, regardless of the news. I remember getting caught in the emotion of a bullish corn report in January of 1994. Looking back, this news was the very top. An opposite (very bearish) report the following year made a significant bottom, which turned out to be the springboard for the biggest corn bull market in history. The move wasn't over until corn prices doubled a year later.

  Consider this breaking news from 2003—March 18: BAGHDAD (AP)—"Iraq's leadership on Tuesday rejected the U.S. ultimatum that Saddam Hussein and his sons leave Iraq or face war, and the United Nations pulled its weapons inspection staff out of the country as battle appeared inevitable." On that day, world oil prices collapsed by 10% (before the war had even started), because the market had already discounted the worst outcome.

- When unexpected news occurs (news that the market has not had time to prepare for), and the market opens in a wide range, or gaps, lower or higher, sell out your longs, or cover your shorts and wait. Watch the market for 30 minutes to an hour. If the market opened sharply lower with heavy selling and was not able to trade much lower than that, it's into support and can be bought at the market with a tight risk point. Watch the market closely at this point. Note the tone of the rally. If it is small and the market is able to again fall under the levels made when the bad news came out (or above the good), it is safe to assume the market is going lower (higher).

eg I remember the big bull coffee move of 1994. When the market was trading in the mid-80¢ level, I was long. Unexpected news hit the wires, something about the release of massive Brazilian stockpiles of coffee. These stocks were supposed to be held in reserve and off the market, but Brazil needed foreign exchange and changed its policy. The market gapped open lower and proceeded to trade down 400 points, stopping me out in the process. It remained weak for a day or so, but mark my words, as soon as the market was able to cross above the mid-80¢ level again (the price registered before the unexpected bad news hit), it basically went straight up. This was the time to re-enter. It was about $1.40 *before* the first freeze hit. The move wasn't over until coffee prices hit close to $2.75—and it all started when the market, on *no* news, crossed the level made prior to the bad news.

Secret 15
Never trade when sick or tired

Good health is essential to success. If you don't feel well, then close out your positions and start over again when you do. Rest is equally essential to success. It is a good idea to close out all your trades periodically, get entirely out of the market, and go on vacation. The market will still be there when you return; trust me. I've heard over and over again from some of the most successful traders that they trade their best right after a vacation. If you stick to something too long without rest, your judgment becomes warped. Traders who are continually in the market day in and day out lose their perspective and ultimately lose.

Secret 16
Overtrading is your greatest enemy

Gann called overtrading the "greatest evil." He felt it was the cause of more losses than anything else, and who am I to disagree with one of the masters? The average novice trader really doesn't have a clue as to how much money is needed to be successful, and he invariably buys (or shorts) more than prudence dictates. He might be right in his analysis or determination of the major trend, but because he takes too big a position, he is forced to liquidate when the margin clerk calls. When he's liquidating, so are the other novices, and that's when the smart money moves in. The money runs out just at that critical time when it's ripest to enter. The over-trader is exhausted and misses the profit opportunity he had once seen so clearly in those more optimistic days.

Be conservative, keep your cool, and avoid the temptation to trade more contracts than your margin can reasonably support in normal markets. This is especially important at tops and bottoms where the excitement, the rumors, and the news are at fever pitch. Human nature has a tendency toward overconfidence at tops and bottoms. Study your charts, and don't let hopes or fears influence good judgement.

Secret 17
Keep a cool head during blow-offs

Markets almost always seem to top out in the same way. When close to the end of a major move, markets become wild. Volume is huge, activity is feverish and erratic, and the imagination of most traders blossoms. If you've had the vision to ride the trend to this point, your payday has come; however, in extreme markets, men and women of reason lose all sense of proportion. They start to believe the propaganda that the world will literally run out of this or that, but it never happens. The Hunts ran silver from $5 an ounce to more than $50. They felt it would go up forever, but they forgot that at some price Grandma's silver candlesticks come out of the cupboard and drop into the smelter. The richest men in the world (at that time) lost all sense of reason and proportion and lost $2 billion in the process. The history of the world has shown that there has never been a time when there was a great demand for anything that a supply in excess of demand didn't develop.

Extreme markets are not the time to pyramid—they are the time to become alert for the end. All good things come to an end, and your mission is to jump before the big bump. At some point, all "the herd" will want to exit the same door at the same time—just make sure you've already left the room. When everyone wants to sell and all buying support disappears, profits can run into losses fast. In the stock market crash of 1987, profits made in the first 10 months of the year were wiped out in two days, and this was repeated in the dot-com mania in early 2000.

How do you turn your paper profits into cash during a runaway market? In blow-off markets, the corrections are generally short and sweet. The market is feverish, and everyone is bullish. (The bears have already thrown in the towel.) The public is buying madly. Weeks might go by without a major correction. You'll hear of fortunes being made, and if you are fortunate enough to be on the move, your paper profits will grow geometrically. The end might be near, but in fact, nobody can see the forest for the trees. Only about 10% of those with big paper profits ever cash in near the top.

Here's my first rule: In this type of market, it does not pay to take a loss amounting to more than two consecutive days' fluctuations. If the market goes against you more than two days, it's likely to go more. Second, be alert for a morning when the market opens off dramatically without news to account for the break. It might rally weakly, but the rally will fail. This is your first sign of the end. The market has reached the saturation point where it's run out of buyers; supply has finally overwhelmed demand. Third, watch for a failure test of the high. Many times after the first break, the market has a secondary rally that fails *under* the high. If you failed to get out on the first break, this is your last good chance.

Secret 18
Never let a good profit turn into a loss

This is one of those trading sins that have ruined many a hope. If you have a decent profit in any position and you are absolutely sure it is going to grow larger, at the very least, place a physical stop where (in the worst case) you'll break even. If the market is any good, your stop won't be hit. Should the market continue to move in your favor, keep moving your stop to lock in at least some profit. The objective is always to protect your principal in every way possible, and when you are fortunate enough to start accumulating paper profits, lock them in.

Secret 19
When in doubt, get out

If the market is not acting right according to your plan, get out. If the market has not started to move in your favor within a reasonable amount of time, get out. Your judgment deteriorates the longer you hang on to a losing position, and at extremes, you will do the wrong thing. One of the old timers once said something like this, "I am prudent enough not to stand in the middle of the railroad tracks while I try to decide if the headlight I think I see is a freight train or an illusion."

Secret 20
Spread your risks through diversification

Distribute your risk among a variety of trades and markets. Divide your capital into tenths, and never risk more than a maximum of 10% on any one trade. One good profit often totally erases four or five small losers. On the other hand, if you take big losses and small profits, you have no chance of success. I also suggest concentrating on active, liquid markets, those that allow you to enter and exit when you want to with a minimum of slippage.

Secret 21
Pyramid the correct way

The big money is made only by pyramiding a good position in a trending market. You have an excellent opportunity to use leverage with your unrealized profits to create a larger position than otherwise possible. Pyramiding takes both courage and self-control. The "weak hands" seldom make the big money, primarily because they do not have the guts to pyramid and maximize the opportunities they are right about (or they do not have the smarts to do it right). Please be advised, there is a right way and a wrong way to pyramid.

The masters suggest you never reverse pyramid (that is, add a greater number of contracts than your initial position while the market moves your way). Your first risk should be your greatest risk. It is generally better to decrease the size of your position throughout the ride, not increase it. In this way, you have the opportunity to increase your profitability without dramatically increasing your risk.

eg **Let's look at a hypothetical example. If you start out with a purchase of ten cocoa contracts at 1300, the way to add to this position is five contracts at 1350, three at 1400, two at 1450, and one every additional 50 points up indefinitely until the move is over. Of course, you follow up this position with a moving stop loss. In ▶**

this way, your last trade or two shows a loss, but all the others show big profits. The point here is that by pyramiding with the larger position underneath (for longs) or above (for shorts), your average price is always better than the market. When trading this way, a correction is more likely to show bottom-line profitability.

Two additional (and useful) pyramiding rules:

- Never try to pyramid after a long advance or decline. The odds are against you. I did this in soybeans during the floods of 1993. I started to be a buyer at just the right time and close to the lows, but I got too bullish at the top, added too many contracts, and never made any real money out of that one. The time to begin a pyramid is when the trend first turns up or down after a long move. Your technical indicators can help you here.

- It is always safer to pyramid after a market moves out of accumulation or distribution—in other words, a breakout from consolidation (see the next secret). The longer the time it takes prior to the breakout, the greater the move you can expect.

Secret 22
Watch for breakouts from consolidation

I've discussed this before, but this secret is powerful and cannot be overemphasized. You need to know what kind of market you are in. In a consolidating market, you can make money by scalping small moves back and forth. However, you won't make the big money in this kind of market, and you never should attempt to pyramid in this kind of market. Big profits are made in the runs between accumulation and distribution. I've found you can make more money by waiting until a commodity plainly declares its trend than by getting in before the move starts. Too many traders are fixated on picking the top or bottom, and as a result, they miss the big picture. What difference does it make if you buy 10, 20, or 30 ticks off the lows as long as you make money? Get the idea of price out of your head and concentrate on market action. Just forget about picking tops and bottoms!

The longer the consolidation, the better. When a market has remained in a narrow range for a long time, a breakout out of that range becomes more significant. The market is telling you that a major shift in the supply and demand fundamentals is taking place. Because it has taken a long time to form, there is more fuel available for the coming move, and this is the best type of market to play to the hilt!

One last point: At times, there are false breakouts, so watch for them. You know it's most likely a false breakout if the market again trades back into the consolidation range. The best breakouts from consolidation never retrace into the breakout range, but it is okay for a market to trade back to the upper or lower edge of the range before resuming new trend action. After it breaks through to the other side, however, there is no question that it was false. When this happens, a reversal play will likely be the best course of action.

Secret 23
Go with the relative strength

I'm not referring to the RSI (relative strength index, a popular indicator of over-sold/overbought). What is important is that you follow the trend of each market and always buy the strong one and sell the weak one. This is especially important for related markets. Silver and gold are both precious metals and generally move in the same direction; however, they move at different *speeds*. In early 1987, silver started to run, and in a short time, it ran up almost $6 per ounce, representing profits of close to $30,000 per contract. We had clients who did not want to "chase the market" after silver made its first $1 run-up, but they had no hesitation buying gold. It was, after all, cheap in relation to silver and would have to catch up eventually, right? Gold did run up, about $60 per ounce, or $6,000 per contract. Not too bad, but you would have made five times more by buying the strong one instead of the weak one. Moves of this nature don't come along very often.

If hogs are going up and bellies are heading down, you should sell the bellies if your trend indicators tell you to do so. It doesn't matter that they're both pork products; the markets are telling you no one is eating bacon—at least not now. When I first started in the business, I remember bellies (which usually trade at a 10¢ to 20¢ premium to the hogs) were trading at the same price as hogs. All the boys at Merrill Lynch said this was a slam-dunk—you just had to make money spreading bellies and hogs. (Buy the bellies and sell the hogs.) This made perfect sense. The logic was sound: How could a finished product ever sell for less than the raw material? We all piled on this one, and you probably can guess what happened. The bellies continued to head south and the hogs north until the bellies were selling at a $5 *discount* to the hogs. This was a loss of $2,000 per spread at the time in a "no risk" trade (and, of course, we overtraded this one because it "couldn't lose").

The point is that you need to judge a market by its own signs. Always sell the weak one and buy the strong one.

Secret 24
Limit moves are important indicators of support and resistance

When a market is bid limit up or offered limit down (for those markets that still have limits, for example the cattle or corn), this is a level where you could be unable to buy or sell. There is more demand at the limit-up price than available supply or vice versa. The market "should" continue in the direction of the limit move. On corrections, it should find support above the limit price (or below if a limit-down move). Watch for this. If a market again trades under the limit bid price or above the limit offered, go with the flow. These are trades that possess reasonable risk, because they indicate the previous support or resistance is now absent. If anyone can now buy a market where it previously was unable to be bought (or sell where you previously couldn't), this is a major sign of weakness or strength.

Here's one example from my memory: The day before the high price was hit in the big bull corn market of 1996, a trader was unable to buy corn. It was not only limit bid, but there were more than 30 million bushels wanted with no sellers at the limit price. A few days later, the market crossed under the limit bid price, and anyone could buy as much as he wanted. After it crossed that price, the market never saw the light of day. It started on a bear-route, one that lasted for six months and didn't end until prices were $1.50 per bushel lower.

Secret 25
Never average a loss

This is critical. I've talked to stock investors who have had great success averaging down. When a stock they liked got cheaper, they bought more. When the long-term trend turned back up, they made out like bandits. A leveraged market, however, is different. Averaging a loss might work four times out of five, but that fifth time will wipe you out, and it is a bad habit to get into.

Look at it this way: If you make a trade and it starts to go against you, then you're wrong—at least temporarily. Why buy or sell more to average the loss? When it's getting worse day by day, why do your best to potentially compound the problem? Stop the loss early before it is eternally too large, and don't make it worse.

Gann felt if you could avoid three weaknesses—overtrading, failing to place a stop loss, and what he called the "fatal" mistake, averaging a loss—then you would be a success. This is good advice. I believe there is one final essential requirement for success, which we will discuss in the next chapter.

14

Jesse's secret

Many market axioms sound terrific in theory but really don't help you much in practice. ("Buy low and sell high" is one good example of this.) Although what is presented in this chapter might sound simplistic, it's not.

The secret to making the big money is to maximize the big move

This principle took me a long time to learn, and most traders never will understand it. You might not have many trades that turn into big movers. The big movers are rare. Generally, just one or two trades will make a big year for you. Capitalizing on only two or three major trading campaigns could mean a lifetime of difference for you!

When I first started working on the floor of the Grain Exchange, I would see this one member, a relatively young man at the time, who'd visit every so often. He'd appear maybe once or twice a week, joke with some of the traders, check the markets, and at times, place a few orders. Then he would disappear for weeks or months. Over time, I got to know him better and learned he lived a happy life. The reason we would not see him for months was because travel was his passion. He could well afford to pursue his passion, because he was independently wealthy. It wasn't inherited money; he came from modest means.

Basically, his story involved the "Russian grain steal" markets of 1973 and 1974. He was working for a living back then like most of us have to today and trading on the side. I don't know exactly how much money he finally took out of the markets, but judging by his lifestyle, I believe it was substantial. I do know he started with a modest sum and made his big money in the soybean market. He was fortunate to be on the right side of one of the biggest soybean moves in history. He was smart enough to have a vision, had the guts to pyramid his position, and was disciplined enough to stand firm until the market told him the move was over. This was the market where soybeans ran from less than $4 per bushel to nearly $13. Bottom line, *in less than two years*, this man was able to change his life dramatically for the better. What he did is quite rare, almost impossible, but he is living proof it is possible.

Think about how tough it must have been to do what he did, to constantly avoid the burning temptation to cash in on what must have been huge paper profits during the move. Human nature would have urged him to "book the profit" every time the market rallied to new highs. After all, you can always "get back in" and reestablish a position on the next correction, right? Taking profits is pleasurable behavior and the easiest road to follow. After a big run, when the correction does materialize, a trader can pat himself on the back. Profitability is enhanced every time you book a profit and are then able to buy back cheaper. After all, "you never go broke taking a profit," isn't that right?

The truth is, you never get rich this way either. The only major glitch in "taking profits" has to do with the corrections. Although the corrections will come, they don't always occur on schedule or from the level you decided to exit. This man, unlike most, had the discipline to forego normal profits and hold out for "life-changing" profits. How did he do this? I believe he had a vision. He had to believe prices could do what others could never envision.

A vision is the key, but this man also must have had the patience to hang in there until the trend absolutely changed direction. This isn't easy to do, and it's not always that easy to see. He had to have the courage to hang on during what looked like vicious shakeouts to me on the charts. (Take a look at a chart of this move; like all the major moves, this one had sharp and deep shakeouts even while the major trend continued to point north.) He must have had the guts to pyramid his position for maximum profitability, and this isn't all that easy. It takes "smart guts." If he was too timid, he could never have achieved life-changing profitability. If too bold, he would have over-traded and become under-margined, unable to hold his position.

Jesse Livermore

Jesse Livermore, the legendary trader of the 1920s, made and lost mega-fortunes countless times over his trading career. At the height of his success, this was a man who made more than $15 million in the crash of 1929, a mega-fortune at the time. Unfortunately, he also must have possessed a fatal flaw, because he somehow lost these multi-fortunes. Jesse was a compulsive gambler, and at the end of his life, he died penniless. He was found dead in the early 1940s in a fleabag hotel room with a self-inflicted bullet wound through his head. Apparently, he did not follow his own advice. In his writings, he cautioned traders to always lock away half of any big profit for retirement and to keep it unavailable for trading. He told us in his book that he actually did this (put half his profits in an irrevocable trust for his wife and kid), but I guess he must have taken out the key and used it in a weak moment. Still, to his credit, he developed the amazing ability to take millions out of the markets after starting with relatively modest sums. This wasn't a one-time fluke either—he made (and lost) literally millions numerous times throughout his career. The high point was his huge short position in 1929, which he covered in full at the lows on the day of the famous crash.

What was Jesse's secret? In *Reminiscences of a Stock Operator,* published in 1923 (a semi-autobiographical account of Livermore's trading career to that time), the hero shared his secret of how to make the big money. In today's world, we have the advantage of computerized trading and financial futures, but the basics of trading and winning haven't changed, simply because human nature hasn't changed. Early in his career, Jesse suffered from the same malady most of us have. Unlike most of us, however, he was able to unlock the secret of making the big money. He shares this early in the book, but this lesson is easy to miss. As a young man, Jesse missed it also as he relates the tale of old Mr. Partridge, a trader who was not as frenetic as most. (Recall in the 1920s, stocks were traded like commodities are today: highly leveraged on small margin.) In this excerpt from the book, feel free to substitute the words "Wall Street" with "LaSalle Street" or the word "stock" with silver, cotton, S&Ps, or whatever it is you're trading now:

"You find very few who can truthfully say that Wall Street doesn't owe them money. Well, there was one old chap who wasn't like the others. To begin with, he was a much older man. He never volunteered advice and never bragged of his winnings . . . Time and again I heard him say, 'Well, this is a bull market, you know!' as though he were giving you a priceless talisman . . . and, of course, I didn't get his meaning . . .'But I couldn't think of selling that stock,' Mr. Partridge would say. 'Why not?' I would ask. 'Why this is a bull market. My dear boy, if I sold that stock now, I would **lose** my position, and then where would I be? And when you are as old as I am, and you have been through as many booms and panics as I have, you'll know that to **lose** your position is something nobody can afford—not even John D. Rockerfeller. I hope that stock reacts and that you will be able to repurchase your line at a substantial concession, sir. But I myself can only trade in accordance with the experience of many years. I paid a high price for it, and I don't feel like throwing away another tuition fee.'

"The more I learned, the more I realized how wise that old chap was. He had evidently suffered from the same defect in his young days and knew his own weakness. I think it was a long step forward in my trading education when I realized at last that when old Mr. Partridge kept on telling the other customers, 'Well you know this is a bull market,' he really meant to tell them that the big money is not in the individual fluctuations, but in the main movements—that is not in reading the tape, but in sizing up the entire market and its trend.

"After spending many years in Wall Street and after making and losing millions of dollars, I want to tell you this: It was never my thinking that made the big money for me. It was always my sitting. Got that? My sitting tight! You always find lots of early bulls in bull markets and early bears in bear markets. I have known many men who were right at exactly the right time and began buying or selling when prices were at the very level that should show the greatest profit. And their experience invariably matched mine—that is, they made no real money out of it. Men who can be both right and sit tight are uncommon. I found it one of the hardest things to learn. But it is only after a speculator has firmly grasped this that he can make big money.

"It is literally true that millions come easier to a trader after he knows how to trade than hundreds did in the days of his ignorance."
(Reprinted from Jesse Livermore, *Reminiscences of a Stock Operator,* Traders' Library Publications 1993, by permission of John Wiley & Sons, Inc.)

Those who can be right and sit tight

At times, I've had clients make big scores in the markets we trade. I've been fortunate enough to do the same at times, but I admit not as often as I could have or should have. When I go back and look at my "Purchase and Sale" statements from the clearinghouse, I generally see the same pattern for the "'best of the best" trades. I see a position entered into when it was not the popular play. I see a position held for a greater period of time than most, held through major shakeouts or sharp short covering rallies. These were generally pyramided but not always the largest positions in terms of size. Substantial money can be made with a fairly modest position, if the position is entered relatively early in a major move and held for a good portion of that move.

To achieve ultimate success, you are required to resist your human weaknesses. Human nature provokes us to take premature profits, because it's pleasurable. The major moves, the ones you want to maximize, are those that are the hardest to endure. Your technical tools can help here. Consider using moving averages (which I personally believe are the best technical tool); however, any tool that helps you determine the trend and maximize profits in a systematic manner is better than thinking too much or too emotionally. Technical tools can provide you with the discipline to stay with moves you otherwise would cash in on prematurely. These big moves are always out there and always will be, but most of us never see the forest for the trees.

As I write this edition, once again I see many markets that have trended for big moves in recent months. You don't need a large bankroll to capitalize on many of them. Consider orange juice, a market with one of the cheapest margin requirements of any we trade, having once again crossed its 30-day moving average to the downside at 7900 about five months ago. Since then, it hasn't been able to close above its 30-day moving average, and as we go to press, it is trading at 6100. This is an 1800 point move (and counting), a return of about $2,700 per contract for just a measly $700 margin deposit. We're talking a greater than 800% annualized return on margin here in a low-priced market and without pyramiding. With a relatively modest account, you could have added one contract short at, for example, every 200 points lower during a move like this, while never being under-margined and always being able to trail a reasonably positioned stop loss. In this way, you could have built a position of more than 10 contracts and accumulated significant unrealized profits. Although this was a nicely trending market, it was quite orderly but by no means abnormal.

Consider crude oil, having crossed its 30-day exponential moving average to the upside at $25.50, and just about the same time OJ crossed its average to the south. Four months later, oil was trading as high as $40 without ever once closing below this average. This was a move equivalent to more than $14,000 per contract for just a $3,000 margin requirement. Think of the fortune that could have been accumulated with just a modest pyramid here.

Sun Apr 25 2004 16:03:12   CQG © 2004

■ **Chart 14.1**   Markets do move in down-trends

Sun Apr 25 2004 15:57:42   CQG © 2004

■ **Chart 14.2**   Markets do move in up-trends

Sun Apr 25 2004 16:02:09   CQG © 2004

Chart 14.3   Markets do move in up-trends

Take a look at the soybeans, crossing their 30-day exponential moving average in August at 539, while not experiencing more than a two-day close below the 30-day exponential until eight months later at 965. This represented more than $20,000 per contract for just a $2,000 margin requirement.

Moves just like this take place every year over a variety of markets and in both directions, but most of us see them only in hindsight. Look at any chart book, and you will see plainly these big moves are there for the taking, available to me and to you. In a free capitalistic society, they are available to us all. What's really exciting is that they continue to develop each year. You can start today, and you can be successful beyond your wildest dreams. You'll require discipline, guts, and courage, and you'll need to take the road less traveled. It's not easy, but the opportunities are out there. Good luck and good trading!

Appendix: World futures and options exchanges

The following information is subject to change and provided without warranty of any kind. For charts, quotes, futures, and commodity-related advice, log onto Commodity Resource Corp: www.commodity.com

Argentina

Buenos Aires Futures Exchange
Mercado a Término de Buenos Aires
Mario Wolberg, Bouchard 454, 5°
1106 Buenos Aires, Argentina
www.matba.com.ar

Australia

Sydney Futures Exchange (SFE)
30 Grosvenor Street, Sydney, NSW 2000, Australia
61-2-9256-0555 Fax 61-2-9256-0666
www.sfe.com.au

Austria

Austrian Futures & Options Exchange (OTOB)
Wallnerstrase 8, P.O. Box 192, A-1014 Wien, Austria
43-1-531-65-0 Fax 43-1-532-97-40
www.wienerboerse.at

Belgium

Belgian Futures & Options Exchange (BELFOX)
Palais de la Bourse Rue Henry Maus, 2, 1000 Brussels, Belgium
32-2-509-1211 Fax 32-2-509-1212
www.belfox.be

Brazil

Bolsa de Mercadoris & Futuros (BM&F)
The Commodities & Futures Exchange
Praca Antonio Prado, 48, Sao Paulo, SP, Brazil 01010-901
55-11-3119-2000 Fax 55-11-3242-7565
www.bmf.com.br

Canada

Montreal Exchange (ME)
The Stock Exchange Tower, 800 Victoria Square, Montreal, Quebec, H4Z 1A9 Canada
514-871-2424 Fax 514- 871-3514
www.me.org

Toronto Futures Exchange (TFE)
P.O. Box 450, 3rd Floor, 130 King Street W., Toronto, Ontario, M5X 1J2 Canada
416-947-4670 Fax 416-947-4662
www.tse.com

Winnipeg Commodity Exchange (WCE)
400 Commodity Exchange Tower, 360 Main St., Winnipeg, Manitoba, R3C 3Z4 Canada
204-925-5000 Fax 204-943-5448
www.wce.ca

Chile

Santiago Stock Exchange
Calle La Bolsa 64, Casilla 123D, Santiago, Chile
56-2-695-8077 Fax 56-2-672-8046
http://www.bolsadesantiago.com/

China

Shanghai Futures Exchange
500 PuDian Road, Shanghai 200122
Tel: 68400000 Fax: 68401198
www.shfe.com.cn

Dalian Commodity Exchange (DCE)
No.18 Huizhan Road, Dalian, China P.C:116023
86-0411-84808888 Fax 86-0411-84808588
www.dce.com.cn

Hong Kong Exchanges and Clearing Ltd.
12/F One International Finance Centre, 1 Harbour View Street
Central, Hong Kong
852-2522-1122 Fax 852-2295-3106
www.hkex.com.hk

Denmark

Futop Market
Copenhagen Stock Exchange, Nikolaj Plads 6, Box 1040
DK-1007 Copenhagen, Denmark
45-33-93-3366 Fax 45-33-12-8613
www.xcse.dk

Finland

Helsinki Exchange (HEX)
P.O. Box 361, FIN-00131, Helsinki, Finland
358-9-616-671 Fax 358-9-6166-7368
www.hex.com

France

Marche a Terme International de France (MATIF)
39, rue Cambon, 75001 Paris, France
33-1 49-27-10-00 Fax 33-1-49-27-11-15
www.matif.fr

Germany

Frankfurt Stock Exchange
Neue Börsenstr. 1, 60485 Frankfurt, Germany
49-69-2-110 Fax 49-69-2-111-1021
www.deutsche-boerse.com

Greece

Athens Stock Exchange (ATHEX)
10 Sophocleous Street, 105 59 Athens, Greece
302-10-32-66-800 Fax 302-10-32-13-938
www.ase.gr

Hungary

Budapest Commodity Exchange (BCE)
P.O. Box 1373, Budapest 495, Hungary
36-1-450-0860 Fax 36-1-450-0859
www.bce-bat.com

India

National Stock Exchange of India Ltd.
Exchange Plaza, Plot no. C/1, G Block, Bandra-Kurla Complex, Bandra (E), Mumbai
400-051, India
22-26598100 Fax 22-26598120
www.nseindia.com

Israel

Tel Aviv Stock Exchange (TASE)
54 Ahad Ha'am St., Tel Aviv, 65202, Israel
972-3-5677411 Fax 972-3-5105379
www.tase.co.il

Italy

Italian Stock Exchange
Piazza degli Affari, 6, 20123, Milan, Italy
39-2-724261 Fax 39-2-72426279
www.borsaitalia.it

Japan

Kansei Commodities Exchange (KANEX)
1-l0-l4 Awaza, Nishi-ku, Osaka 550, Japan
8l-6-531-7931 Fax 81-6-541-9343
www.kanex.or.jp

Osaka Securities Exchange (OSE)
8-16, Kitahama, 1-chome, Chuo-ku, Osaka 541, Japan
81-6-229-8643 Fax 81-6-231-2639
www.ose.or.jp

Osaka Textile Exchange
2-5-28 Kyutaro-machi, Chuo-ku, Osaka 54l, Japan
81-6-253-0031 Fax 81-6-253-0034
www.osamex.com

Tokyo Commodity Exchange (TOCOM)
10-8 Nihonbashi, Horidome-cho, 1-chome, Chuo-ku, Tokyo 103, Japan
81-3-3661-9191 Fax 81-3-3661-7568
www.tocom.or.jp

Tokyo Grain Exchange (TGE)
1-12-5 Nihonbashi Kakigara-cho, 1-Chome, Chuo-ku, Tokyo 103, Japan
81-3-3668-9321 Fax 81-3-3661-4564
www.tge.or.jp

Tokyo International Financial Futures Exchange (TIFFE)
Ichiban-cho Tokyu Building
21 Ichiban-cho, Chiyoda-ku, Tokyo 102-0082, Japan
81-3-3514-2400 Fax 81-3-3514-2425
www.tiffe.or.jp

Korea

Korea Stock Exchange
33, Yoida-dong, Youngdeunpo-ku, Seoul 150-977, Korea
82-2-3774-9127 Fax 82-2-3774-9138
www.kse.or.kr

Korea Futures Exchange (KOFEX)
17th Floor, Allianz Tower, 45-21, Yeouido-dong, Yeongdeungpo-gu, Seoul, 150-978
Korea
82-2-3787-7400 Fax 82-2-3787-7430
www.kofex.com

Malaysia

Malaysia Derivatives Exchange (MDEX)
Kuala Lumpur Stock Exchange
Group Marketing, 10th Floor, Exchange Square
Bukit Kewangan, 50200 Kuala Lumpur, Malaysia
603-2026 7099 Fax 603-2710-2308
www.mdex.com.my

Netherlands

European Options Exchange (EOE)
Financiee l Nieuwscentrum, Beursplein 5, 1012 JW Amsterdam, The Netherlands
20-550-5505 Fax 20-550-5515
www.aex.nl

New Zealand

New Zealand Exchange (NZX)
New Zealand Futures & Options Exchange (NZFOX)
9th Floor, ASB Tower, 2 Hunter Street, PO Box 2959, Wellington, New Zealand
64-4-472-7599 Fax 64-4-496-2893
www.nzx.com

Norway

Oslo Stock Exchange (OSLO)
P.O. Box 460, Sentrum, N-0105 Oslo, Norway
47-22-34-1700 Fax 47-22-34-1925
www.oslobors.no

Singapore

Singapore Commodity Exchange Ltd. (SICOM)
111 North Bridge Road #23-04/05, Peninsula Plaza, Singapore 179098
65-6338-5600 Fax 65-6338-9116
www.sicom.com.sg

Singapore Exchange (SGX)
2 Shenton Way, 19-00 SGX Centre 1, Singapore 068804
65-6236-8888 Fax 65-6535-6994
www.sgx.com

Spain

Spanish Exchange for Financial Futures & Options (MEFF)
Torre Picasso, Planta 26, 28020 Madrid, Spain
91-5850800 Fax 91-5719542
www.meff.com

Sweden

OMHEX
Tullvaktsvagen 15, SE 105 78 Stockholm, Sweden
46-8-405-60-00 Fax 46-8-405-60-01
www.omhex.com

Switzerland

Swiss Exchange (SWX)
Selnaustrasse 30, CH-8021 Zurich, Switzerland
41-58-854-54-54 Fax 41-58-854-22-33
www.swx.com

United Kingdom

International Petroleum Exchange (IPE)
International House, 1 St. Katharine's Way, London E1W 1UY, U.K.
44-20-7481-0643 Fax 44-7481-8485
www.theipe.com

London Int'l Futures & Options Exchange (LIFFE)
Cannon Bridge House, 1 Cousin Lane, London EC4R 3XX, U.K.
44-20-7623-0444 Fax 44-20-7588-3624
www.liffe.com

London Metal Exchange (LME)
56 Leadenhall Street, London EC3A 2DX, U.K.
44-20-7264-5555 Fax 44-20-7680-0505
www.lme.co.uk

London Equity Derivatives Exchange (EDX)
131 Finsbury Pavement, London EC2A 1NT, U.K.
44-20-7065-8500
www.londonstockexchange.com/edx

United States

Chicago Board Options Exchange (CBOE)
400 S. LaSalle Street, Chicago IL, 60605
312-786-5600 Fax 312-786-7413
www.cboe.com

Chicago Board of Trade (CBOT)
141 W Jackson Blvd., Chicago, IL 60604-2994
312-435-3500 Fax 312-341-3306
www.cbot.com

Chicago Mercantile Exchange (CME)
20 S. Wacker Drive, Chicago, IL 60606
312-930-1000 Fax 312-930-3439
www.cme.com

Kansas City Board of Trade (KCBT)
4800 Main St., Suite 303, Kansas City, MO 64112
816-753-7500 Fax 816-821-5228
www.kcbt.com

Minneapolis Grain Exchange (MGE)
400 S. Fourth St., Minneapolis, MN 55415
612-321-7101
www.mgex.com

New York Board of Trade (NYBOT)
One North End Avenue, New York, NY 10282-1101
212-748-4000
www.nybot.com

New York Mercantile Exchange (NYMEX)
World Financial Center, One North End Avenue, New York, NY 10282-1101
212-299-2000
www.nymex.com

One Chicago
141 W. Jackson Boulevard
Suite 2208-A
Chicago, IL 60604
Fax: 312-424-8529
www.onechicago.com

Index

Symbols

U-V

W

X-Z